Pants FOR Real People

FIT AND SEW FOR ANY BODY!

BY PATI PALMER & MARTA ALTO

Fourth revised expanded edition
of Pants for Any Body

Designed by Linda Wisner
Photography by Pati Palmer
Illustrations by Kate Pryka, Jeannette Schilling,
  and Theresa O'Connell
Styling and Sewing by Marta Alto
Cover by Linda Wisner and Pati Palmer
Edited by Sue Neall and Connie Hamilton
Technical and Copy Editing by Ann Gosch

Acknowledgements

Without our students, we wouldn't have had a "living research laboratory." Thanks to them we have evolved from determining alterations from measurements and pre-made gingham pants in our days teaching at Meier & Frank department store to tissue-fitting today's students.

We also thank those who graciously volunteered to be models for this book in hopes of sharing their challenges so you could benefit. Some of our models are Certified Palmer/Pletsch Instructors who were taking workshops here in Portland and offered to be in the book. Models are Marta Alto, Jean Baxter, Connie Hamilton, Sue Neall, Alicia Panetta, and Melissa Watson. On the cover left to right are Susie Brown, Nancy Seifert, Melissa Watson, Verna Day, and Ethel Harms.

Also, a special thank you to former Palmer/Pletsch traveling associates Lynn Raasch, Karen Dillon, Leslie Wood, Kathleen Spike, and Barbara Weiland who contributed to ideas for our books over the years.

The pattern companies have always been open to our "opinions," such as putting the finished garment measurements on the pattern envelope. We have loved the connection. Thanks to Bob Hermann, Sidney Tepper, Carl LaLumia, Kathleen Len, and Nancy DiCocco from McCall's and to Karen Burkhart, now with Simplicity, whom we worked with on our very first pant pattern for Vogue and then at McCall's.

Also, a special thanks to the technical people at McCall's, who have helped build fit information into the tissue and guidesheets and, on occassion, know our techniques so well, they just do the patterns: Benhaz Livian, Charlotte Schulze, Christine Carballeira, Pamyla Brooks, and Stacy Wood.

Without our talented production team and their long, intense hours of work, this book would not exist. Our artists, some of whom we've worked with for 25 years, often even made samples to test the instructions. Our most sincere thanks to Linda Wisner, Jeannette Schilling, Kate Pryka and Theresa O'Connell. Also, several people read the book one or more times during its re-creation including Connie Hamilton.

Thanks to all Palmer/Pletsch teachers world-wide who are spreading their fashion sewing passion. This also includes Sue Neall, who flew to Portland, Oregon from Sydney, Australia last September to give us that much needed push and motivation to finish in less than four years.

Lastly, thanks to our families who've been so supportive over the years and especially during the final production of this book, including Melissa Watson, Cleo Cummings, and Anastasia, Jerry, and Chris Alto. At our warehouse, for support while we were away writing, a thanks to Jeff Watson, George Palmer, Sean Peters, and Bill Reavis.

Pants for Real People — Fourth Revised and Expanded Edition of *Pants for Any Body*
Copyright © 2003 by Palmer/Pletsch Incorporated. Third Printing Summer 2009.

Pants for Any Body First Edition copyright © 1973 by Pati Palmer. Revised edition copyright © 1976 by Pati Palmer and Susan Pletsch. Revised expanded edition copyright © 1982 by Pati Palmer and Susan Pletsch. Fourteenth printing 1999.

Library of Congress Catalog Control Number: 2003103596
Published by Palmer/Pletsch Incorporated, 1801 N.W. Upshur, Suite 100, Portland, OR 97209, U.S.A.
Printed by Quebecor World, Dubuque, IA, U.S.A.
Fashion illustrations on pages 19 and 74 created by Patty Andersen for the original *Pants for Any Body*.

ISBN 9780935278576

Contents

About the Authors

The previous editions of this book included co-author Susan (Pletsch) Foster, Pati's former business partner. Before computers, Pati typed, Susan drew, and everything was carefully pasted up by the team and sent to the printer. After Susan retired into a blissful marriage, Marta picked up where Susan left off, though not in drawing–not her forte–but in sewing. Marta is an R & D sewer, always testing new and better techniques. She also did all of the sewing for the REAL PEOPLE sections in this book. Here is a little more about Marta and Pati.

Marta Alto

Marta's career as a sewing expert began during her summer "vacations" from studying at Oregon State University, when she sewed costumes at the Oregon Shakespearean Festival in Ashland. That led to a job at San Francisco State University teaching drama students how to sew costumes. As a result, Marta learned how to sew without patterns and to fit many actors' figures.

Marta's unconventional problem-solving approach to fit grew out of this experience. Pati used to cringe at Marta's less-than-technically-correct solutions to fit. Now Pati enjoys Marta's creative problem solving, including the coining of new fit terms such as "smooshing out a dart" and "taking a little here and putting a little there."

After five years in San Francisco, Marta returned to Oregon in 1972 with her 4-year-old son and became a custom dressmaker at a major Oregon department store. She sewed for designer-clothing customers who couldn't find the right silk blouse, for mothers of brides who wanted a special dress that fit, and for people wanting outfits out of that wonderful "new" fabric, Ultrasuede®. Marta then became an assistant buyer and later managed the store's sewing school. After the birth of her second child in 1977, she "retired" to teaching sewing in Portland, then Seattle. In 1981 Marta joined Palmer/Pletsch and traveled throughout the United States, Canada, and Australia teaching Ultrasuede, fit, tailoring and serger seminars.

In 1986 Marta became a Palmer/Pletsch corporate workshop educator. She is also co-author of *Fit for REAL People, The Serger Idea Book* and *Sewing Ultrasuede* and has made four serger videos and one on Ultrasuede. She currently teaches at the Palmer/Pletsch school in Portland and does writing and research on sewing trends.

Pati Palmer

Fit has always been Pati's specialty. After she earned a degree in clothing and textiles from Oregon State University, one of her first jobs was to start a sewing school at Portland's Meier & Frank department store. That was only the beginning of her experience fitting thousands of women. As a result, she has developed workable techniques that any size sewer can use with commercial patterns.

Pati is billed as the "Fit Expert" in the McCall's pattern catalog, which has featured nearly 100 of her designs. Besides conceiving the designs, Pati and her staff write the sewing and fitting instructions themselves.

Palmer/Pletsch was formed in 1973 when Pati and her then-partner, Susan Pletsch, merged their writing and speaking talents. After co-authoring four books, they traveled throughout the United States and Canada teaching seminars based on the books. By 1980, nine Palmer/Pletsch associates were teaching 900 sewing seminars a year.

Pati and Susan approached Vogue Pattern Company in 1975 and became a licensee, the first time an educator had signed on with a pattern company. Five years later, Pati and Susan switched to The McCall Pattern Company. Now McCall's president Bob Hermann tells Pati she is the company's longest-running licensee, beating out the previous titleholder, Marlo Thomas!

In 1986, after buying Susan's share of the business, Pati established four-day workshops in Portland. Sewing enthusiasts have come to the workshops from around the world to learn the latest techniques. In 1990, Palmer/Pletsch added teacher training and in 1994 initiated a certification program, the first to be developed for sewing instructors. To date, more than 500 teachers have graduated and more than 100 have become certified.

Pati and Marta with Palmer/Pletsch trained instructors, left to right: Janet Dapson (Michigan), Sharon Blair (Oregon), Pati Palmer, Verna Day (Montana), Marta Alto, Nancy Seifert (Washington).

A Little History
by Pati Palmer

In 1973, while teaching pant fitting classes at Meier & Frank department store in Portland, Oregon, I decided to write about the subject. There was virtually nothing written about sewing and fitting pants. My students encouraged me. One night I was lying in bed and closed my eyes to visualize how this book could be laid out. I even dreamed up the title and the cover design. It just came to me. I have always said that this book, and maybe Palmer/Pletsch, would never have been if I had fallen asleep that night. Thank goodness I turned on the light, grabbed a tablet, and started writing. Three hours later, I had outlined the entire book and written *Pants for ANY Body* on the first page.

I got up at 5:00 every morning for months to use the executive secretary's IBM Executive typewriter before she arrived at work. I then went back to it after 5:00 p.m. until I had to leave when the store was locked up. Then at home I would do art and paste-ups. We all laughed later when Susan Pletsch first noted that I had drawn a hand with the thumb on the wrong side. If you have the original

80-page book, it is on page 15. (Susan redid all art in the next version. She was better at it, and as long as she didn't drink coffee, her lines were smooth.)

Finally the book was done, but when my students read it, they said it didn't "sound" like me. What a revelation! You mean you can write like you talk? I went through the book again and made it more fun. Meier & Frank's print shop printed the book for me. The pages were collated with the help of my family. Then I took boxes of books into the store to use its saddle stitch machine to staple them together. Of course, the middle pages stuck out when the book was folded. No problem, we just made the cover larger. Only 500 of those were printed. Fortunately, I was the notions buyer as well as sewing instructor, so I sold myself books to pay for the printing. Finally, I had books to go along with my classes.

I started traveling the country on weekends and during my vacations to teach pant fitting classes at other department stores. This was the beginning of the Palmer/Pletsch traveling seminar business.

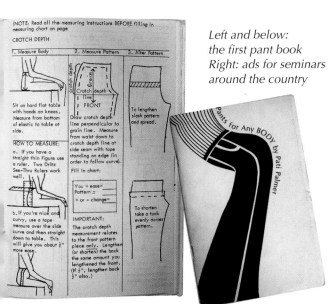

Left and below: the first pant book
Right: ads for seminars around the country

5

When Susan and I got together and wrote *Painless Sewing, Easy, Easier, Easiest Tailoring,* and *Sewing Ultrasuede Fabric,* we decided to revise *Pants for Any Body* together. We did this three times, first expanding it from its original 80 pages to 128, then later updating and expanding it after years of teaching experience.

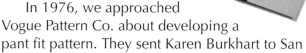

The original Vogue pant pattern catalog page and guidesheet from 1976.

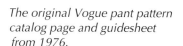

In 1976, we approached Vogue Pattern Co. about developing a pant fit pattern. They sent Karen Burkhart to San Diego to watch me teach a pant seminar to determine whether they should let us do a pattern for them. Until that point, only ready-to-wear clothing designers, never teachers, were licensees of a pattern company. When we were accepted, we wrote the fit portion of the guide sheet and then flew to New York to photograph a model being fitted. The pattern became a Vogue best-seller, selling

our old and new pant patterns from 1980 to present

150,000 copies the first year. It was in their catalog until 1985, five years after we had moved on to McCall's.

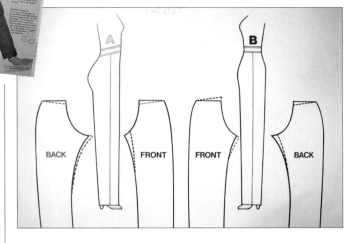

In 1980, we switched to McCall's and were allowed to write not only the fit instructions but the sewing directions as well. They let us change to 1" side seam allowances from the normal 5/8" in fitted garments. By 1990, we were adding alteration lines on the tissue. We were pretty revolutionary and McCall's liked the sales results. One of our first patterns, the 8-hour blazer, which was featured in *Family Circle* magazine, sold more than one million copies in one year—a record-breaker at that time.

During the past 30 years, Palmer/Pletsch has been continually redefining how to fit pants. Our first edition of *Pants for ANY Body* emphasized measuring as a way to achieve perfect fit. But we found that the only measurements that were accurate were length and width; crotch measurements were impossible.

We even tried unique tools, to no avail. One of the first was our handy-dandy crotch-o-meter—two tape measures tied together with a weight tied at the joint. Others refined the concept. See the one at the right and below.

Why didn't these tools work? If you measured the women in the drawing below, how would you know WHERE to add or subtract to the crotch length?

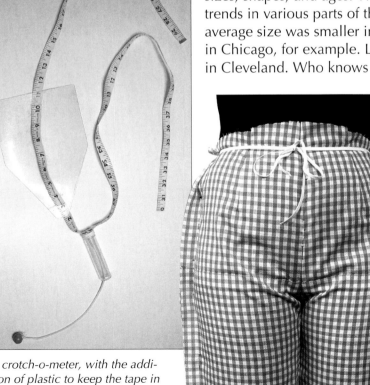

We found a better way! We made 1/4"-check gingham pant-fitting shells in all sizes for our students to try on. No more measuring. We let the pant tell us the size and let the checks give us the fit clues! Throughout the 1970s, '80s, and '90s, we fitted more than 100,000 women in gingham shells all over North America. Gingham took away the guesswork!

We learned a lot by seeing so many sizes, shapes, and ages. We even saw size trends in various parts of the country. The average size was smaller in San Diego then in Chicago, for example. Lots of high hips in Cleveland. Who knows why!?

gingham reveals smiles

A crotch-o-meter, with the addition of plastic to keep the tape in proper place in back and a plumb line with a vial attached. Not sure why.

7

In 1986 Palmer/Pletsch began teaching four-day workshops in Portland. Pant Fitting and Sewing was one of our earliest. We had long since stopped taking crotch measurements because they just didn't work. But we did have our first students make a gingham shell to perfect their pants pattern. Eventually, we started tissue-fitting, thanks to our friend Terri Burns. She said that we tissue-fitted everything else, so why not pants? She simply taped the crotch of the tissue to strengthen it.

By the mid-1990s we were letting our students try on the tissue pattern after we first checked out their fit in gingham. In 2002, we dropped the gingham entirely and went directly to the tissue. It was a big step, but we tested the process in a workshop and we got people in the right size every time. (Our new multisize pant fit patterns helped a lot!) Now all of our McCall's pant patterns have alteration lines on the tissue to make tissue-fitting easy.

With Susan no longer in the business, I teamed with Marta Alto to revise and expand our pant book. Marta assists in the pant workshops, but is the first to admit she is not a pant fit expert, though she is learn-

ing. Marta's talent is in sewing pants and perfecting techniques such as the no-gap welt pocket. She is also a great judge of pattern markings and anything that makes the fit process easier. Marta enjoys sewing so much that she volunteered to help our models sewing their pants during photography.

As you can tell, when we write books, we write from experience, not research. If we write about it, we've done it. We finally can say that pant fitting is easier than it has ever been. When you tissue-fit, you need only your hip measurement to get the right size pattern. From there, what you see is what you get.

Above: These five women all started with a size 18 pattern, yet look how different their shapes are. Some people want us to design one pattern that would fit everyone better. Which of these size 18's would you pick? That is why we put alteration lines on our patterns instead.

Top of page: Pati and Marta teaching a workshop in 1984

Left: Pati and Marta during their Meier & Frank days in 1974. They can't believe they put plaid and tweed on their bodies once.

Far left: Marta teaching a workshop in 1994.

Our pant fitting philosophy is different from most:

1. We use commercial patterns rather than teaching you to draft your own.

After all, patterns are one of the least expensive ingredients in sewing pants, and the most time consuming if you were to draft your own. All of the major pattern companies use a "sloper" or master pattern to develop their fashion patterns and all are similar in shape. They all start with the same standard set of body measurements. Once you find your alterations, some or all will be needed on any pant pattern depending on the design. Your high hip won't disappear just because you sewed a Butterick instead of a McCall's. Patterns are hand drafted then computer graded to create multiple sizes, so there is always that human element and judgment involved. This is why we teach tissue-fitting before cutting out your fabric.

McCalls tests every design in half plaid, half muslin.

2. We don't promise you a perfect pattern

that you can cut, sew, and wear without ever trying it on. That's impossible unless you never fluctuate one ounce in weight, never make a cutting error (an 1/8" error times eight seam allowances around a pant can make each pair 1" different in width), and always use exactly the same fabric (every fabric fits differently). You can, however, alter a pattern to be close to your size and shape and then use our fit-as-you-sew system to create **PERFECT PANTS**.

3. You can use ANY fabric with ANY pattern.

You don't need a special pattern for knits and another for woven fabrics. Using our fit-as-you-sew system, you can get good fit with any fabric.

4. Great looking pants go beyond good fit!

It is also selecting the best style for your figure and the best fabric for that style, and sewing beautiful pant details. Pockets that gap, zippers that pucker, and pleats that pooch all detract from good fit. We think choosing the right pattern, fabric, and sewing techniques form the "great pants package deal." We'll even share some of our favorite tips for FAST pant sewing – how about "Great Pants in Three Hours!!"

We often tell our students to go home after a workshop and sew a dozen pairs of pants right away in different styles and fabrics to really get the fit down. Jacky Crawford from Wisconsin took us literally. She says, "What 'twill be 'twill be!"

Happy Fitting,

Pati Palmer

Pati Palmer

Jackie Crawford, from West Allis Wisconsin, sewed a dozen pairs of pants during a three-week workshop marathon in Portland one summer.

The Palmer/Pletsch Approach to Pant Fitting

- **IT'S EASY!**
- **IT'S PRACTICAL!**
- **IT APPLIES TO ALL PATTERN COMPANIES!**
- **IT'S NEARLY MEASURE-FREE!**
- **THERE'S NO NEED TO DRAFT PANTS FROM SCRATCH!**
- **THERE'S NO NEED TO MAKE A MUSLIN!**

Does the fitting approach described here sound too good to be true? After fitting thousands of women in pants since the '70s and perfecting pant fitting techniques, a proven method is now taught by Palmer/Pletsch instructors worldwide. For the first time, they will share what they've learned about tissue-fitting pants with YOU!

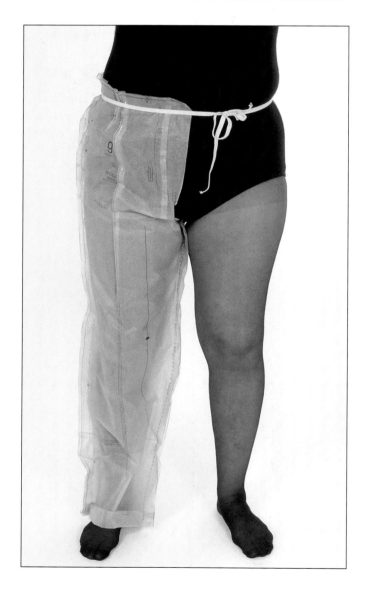

1. **Buy the right size pattern.**
2. **Tissue-fit the pattern.**

3. **Alter and refit the pattern.**

Learning to fit pants is a process. The more you do it, the better you get. Once you get a pattern to fit, all you will have to do is to pin-fit each fabric you sew. Fabrics all drape differently, so "tweaking" the fit on your body will always be necessary.

4. Pin-fit the fabric.

5. Enjoy the final pair of pants.

Pants Can Flatter You

What style pant is best for your figure? Our philosophy is that any figure type can wear any style as long as it fits properly. Even a person with a large tummy can look nice in a pant with a waistband and a tucked-in blouse. Good fit can make you look 10 pounds thinner! With pants that fit, you will be liberated to wear more variety and to look more fashionable!

Which Pant Styles are Most Flattering?

Tight pants show off your shape, so unless your shape is perfect, looser pants are universally better for both thinner and heavier bodies. Even a narrow-leg pant will

looser here de-emphasizes shape

be more flattering if the narrowing is gradual rather than beginning just below the tummy and derriere.

Trousers are a very flattering style as they are not fitted and have vertical lines that make you look taller and slimmer. Jeans on the other hand are designed to fit tight, often with no "ease" in the hips. See page 21 for information on ease.

More ease isn't always more flattering, however. A full pant on a petite person can be overwhelming and a full pant on a large person can make her look larger.

The good news is that ANY style of pants will be flattering IF THE PANTS FIT. Ease is a personal preference and can be changed to suit the wearer, however, it is good to know the amount of ease built into the various styles available so you will know what to expect when you buy a pattern.

Pant Styles and Standard Waist, Hip, and Crotch Depth Ease

  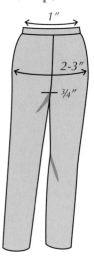  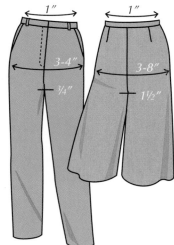

Leggings—knit pants that stretch to fit the body. Originally they were used for exercising, but moved into fashion in the 1990s. Unless you have a perfect shape, avoid them without a long top worn over them.

Traditional jeans —very fitted except in the waist (so you can bend over!). Originally a functional pant for riding horses. Extra crotch ease would cause chafing and saddle sores!

Plain fitted pants —a nice basic, especially to wear with sweaters or overblouses where waist details wouldn't show.

Classic trousers — have slanted pockets, fly-front, pleats, and a front crease pressed up to one of the pleats...lots of vertical lines. For the most flattering look, press the deeper pleat and crease flat to the thigh.

Modified trousers—may have slanted trouser pockets and a fly- front zipper, but no pleats or crease. Nice if you want a fitted pant with pockets.

Culottes—pants with a longer crotch. They look like a skirt, so the longer crotch just adds comfort without looking baggy.

Full evening pants—these must be made of very soft drapey fabrics to be flattering. If you are heavy or petite, buy a smaller size with less ease for the most flattering look.

Flattering Fabrics

If you are heavy and/or short, avoid bulky or stiff fabrics, tweeds, plaids, and wide-wale corduroy. They add visual weight. Wool gabardine or wool crepe, microfiber polyester gabardine, and linen-like fabrics are universally flattering pant fabrics. They are heavy enough to drape over and camouflage body bulges, yet not so heavy or textured that they add bulk. Our favorite pant fabric is wool crepe because it is easy to sew, drapes well, and just seems to mold to fit your body.

Pant Colors

The most versatile colors are the basics: taupe, beige, black, brown, ecru, gray and navy. You can wear many colors of tops with them. They are also seasonless. If you have a navy wool gabardine pant, you can wear it all year round in most climates. Wool breathes. If you make fuchsia pants, you will probably need to plan ahead to make a coordinating top. If you don't have something to wear on top, you won't wear the pants.

Use Color to Your Advantage

Your eyes see light, bright, and shiny colors first, so if you want to de-emphasize your hip width, avoid these colors on the bottom. Use them to call attention to your face. Study these drawings to see how color can enhance your figure:

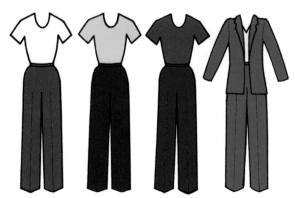

Very light top and dark bottom with strong contrast shortens figure with horizontal line.

Medium light top and medium dark bottom won't cut the figure in half, yet it still draws the eye to the face.

Monochromatic (same color) top and bottom is elongating. Colors can be of slightly different shades.

Jacket and pant in same color create a full length vertical line. Light blouse draws eye to face. This is the most slimming look of all.

Building a Pant Wardrobe

Carry swatches of your wardrobe fabrics on a card in your purse to use for color matching while shopping. You will plan better and will look smarter on a much smaller budget.

tan jacket	yellow striped shirt
white pants	navy jacket
navy print blouse	navy pants

Also, keep in your wallet the amount of yardage you need for 45", 54," and 60" fabrics for a plain pant and for trousers.

For example, possible yardage needed for size 10:

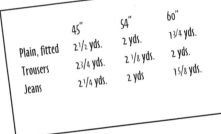

	45"	54"	60"
Plain, fitted	2 1/2 yds.	2 yds.	1 3/4 yds.
Trousers	2 3/4 yds.	2 1/8 yds.	2 yds.
Jeans	2 1/4 yds.	2 yds.	1 5/8 yds.

When you buy fabric for pants (see more about fabric, pages 15-16), decide if it would be a good fabric for a jacket, then buy it all at one time as dye lots vary. There are so many different blacks, whites, and navies that you may never match the pants. We go one step further. We buy enough for pants, skirt, and jacket at one time. The cutting advantage gained will often leave enough fabric for a free vest or skirt to be added.

Waistbands Designed to Flatter

If you are short waisted and/or have a full and low bust, a narrow waistband will be more comfortable and flattering.

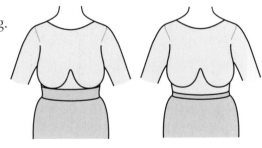

Contour waistbands require tissue-fitting as they must fit well to look good.

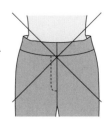

Low riding pants are more flattering if you have a small waistline with a fairly flat tummy.

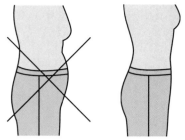

Pull-on pants fit more smoothly around the waistline if you have little difference between the size of your waist and hip.

If your waist is a lot smaller, you will end up with more gathers. A zipper might be more flattering.

Jackets With Pants

If your pants fit well, jacket length can vary. However, if they stop at the fullest part of the hip, they will emphasize hip width. Overall proportion must also be considered—a short person may look better in a shorter jacket. Before making a jacket, pin the pattern pieces together and try on with the finished pants. A full-length mirror will give you your answers.

If the proportion doesn't seem right, try one of the following:

- Change shoes (shape and heel height).
- Change jacket length.
- Pin pant legs narrower.
- Match jacket and pant colors.

Pant Shoes and Stockings

The wrong shoe can throw off the whole proportion of your outfit. Stockings are important too. If you want your legs to look their longest, ALWAYS blend your stockings and shoes with your pant color. The stockings can be opaque in the winter, but should be sheer in the summer. A closed toe pump with a 1½-2" heel is a universally safe year-round shoe that can be worn with both pants and skirts, so if your budget is tight, this is a great way to go. Avoid wearing out-of-date shoes and stockings. Flip through fashion magazines looking at nothing but shoes and stockings for a quick way to be fashion savvy.

Watch Out for "The Tacky Look!"

Panty lines—Look in the mirror before you go out. Any lines? French cut panties (high side legs) with wide elastic that comes to the waist work well. It is usually the bikinis that hit you at the middle of your tummy that create major dents. Or, try pantyhose with built-in panties.

Blouse lines—Pati simply pinks the lower edges of shirts so they are flat when tucked in. Marta serges hers. Also, try tucking blouses into panties or pantyhose. You will be less likely to have panty or blouse lines with looser pants, firmer fabrics, or with lined pants.

Style Changes Affect Pattern Drafting

When pants go from very fitted to a wide-legged trouser, the shape and length of the crotch changes. Some of your needed alterations may even go away! Here is what happened in the 1970s when the first trousers reappeared since the 1940s. (Pink is a fitted pant and black is a trouser.)

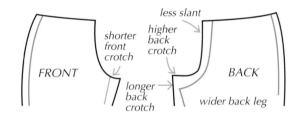

Can We Change Our Shape?

Yes! We can change in weight. One of our favorite sayings is "a moment on the lips, a lifetime on the hips." We can also exercise and smooth out the figure. One of Pati's favorite pant exercises is to do side leg lifts while she is brushing her teeth, washing dishes, or fusing interfacings.

But the easiest way of all to change our shape is to create the illusion of svelte by wearing pants that fit!

CHAPTER 3
Pant Fabrics & Notions

Fabric Choices

Wool Gabardine—comes in various weights. It is a tightly woven twill. If the quality of the wool fiber is good, you can grab a handful of fabric and crush it and when you let go, it will spring out flat without wrinkles. Sometimes color will change depending on the direction, so check before cutting. A hot iron can cause shine on dark colors. Test. If it shines, use a press cloth when pressing on the right side. Long seams tend to pucker. Use "taut sewing," page 40, to prevent puckered seams. Lining is optional.

Wool Flannel—can be wonderful to sew unless it is really dense and tightly woven. Then puckered seams can be a problem. Also, do the wrinkle test mentioned above to determine the quality. Lining will help prevent wrinkles and make the pants feel wonderful.

Wool Crepe—is our number one favorite pant fabric. The wool filling yarns are tightly twisted, making the fabric very springy and wrinkle resistant. Wool crepe just molds to the body while also being very easy to sew and press. There will be no color difference if you reverse pattern pieces. Lining will help prevent wrinkles and make the pants feel luxurious. Wool crepe works in both fitted and trouser styles.

Linen—Unfortunately, today's linens seem to wrinkle more than some brands we used to have, so we reserve linen for jackets where fusible interfacings lessen wrinkling. Or, you can just wear the wrinkles and call them "status wrinkles." Looser styles and lined pants will wrinkle less.

Synthetic Linens—Rayon and polyester blends are woven into fabrics that resemble linen. Some will pill and others lose color if not washed properly. Ask the store which brand they have found performs the best. These fabrics can also be a blend of linen or cotton and polyester.

Denim—is always popular and comes in many weights and styles. It is 100% cotton woven in a twill weave that has a mind of its own. Don't try to straighten denim as it will revert to its original state after washing and you will have twisted side seams. It is recommended to preshrink it three times to remove all shrinkage. Some denims are a blend of cotton and spandex. Denim is easy to sew. A "denim needle" can be used if you get skipped stitches. Be sure to use a size 14(90) or 16 (100) needle if you are sewing through several layers of heavy denim. Some denim looks are made from Tencel® and are more drapey than cotton.

Cotton and Poly/Cotton Sportswear Fabrics—are durable for play pants, but they don't drape very gracefully, so may not be the most flattering pant fabric category. But when a workhorse fabric is needed, you'll have play pants that fit. These fabrics can be a plain weave poplin or a twill weave gabardine. Some stretch because a spandex fiber has been added. Use "taut sewing" to avoid puckered seams.

Chino—is a sateen-surface, combed cotton. It is best dry-cleaned if you want to keep the shiny surface. Although we often call sporty pants "chinos," they are usually a cotton fabric made with a plain or twill weave rather than a sateen weave.

Crinkle Gauze—Some are cotton, others rayon. They can grow while you wear them. We recently experimented—after preshrinking, we ironed most of the crinkles out, cut out pants, and sewed them up. They were perfect. They still grew a little, but not so much we couldn't wear them.

Polar Fleece—is a deep-pile polyester. It is very easy to sew and warm to wear. Pati has a pull-on polar fleece pant with elastic at the ankles so no cold air can get in. One cold winter, they were the only thing that kept her warm. A quality brand from Malden Mills called Polartec® comes in a lightweight 100, medium weight 200, and heavyweight 300.

Silk and Silkies—make wonderful dressy pants. Depending on the weight of the fabric, they can be made into trouser styles or soft full pants. Use "taut sewing" to prevent puckered seams.

Silk Suitings—are easy to sew because pressing will remove any puckering. You will have less wrinkling with a trouser style pant. Lining also helps prevent wrinkling and feels good next to your skin. Silk suitings come in solids and tweeds; avoid tweeds if you are heavy on the bottom.

Corduroy—is a cotton fabric with a nap. Wide-wale corduroy is very sporty and a great look, but does add pounds to the figure. Looser styles work best because corduroy will stretch out during wearing. Some corduroy now has spandex fibers added to the cotton for crosswise stretch.

Microfiber—is the term for a fiber that is very thin, a denier of 1.0 mm or less. Most clothing fibers have a denier of 7.0 mm. Microfibers are made from polyester, nylon, acrylic, and rayon. They can be blended with other fibers such as cotton, linen, wool, and spandex.

Doubleknits—are generally polyester or wool. Polyester doubleknits wear like iron and are easy to sew. Wool doubleknits used to be very heavy, but they are lighter and drapier today.

Stretch-Woven Polyesters—stretch because the polyester fiber has been heat-set into a crimp.

Cotton Knits—are best for pants when combined with spandex (Lycra) for better stretch recovery. Be sure to preshrink the fabric before cutting. Using cold water and a short washer and dryer cycle will help them retain their color.

Stretch Velvet—is a wonderful napped polyester knit that is luxurious and soft. It also washes very well and never seems to lose its color brilliance.

Ultrasuede®—can be found in soft chamois weights that make a beautiful washable suede-like pant. Cut using the "with nap" direction. If the nap runs down, you will see a lighter, silvery shade. If the nap runs up, the color will be richer and darker.

Ultraleather®—This leather look is wonderful for pants, even a simple pull-on with an elastic waist. See the Palmer/Pletsch book on Ultrasuede and Ultraleather for sewing and care instructions.

Polyester/rayon gabardine—These fabrics drape well, are usually 60"-wide and are inexpensive. Use cold water and a short washer and dryer cycle to keep them looking newer longer.

Tencel®—This popular fabric is an environmentally friendly rayon that is sporty like cotton and linen, but wrinkles less.

How Can I Tell If a Fabric Will Make Nice Pants?

1. Fabric Drape

Nearly any fabric can be made into pants today. In ready-to-wear you'll see double layers of chiffon, shiny or dull microfiber fabrics, wovens that stretch because they have a spandex fiber blended with wool, rayon, or cotton, or because the synthetic fiber has been crimped with heat.

The most important feature for a good pant fabric is good drape. Grab the middle of a yard of firm cotton fabric and do the same with a soft rayon. The cotton will fan out and the rayon will hang straight to the floor. Hold a length of fabric up to your body and make it look like pants. Take a step or two to see how it "moves." How does it look as a pant?

2. Will it wrinkle?

Perform the wrinkle test by holding a 5" square in your hand and squeezing it for five seconds. Do the wrinkles come out quickly? The higher the natural fiber content, the more it will wrinkle. Wovens wrinkle more than knits. Stretch wovens wrinkle less than regular wovens. Expect pants to wrinkle a bit where your body bends—knees and hips—but minimize wrinkles by testing fabric first. Lined pants will wrinkle less and feel luxurious.

3. Will it hold its shape?

The "thumb test" is taken by pulling on a small section of the fabric with your thumbs and holding for five seconds. If it recovers quickly from the warmth and stress of your thumbs, it will hold its shape in wear. The tighter the knit or weave, the heavier the fabric, and the less absorbent the fiber, the better it will hold its shape. Generally, double knits hold their shape better than single knits, wovens better than knits, and synthetics better than natural fibers. A fabric that fails the "thumb test" will leave you with baggy knees and derriere.

4. Will it pill?

The shorter the fibers (fuzzy surfaces), the more the fabric is likely to pill. The higher the synthetic fiber content, the drier and more static-prone it will be and thus the short fibers will cling together, or "pill," more easily. Pants will pill in the thigh area between the legs and where a handbag rubs.

5. Will it sew easily?

Knits don't ravel, so seam finishes are unnecessary. Very stretchy fabrics may be harder to handle as will fabrics made from slippery yarns. Synthetic fibers and fabrics with permanent press finishes may not press as easily as natural fibers.

6. Will it be comfortable?

Fabrics that are lightweight and high in natural fiber content are often more comfortable to wear. Thick knits and synthetics are often warmer. Some synthetics can feel clammy.

What Fabric Should I Use for My First Pair of Pants?

We'd love to have you use wool crepe for your first pair as it sews well and just seems to mold to your body. However, you may feel it's too expensive for a first pair. An alternative fabric that drapes well is poly/rayon gabardine. It is usually 60" wide and inexpensive. If you sewed pants in wool crepe, you'd be copying a $150 to $500 ready-made pant. If it is made from poly/rayon gabardine, you'd be copying a $20 to $80 ready-made pant. If your time is really valuable, which pair makes the most sense? When taking a sewing class, ALWAYS sew the most expensive fabric you can afford as you will be in the hands of a pro.

Do I Need a Special Pattern for Knit Fabrics?

If you use our "Fit-As-You-Sew™" system to fine-tune fit in your pants, you can use any pattern for knit fabrics. A pattern that is designed "for stretch knits only" has less ease than a pattern cut for all fabrics, so just fitting the knit pant a bit tighter will accomplish what the "for knits only" pattern would do. But use caution—that tighter fit is more revealing and some bodies are best when hidden with a looser fit!

NOTE: Learn how to sit in pants!

Take a lesson from men. Pull up the front of your pants at the knees before sitting. This prevents pants from pulling down in the back, and minimizes baggy knees. It also lessens wrinkling in the front, because softer folds will form when you sit.

Fabric Care Guide

1. **Read the bolt-end label for fiber and care information.**

2. **Preshrink your fabric, zippers, and linings if you plan to wash the finished garment.**

3. **Preshrink in the same manner you would wash:**

   - Don't overcrowd the washing machine

   - Use short, cold water cycles to preserve colors.

   - Use detergent when preshrinking.

   - Use a cool rinse with synthetic fibers to minimize wrinkling.

   - Don't over-dry fabrics or they will pill and fade.

4. **Preshrink fabric to be dry-cleaned** by having the dry cleaner steam the fabric, or steam it yourself with a "shot-of-steam" type iron. Place fabric on a padded pressing surface or on a bed. First, place the iron in one spot on the fabric and steam. If the fabric puckers around the sole plate imprint, it needs shrinking. Slowly and thoroughly steam every inch of the fabric. Allow to cool and dry before moving.

Great Notions for Pant Sewing

(NOTE: See chapter 5 for fitting notions.)

1. **Cutting board**—Make a "cut 'n press" board, page 100.

2. **See-through ruler**—for placing pattern onto fabric on grain.

3. **8-9" bent-handled shears**—(in good sharp condition). The blades glide along the table as you cut.

4. **Tracing paper**—page 99. (Make sure it will wash out.)

5. **Water-soluble or air-erasable marking pens**—for marking. Be sure to read the directions to avoid permanent staining. Or, use hard tailor's chalk or a chalk wheel. The hard chalk is more lasting, so use it to mark seamlines. The chalk wheel is easier for marking waist seamline, but immediately stitch on the line to mark it permanently.

6. **Basting tape**—1/8"-wide double-faced tape used in place of pins or hand basting.

7. **1/4", 3/8", or 1" elastic**—to hold pants up while you fit.

8. **A full-length mirror and a hand-held rear-view mirror**—Save fitting time by having them in your sewing room.

9. **Seam ripper**—the best friend flattering pants can have!

10. **Stay-tape®**—a lightweight stabilized tricot used to prevent the bias edges of trouser pockets from stretching. It is also used to stabilize faced waistlines.

11. **Steam iron**—We like the "shot-of-steam" type irons for faster, better pressing.

12. **Steam generator irons**—hold more water and offer continuous steam when holding the iron in any position. Gives you the best pressing option.

13. **Serger or overlock machine**—finishes seam allowances quickly and neatly.

14. **Pounding block or clapper**—made of wood and essential for getting a sharp crease. It also helps seams stay pressed open.

15. **Seam roll and ham**—for pressing long seams, darts, and curved seams.

CHAPTER 4

Buy the Right Size

Take only ONE measurement (hip) to buy the right size pattern. No more measuring every inch of your body. No more sitting on a chair to take the crotch measurement. Why? Because it doesn't work.

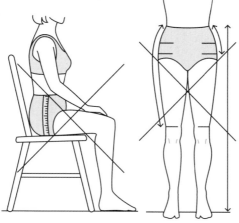

Rules for Measuring

- Measure the fullest part of the hip above the crotch, usually about 7-9" from your waist. Use a reinforced fiberglass tape measure that won't stretch.

- Measure over the underwear you plan to wear with your pants. If you plan to wear pantyhose, measure over them. They can change your size and shape. Also, do all of your fitting with them on.

- Measure, making sure your fingers are not under the tape. This is a snug, SKIN measurement.

TIP: Don't measure the tummy area, because even if it is larger, you can leave out the darts and add to the waist at the sides and center front.

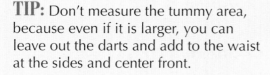

If you are fuller below the crotch, don't worry. In pants you can let out both the side seams and inseams for full thighs.

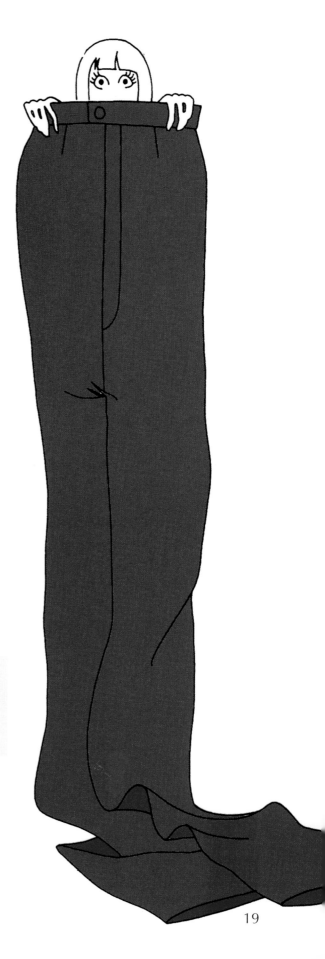

But I'm Between Sizes

If you are between sizes, select the smaller size unless the garment is VERY fitted. Pattern companies generally add enough ease to cover you until you get to the next size.

However, if you are very flat in the back, go to the larger size so you will have enough room to take a tuck out of the back to reduce the back width and still have the side seam at your side. (See page 31.)

SIZE	6	8	10	12	14	16	18	20	22	24	26W	28W	30W	32W
Bust	30½	31½	32½	34	36	38	40	42	44	46	48	50	52	54
Waist	23	24	25	26½	28	30	32	34	37	39	41½	44	46½	49
Hip	32½	33½	34½	36	38	40	42	44	46	48	50	52	54	56
Back Waist Length	15½	15¾	16	16¼	16½	16¾	17	17¼	17⅜	17½	17⅝	17¾	17⅞	18

But the Pattern Doesn't Come in My Size

If the pattern doesn't come in your size or you have bought a coordinates pattern to fit your top and the bottom included in the pattern is not your bottom size, don't worry. Understanding grading should make you more comfortable sewing with any size. True pant grading to enlarge a pattern might look like the illustration below.

Most sizes gain about 2″ in width, but look at how little is gained in the crotch depth or length. If you are LONG in the crotch, you could sew three sizes larger and still not have enough crotch room.

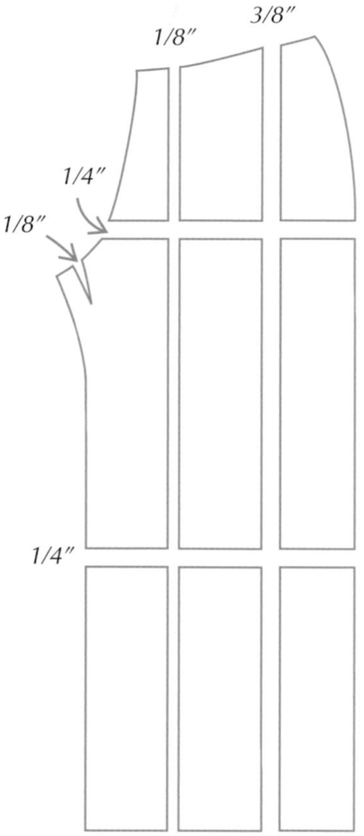

3/8″
1/8″
1/4″
1/8″
1/4″

If the pattern is not large enough, you can add to the sides seams, inseams, and at the top.

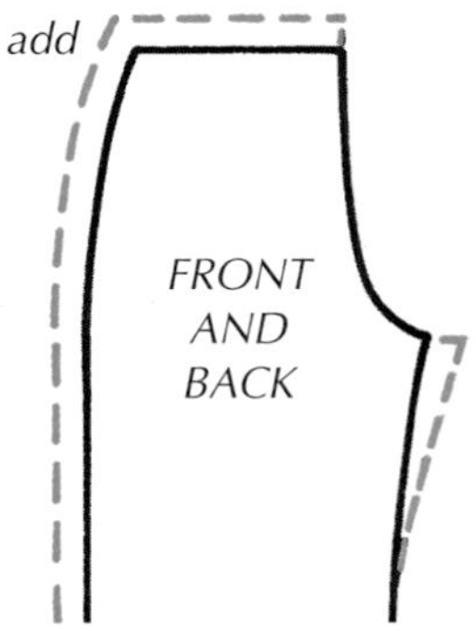

add
FRONT
AND
BACK

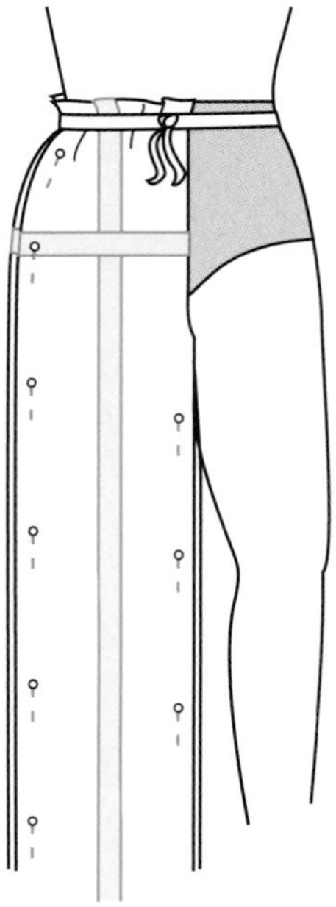

Or, you can cut the pattern and spread it, adding as much tissue as you'd like.

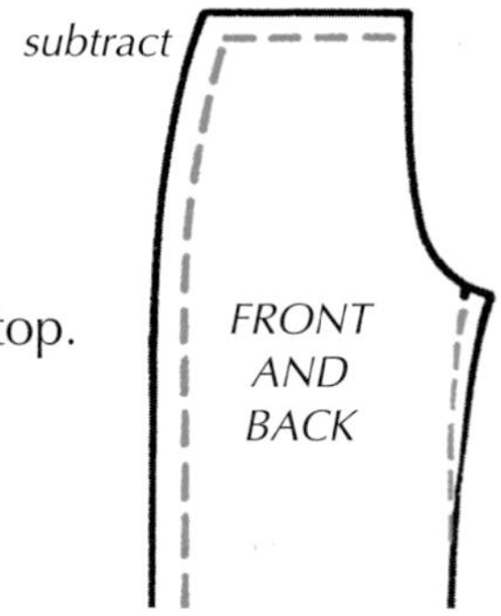

subtract
FRONT
AND
BACK

If the pattern is not small enough, subtract from side seams, inseams, and at the top.

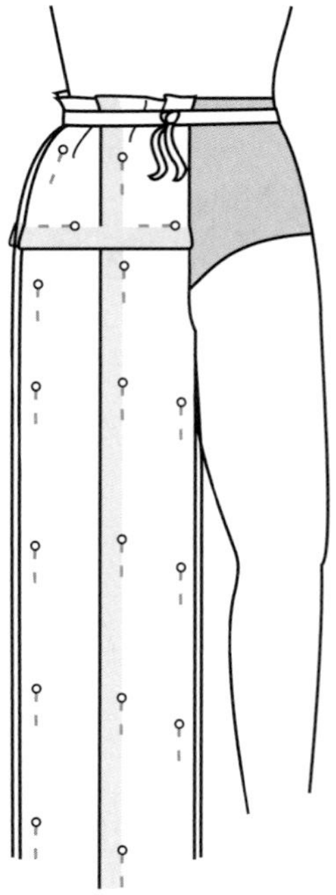

OR you can try on the tissue and tuck it where needed until it fits.

Ease

Ease Is Built into All Patterns

The difference between the size of your pants and your body is called "ease." Pattern companies automatically add ease to body measurements.

Comfort Ease

Width—All pattern companies allow a standard minimum comfort ease of 1" in the waist and 2" in the hips.

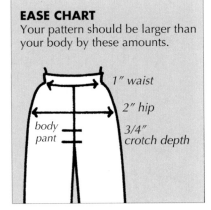

EASE CHART
Your pattern should be larger than your body by these amounts.

1" waist
2" hip
3/4" crotch depth
body
pant

Crotch Depth—

Pattern companies allow a standard comfort ease of 3/4" in the crotch depth. This means pants will hang down 3/4" from the body.

Ease Is Personal Preference

The amount of ease that you find comfortable varies with your size and the way you like clothes to fit. We have found that short people and very large people like less fabric on their body because it overpowers them or makes them look larger.

To find out the amount of ease you prefer, try on various styles of pants in your wardrobe.

Pull all the ease to one side and pinch the excess. If you can pinch 1", you have 2" ease since you are pinching double thickness. If you can pinch 1/2", that is 1" ease.

Do you like the amount of ease in each pant? Do the styles differ in the amount of ease? Now lift the pants up and down to "feel" how far they hang down from your crotch. Do the pants that feel comfortable hang down 1/2", 3/4", or more?

Design Ease

This is the actual amount of ease a designer allows to create a style. Jeans are designed to fit tightly, but for you to be able to bend, the waist has **extra** ease. Trousers must have a minimum of 4" of ease or the pleats will pull. A knits-only pattern has minimal ease and relies on the fabric to give. Most culottes have more ease in the crotch than pants to look more like a skirt. See page 12 for ease amounts in various styles.

Check the Finished Garment Measurements

If you buy a size 16, your hips measure between 40" and 42". A size 16 pant will vary in finished hip measurement, depending on style.

Here is how you use the finished garment measurements printed on some envelopes. If a pattern is designed for a soft fabric and has wide legs, it might be designed with 12" of ease. If you are heavy, short, or using a fabric that is heavy or firm, you may want less fabric around your body.

If you decide 4" of ease would be enough, find the size that gives you your hip measurement plus 4". When finished garment measurements are printed on the back of the envelope, you can make this decision before buying the pattern. It might be two or three sizes smaller than you would usually buy.

Finished Garment Measurements

Size	12	14	16
Hip	36	38	40
Finished Hip	45	47	49

If you are a short size 16, 9" of ease may be way too much fabric for your body. You could buy this pattern two sizes smaller. Five inches of ease may still create the "look" of the design on your shorter stature. You may also choose a smaller size if the fabric you are using would be too bulky with a lot of ease.

Don't Use Ready-to-wear As a Guide to Your Size

The only size standard of pant manufacturers is "the more you pay, the smaller size you can be." Pati's size 18 derriere got into a size 12 Anne Klein. She almost bought them! We call this vanity sizing! Ready-to-wear manufacturers don't have standards, because you can try on the merchandise before you buy it.

Some ready-to-wear manufacturers design their slopers for a specific audience. Have you noticed that pants for the mature woman are fuller in the waist and flatter in the derriere? Pants for juniors are flat in the front, small in the waist, and full in the derriere.

See our book *Fit for REAL People* to read more about size, especially the differences between Women's, Petite, Half, and Misses' sizes.

Small, Medium, and Large Sizes

Patterns sold by small (8-10), medium (12-14), and large (16-18) are cut for the larger of the two sizes. Keep this in mind as you are making your size decisions. Always check to see which sizes are actually in each range of small, medium, and large as they may vary from company to company.

Multisize Patterns

Pattern companies are changing primarily to multisize patterns. These have cutting lines for several sizes in one pattern. They use less paper, give consumers more size choices, AND save the retailer from needing as many patterns in stock.

Palmer/Pletsch McCall's Pant Patterns

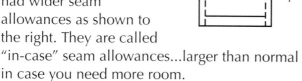

The latest direction for us is to join multi-sizing. We loved single-size patterns as they have all of the seam lines marked. But it just isn't practical any longer, so we are joining the ranks.

All Palmer/Pletsch McCall's patterns have had wider seam allowances as shown to the right. They are called "in-case" seam allowances...larger than normal in case you need more room.

Regardless of the size of the seam allowances allowed on the pattern you are using, we prefer to leave an even 1" on side, inseam, and waist seam after fitting to allow for fabric variables.

Body Shape and Age

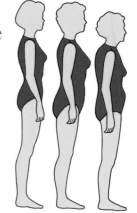

age 20   age 45   age 80

As we mature, our derriere gets lower and flatter due to gravity. Usually our waist thickens due to the space between the vertebrae narrowing. Our tummies get fuller due to relaxing muscle tone. Genetics also plays a role. We decided not to make a flat derriere pattern because the amount of flatness is not standard. Everyone is different!

For these reasons, Palmer/Pletsch patterns have alteration lines on the tissue. In the guide sheet we tell you how to tissue-fit.

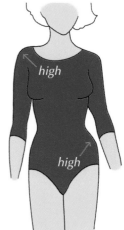

Posture

If you have carried books, babies, or groceries on one hip all of your life, your spine is probably curved and one hip is higher. If you see young people doing this, tell them to switch sides so they don't end up higher on one side.

Do All Pattern Companies Fit the Same?

Pattern companies have standardized sizing because you can't try on a pattern before you buy it. However, the ease and crotch shape will vary with each design. Some styles may require less altering because of the ease allowed. The computer grades the design, but people actually hand draft every design, so you do get that "human touch," which might affect the shape and hence your fit. But we have found that if you have "thighus gigantus" in a pattern from one company, you'll have it in similar-style patterns from another company.

CHAPTER 5
Tissue-fitting Basics

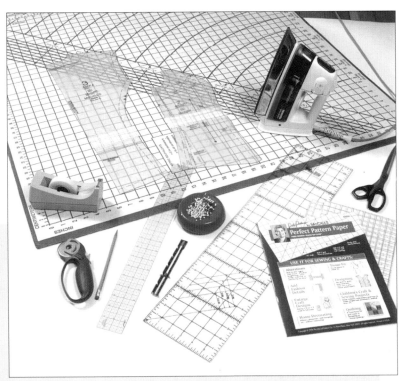

The Ten Steps to Perfect Pant Fit

1. **Press and trim the tissue (page 25).** Mark stitching lines on multi-size patterns. Palmer/Pletsch patterns use varied width seam allowances noted on the tissue.

2. **Tape crotch curve** on the right side of the pattern inside stitching line (pages 26).

3. **Pin tissue WRONG SIDES together** for fitting.

4. **Try on and determine alterations** (Chapter 6).

5. **Unpin; press from the WRONG SIDE to avoid the tape; alter** using a pencil, ruler, pins, tape, and alteration tissue.

6. **Repin pattern together.** BEGIN BY MATCHING HEMLINES to make sure front and back seams end up the same length. If not, trim them until even at the TOP (page 34).

7. **Try on. Check fit** using two mirrors, full-length and hand-held to see your back (see page 25).

8. **Unpin, press, and mark any additional alterations.**

9. **Pin tissue to your fabric.**

10. **Cut out the fabric. Sew crotch seams. Pin inseams and side seams WRONG SIDES TOGETHER. Try on and adjust.** Repin RIGHT SIDES TOGETHER. Finish sewing and pressing (Chapter 7).

Collect Your Alteration Tools

Work On a Gridded Cardboard Surface

You need a large work surface. No part of your tissue should hang off the surface while altering. The surface must be pinnable. Cardboard is the easiest surface on which to work. Place it on your kitchen counter for a comfortable work height.

Buy a gridded folding cardboard **cutting board** or a gridded cardboard **cutting table**. The grid makes altering easier.

To protect the surface when marking tissue patterns with marking pens, place plain paper under the pattern so ink won't bleed onto the table. In our classes we have students use a lead pencil only. They can later mark *final* alterations with a colored pen.

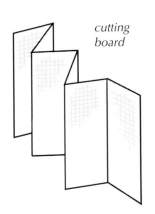

cutting board

Pattern Alteration Tissue

As long as you are "*tissue*-fitting," alter with *tissue*! Heavy paper or non-woven fabrics overpower the lightweight pattern tissue.

You can find brightly-colored tissue in a gift-wrap department or in an art supplystore, or try Perfect Pattern Paper from McCall's, developed by Pati Palmer at the suggestion of her students. It's the same weight tissue used in patterns so it is not over-powering. Since it's white, you can distinguish it from the pattern tissue. It has a handy grid printed on it, from 1/8" to 1", that makes alterations easy and accurate.

Perfect Pattern Paper Uses

• Add the same amount to several pattern pieces following the grid.

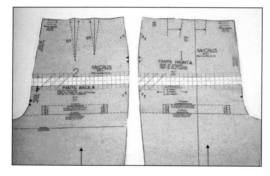

• If a pattern is printed on paper too heavy for tissue-fitting, trace pieces onto Perfect Pattern Paper.

• It's a "ruler."

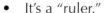

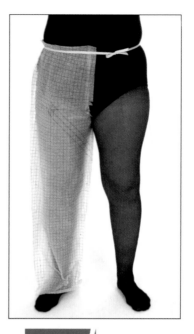

Marta had her body scanned and a pant pattern drafted for her by Unique Pattern Company. We traced it onto Perfect Pattern Paper to test the fit from this new technology. See www.uniquepatterns.com for more information on the body scanning technology.

Also, use this gridded paper to tissue-fit patterns printed on heavy paper.

Quick Tip — Cut tissue into 1", 2", and 3" strips and roll them onto an empty paper towel tube so you have them ready to use. Use strips just barely wider than the opening so you do not have lots of excess tissue under the pattern.

PRO Tip — Start a new habit. Alter with pattern pieces RIGHT SIDE up. Put alteration tissue UNDER the pattern. Tape pattern to alteration tissue from the RIGHT SIDE of the pattern.

Always put tape on the right side of the tissue only. Then always press the WRONG side of the tissue only, so the iron won't directly touch the tape. Make this a habit! Neatness and consistency will prove to be your friends.

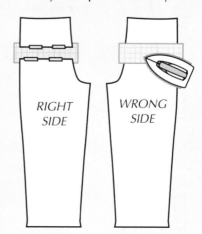

RIGHT SIDE

WRONG SIDE

Tape

Do not use clear cellophane tape! Use 1/2"-wide Scotch® Magic™ Tape, the translucent one. It won't scrunch the tissue or melt under the iron as easily as clear tape does. Using 3/4" tape makes your pattern stiff.

If you need to remove tape, slit tape at the lapping point and gently tear it.

pull up

slit tape

Soft Lead Pencil

We used to use a red, plastic-tip pen to mark alterations on the pattern, but it penetrates the tissue and makes a mess of your cutting board. Now we recommend using a pencil.

Pins

Invest in 1 3/8" extra fine (.5mm) glass-head (won't melt) pins. Dritz, Collins, and Clotilde offer wonderful, quality pins. These pins are made from steel so you can use your magnetic pin cushion to pick them up.

Don't use large quilting pins. They can be painful in tissue fitting. They also make a big hole in the tissue and fall out easily.

Use 1³/8" (.5mm extra fine, glass head pins. Don't use large quilting pins.

Mirrors

For accurate tissue fitting you shouldn't twist or bend to see your alterations. If you have a three-way mirror, great, but it's not necessary. All you need is a full-length mirror and a hand-held mirror for the rear view.

Accuracy, Accuracy, Accuracy

As teachers doing hands-on classes, we've seen it all. But the one thing that impresses us most is the need to be accurate. Otherwise, mistakes multiply. Here is how to avoid them.

Get the Pattern Ready

Press the Tissue

Do not tissue-fit or cut out the fabric using wrinkled tissue!! Press it with a DRY IRON set at the wool setting. A "warm" iron isn't hot enough.

Steam and water drips spoil the pattern tissue. Empty water from the iron if dripping is a problem.

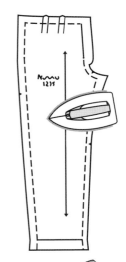

Trim the Tissue

Trimming around the tissue first improves your accuracy when cutting fabric. It keeps the tissue from moving during the cutting process. If using a multisize pant pattern, you can trim on the largest size if you are unsure of your fit.

Do you trim INSIDE or OUTSIDE the black line? On most patterns, from the stitching line to the black cutting line is 5/8". The width of the cutting line is 1/32" - 1/16", depending on the pattern brand.

5/8"

1/16"

Sewing machine companies mark metric measurements on the throat plates and pattern companies use inches for seam allowance widths. The 5/8" seam allowance is slightly more than 1.5 cm marked on your machine as the stitching guide.

To make things even more complicated, each machine is different. Pati's machine has a left and center needle position, but the markings are for the left position.

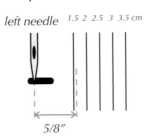

left needle   1.5 2 2.5 3 3.5 cm

5/8"

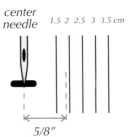

center needle   1.5 2 2.5 3 3.5 cm

5/8"

Pati likes the center needle position and since she trims patterns outside the black line, the 2 cm guide line is her seam allowance guide.

The answer? Cut where you want to, but be consistent. If you like seeing the black line, fine. (We do!) Place a piece of masking tape on the throat plate of your machine. Put your trimmed pattern on your machine and lower the needle into the stitching line. Mark a line on the masking tape at the pattern edge. Now you can sew exactly on the stitching line.

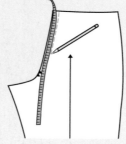

Draw line along edge of pattern for exact seam allowance you cut.

Draw line 1" from needle for the 1" "in-case" seam allowances.

←—1"—→

←5/8"→

wide masking tape

NOTE: Mark Stitching Lines

Multi-size patterns often have no stitching lines printed on the tissue. Mark the stitching lines with a pencil. Most tape measures are 5/8" wide. Use one as a guide when marking stitching lines.

If you have a low derriere, draw two more stitching lines on the lower back crotch curve, each 1/4" lower than the one above it. (Palmer/Pletsch McCall's patterns already have these lines printed on the tissue.)

Tape the Tissue

With tissue RIGHT SIDE UP, pin the front and back to a cardboard cutting board and tape the ENTIRE crotch INSIDE the stitching line.

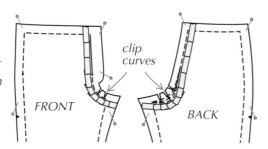

Tape up to the waistline even if your design has a fly front.

FRONT

clip curves

BACK

Tape the back crotch below the LOWEST stitching line. (See note to left, at bottom.) Use 1/2" tape. Lap short pieces of tape in the curved areas. Clip curves to the tape.

Tug lightly on the tissue to see if it is taped securely.

Pin Tissue Together

Pin pattern WRONG SIDES TOGETHER unless your left side is much larger than your right. Then pin right sides together and fit your left side.

Place pattern pieces on a large cardboard surface. Start pinning by matching HEMS FIRST. Put a pin through front and back vertically into cardboard through hemlines on inseam and outseam. Don't pin tissues together yet. Make sure all notches and seams match and that they are even at the top.

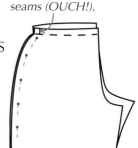

No pins in waistline seams (OUCH!).

Point pins down. (They won't fall out!)

Why might the inseams not match? Some designers make the back inseam shorter and have you stretch the back to fit the front. This puts extra ease in the pant front, which often ends up looking like puckers.

Our theory is that this technique came from men's tailors. Could the extra ease in the front be needed for extra body parts on men? At any rate, women don't need it.

We say trim inseams at the top until they are even and forget the stretch.

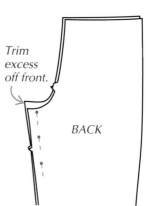

Trim excess off front.

BACK

Pin darts on the outside.

If you have pleats, pin them as they will be sewn. See Tissue-Fitting Trousers for more on pleated styles. (See page 75.)

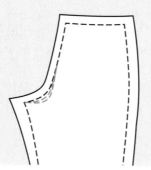

CHAPTER 6

Fit the Tissue

We will start with a plain fitted pant.

Try on the Tissue

Try the tissue on the RIGHT SIDE of your body, right side out with seams sticking out. (However, if your left side is much fuller than your right, pin the tissue so RIGHT SIDES are together and try it on the LEFT side of your body.) **Stand with legs APART so you can get tissue up to your crotch and centered between the legs.** This will help you get the back up to the waistline.

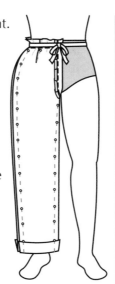

Tie 1/4" elastic around your waist. The bottom of the elastic should rest on the pattern waistline seam where the waistband will be sewn.

> **FIT Tip** Where is your waistline? The top of the hipbone at your sides is the normal location, but some people want to wear pants higher or lower. If you have waist rolls, use 1" elastic and put it where you want to wear your 1" waistband.

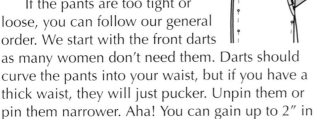

Ways to Gain Width
Eliminate Darts

If the pants are too tight or loose, you can follow our general order. We start with the front darts as many women don't need them. Darts should curve the pants into your waist, but if you have a thick waist, they will just pucker. Unpin them or pin them narrower. Aha! You can gain up to 2" in width. (See chapter 12 for more on darts.)

Straighten Center Front

If the pant center is slanted, straighten it.

Extend grainline to waist. Add tissue creating a new cutting line parallel to the grainline.

For fly fronts, cut on center front and make it parallel to grainline. Insert tissue.

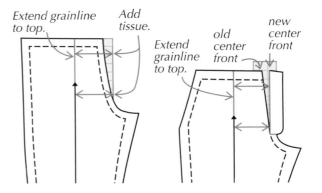

Extend grainline to top. *Add tissue.*

Extend grainline to top. *old center front* *new center front*

Add to the Side Seams

Tape an oblong "chunk" of tissue to the side seam. Make it wider than what you'll need. It can be short if you only need room in the waist or long if you need room in the hip or thigh area as well.

Try on the tissue, matching the center front and back to yours. Pin side seams to just skim your body shape. Leave 1" seam allowances to allow for variations in fabrics.

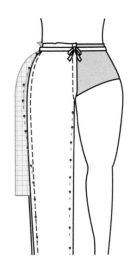

> **TIP:** Tape alteration tissue so the grid is the same on the front and back. This will help you pin accurately, adding the same amount to both front and back.

When you trim, gradually blend the edge of the added tissue into the edge of the original pattern.

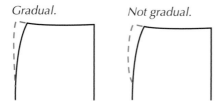

Gradual. *Not gradual.*

Take In the Side Seams

If pants are too loose, pin side seams deeper where you see vertical wrinkles until the tissue skims your body.

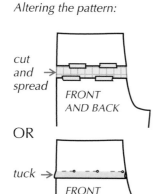

Pin deeper.

Crotch Depth vs. Length

This is crotch depth.   This is crotch length.

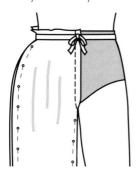 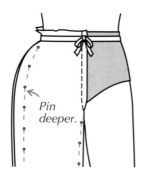

crotch depth

crotch length

pant crotch   *pant crotch*

Altering the pattern:

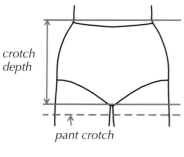

cut and spread

FRONT AND BACK

OR

tuck

FRONT AND BACK

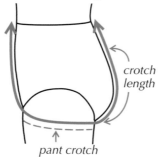

← shorten

shorten

FRONT AND/OR BACK

OR

← lengthen

lengthen

FRONT AND/OR BACK

How to Alter for Crotch Depth

If the crotch seamline is touching your body and the tissue doesn't come up to your waist at the sides, then lengthen the crotch depth.

Measure from pattern waistline stitching line up to bottom of elastic at the side for the amount you will need to add.

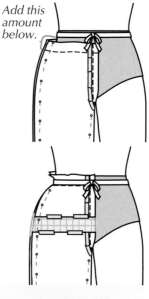

Add this amount below.

To lengthen, add tissue to back and front evenly.

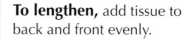

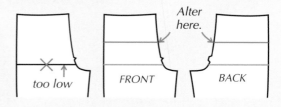

PRO Tip If the pattern's lengthen and shorten line is in the crotch curve, don't use it. Draw another line above the curve on both front and back.

Alter here.

too low   FRONT   BACK

Place alteration tissue under the area to be altered.

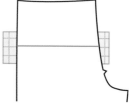

Cut on your alteration line. Anchor one section of the pattern tissue to the alteration tissue along one line on the grid.

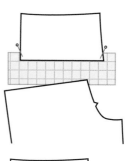

Spread the pattern the desired amount. Anchor the other part of the pattern.

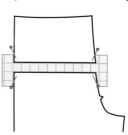

Use the lines on Perfect Pattern Paper as your ruler and to line up cut pattern pieces.

Tape in place and trim away excess tissue. There should be only a 1/4" lap of pattern over alteration tissue.

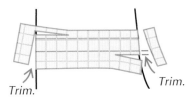

Horizontal lines align with cut edges.

Vertical lines align with cut edges.

Trim. *Trim.*

To shorten,

tuck the front and back the same amount.

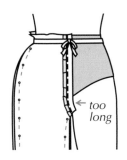

← *too long*

tuck

Tissue seam touches body. It will become longer in fabric.

Draw one line perpendicular to the grainline. If you need to shorten the crotch 1", draw another line 1" away and bring the two lines together.

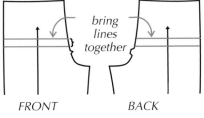

bring lines together

FRONT BACK

 Do not tape as you go. Tape only after all pieces are pinned and lying totally flat.

Pin tuck to board, then crease.

Finally, if the tuck is even all the way across, tape.

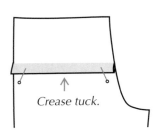

Crease tuck.

Tape.

How to Alter for Crotch Length

You can change crotch length in all of the following ways:

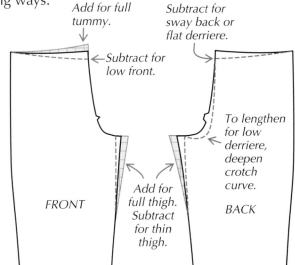

Add for full tummy.

Subtract for sway back or flat derriere.

←Subtract for low front.

To lengthen for low derriere, deepen crotch curve.

Add for full thigh. Subtract for thin thigh.

FRONT BACK

Smiles–Full Thighs

If the tissue pulls ("smiles") in the thigh area, let out the inseam in the front or back or both, depending on where you see the pulls.

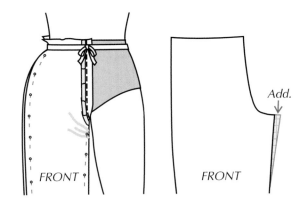

FRONT

Add.

FRONT

Frowns–Thin Thighs

Vertical wrinkles in the front or back mean you need less crotch length. Take in front or back inseam where you see the wrinkles.

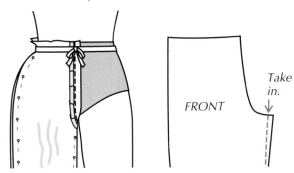

FRONT

Take in.

FRONT

False Smiles

This wrinkle can be removed by putting the center front of the tissue at the body's center front. You may need to unpin side seams or eliminate darts.

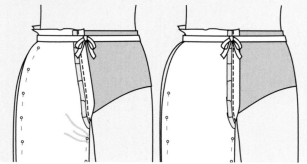

Full Tummy

If you see these wrinkles...

...pull pattern down at the center front until the wrinkles are gone. You'll gain extra length over the tummy.

Mark new waist seamline below the elastic.

Mark new seamline.

Pull down.

Low Front Waist

If you are low-waisted or want to wear your pants below your actual waist, you must fit them that way. (See Chapter 8, page 77 for additional tips for when you have trouser pleats.)

See REAL PEOPLE examples: Verna page 67; Marta page 51; and Jean page 88.

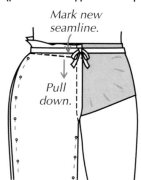

original waistline seam

new waistline seamline

Front Dimples

Even if you have eliminated the darts, you may have too much length in the front below where the darts are marked. This is because you have a hollow on both sides of your tummy.

Pull the tissue up just in that area until the droopiness is gone.

If this causes pulls in the front, let out the front inseam.

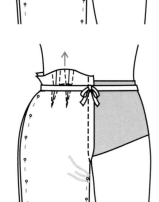

Full Tummy and Flat Derriere Combined—Side Seam is a Clue

If your side seam swings forward and you have these wrinkles:

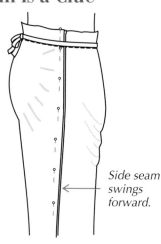

Side seam swings forward.

Pull up.

Mark new seamline.

Pull down.

Pull down in the front and up in the back until side seam is straight. Mark new waist seamline.

PRO Tip

Altering crotch DEPTH changes crotch LENGTH

It is a balancing act between the two that takes some trial and error to get right. Eventually you will develop an eye and just "see it!"

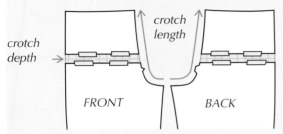

crotch depth →

crotch length

FRONT   BACK

Altering crotch LENGTH affects crotch DEPTH.

Adding or subtracting from crotch length may make crotch DEPTH suddenly comfortable or uncomfortable.

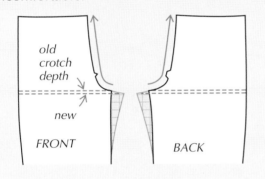

old crotch depth

new

FRONT   BACK

Bagginess in the Back

5-Step Solution to Eliminating the Baggies

Follow this special order. After fitting thousands of people in pants, we FINALLY learned that ORDER is important!!!

1. Pull up pants in the back until wrinkles are gone.

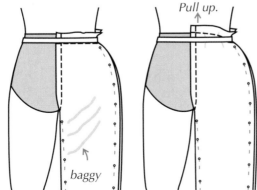

Pull up.

baggy

2. THEN check crotch depth.

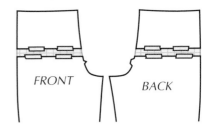

FRONT   BACK

   a. If it feels tight in FRONT and BACK, lengthen evenly, front and back.

   b. If tight (short) in the BACK ONLY, tape tissue to lower crotch seamline and clip to tape.

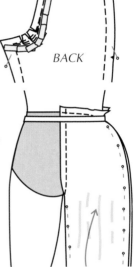

BACK

3. Now, bagginess is gone, but the back still seems FULL. If there is too much width at the lowest part of the derriere take a vertical tuck parallel to the grainline. The tuck needs to be taken EVENLY from **waist** to **hem**, even if this makes the waist too small.

To determine the amount, **pinch out the amount of excess** just below the derriere.

Whatever you can pinch here is the depth of the tuck all the way up and down.

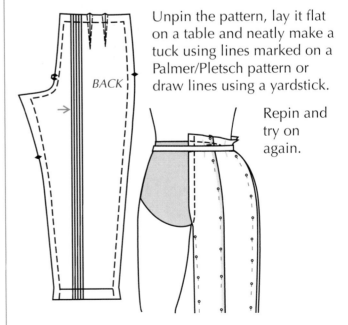

BACK

Unpin the pattern, lay it flat on a table and neatly make a tuck using lines marked on a Palmer/Pletsch pattern or draw lines using a yardstick.

Repin and try on again.

For more waist room, make darts narrower and/or adjust side seams. Add tissue to side seams if necessary.

4. Additional fullness may also be removed by taking in the back inseam.

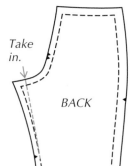

Take in.

BACK

5. NOW, look at the FRONT. Lifting the back often causes the front to smile. Let out the front inseam until the wrinkles are gone and the grain or crease line is straight.

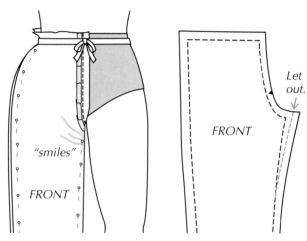

"smiles"

FRONT

FRONT

Let out.

FRONT

Knock Knees

If your inner legs are full or come together just above or at the knees, you may need to widen the inner leg as shown.

Draw a new stitching line. Add tissue to the inner thighs on front and back until you have an even 1" seam allowance. (See Alicia, page 62.)

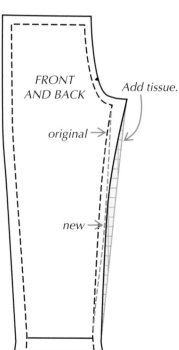

FRONT AND BACK

Add tissue.

original

new

Bow Legs

Usually we do the same thing as for knock knees, but the purpose is to fill in some of that blank space between the legs. Avoid fitted tapered pants if you want to camouflage bow legs.

Swayback

If you are hollow at the waistline at center back, you will see wrinkles puddling below the waistline.

Pull pants up at center back until wrinkles are gone. Mark new waistline seam below elastic. You may also need to sew deeper back darts.

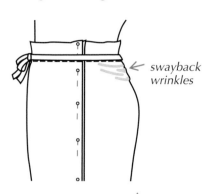

swayback wrinkles

Pull up.

new waist seam-line

Full Derriere

Wrinkles point to the derriere. Pants won't come up to waist in back.

Generally, you only need to add to the back inseam, but occasionally, you need to also add to the top. Deeper, or additional, back darts may also be needed.

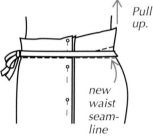

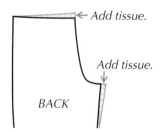

Add tissue.

Add tissue.

BACK

A way of adding length for a full derriere without letting out the inseam is to sew a more acute crotch curve. If you measured the new stitching line, it would be longer than the old one.

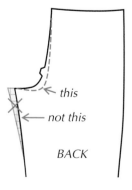

this

not this

BACK

Full Derriere with Flat Front

This is common with slender teenagers. Their almost "hollow" tummies don't need front darts for shaping. We usually eliminate them. More width may be needed across the back. Add to the side seam and inseam.

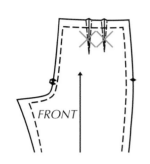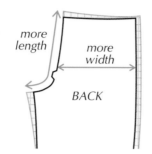

more length *more width*

BACK

FRONT

High Derriere

If you wear control top pantyhose with pants, the back crotch seam may hang too low as the pantyhose lifts the body. Redraw the back curve higher.

Redraw back crotch curve higher.

Length

If the leg is straight, you can change the length at the bottom.

If it is tapered or flared, alter in the knee area.

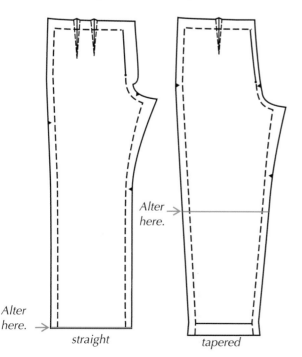

Alter here.

Alter here.

straight   *tapered*

When you shorten or lengthen a tapered leg, be sure to true the lines. As a general rule, mark the midpoint between the two lines. Then draw from one stitching line to the next through the midpoint. Do this for the cutting line as well.

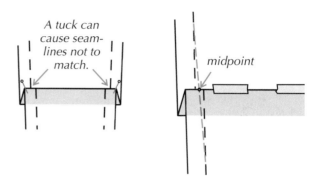

A tuck can cause seam-lines not to match.

midpoint

Leg Width

A straight-leg pant (16"-19" at the bottom) is universally flattering. You can change the leg width while tissue-fitting or, if making it narrower, later in fabric.

Do you want the legs narrower? Repin as shown until you like the width. At the hem, pin in the same amount on inseam and side seam. Taper to original seamlines at the knee, or higher if you have thin legs.

Or, if you have full inner thighs, you may want to take in the inseam beginning below the knee, while starting higher at the side seam.

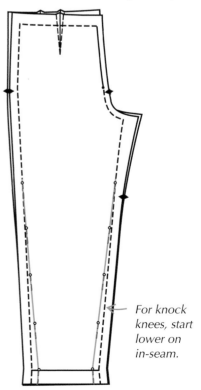

For knock knees, start lower on in-seam.

Extended Calves

If your calves are pulling the tissue to the back, let out side and inseams from just above the knee to hemline on the BACK ONLY.

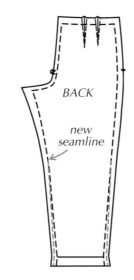

BACK

new seamline

Mark the Tissue

TIP: If the crotch seam in the tissue is touching your body, it will hang down at least 1/2" in most fabrics.

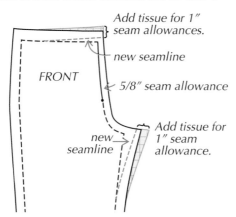

Mark the waist seamline at the bottom edge of the elastic while the tissue is on your body.

Take tissue off and mark pin positions on the rest of the seams if they are not in the original seamlines.

A roller ball pen will penetrate both layers of tissue so you can mark front and back seams at the same time.

NOTE: **DO NOT WORK WITH WRINKLED TISSUE.** Unpin the tissue and press with a dry iron.

Make all seam allowances 1" except crotch. If you have deepened the back crotch stitching line, trim the crotch seam allowance to 5/8".

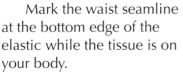

Add tissue for 1" seam allowances.

new seamline

FRONT

5/8" seam allowance

new seamline

Add tissue for 1" seam allowance.

PRO Tip

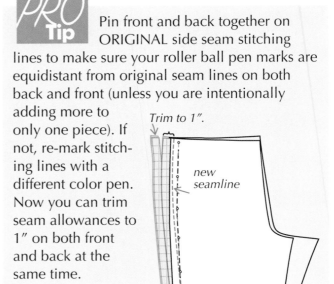

Pin front and back together on ORIGINAL side seam stitching lines to make sure your roller ball pen marks are equidistant from original seam lines on both back and front (unless you are intentionally adding more to only one piece). If not, re-mark stitching lines with a different color pen. Now you can trim seam allowances to 1" on both front and back at the same time.

Trim to 1".

new seamline

Repin pattern together, BEGINNING BY MATCHING HEMLINES to make sure front and back seams are the same length.

If you have added a lot to one inseam and not to the other (see below), match legs at hemline and if uneven at top, trim the longer one to match the shorter (see illustration at right).

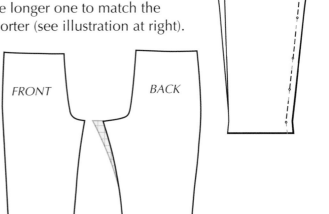

FRONT

trim off

FRONT   BACK

Waistband

Fold the waistband tissue in half lengthwise and wrap it around your waist. Mark where the ends lap. If you don't have 1" left on the ends, add tissue to the ends. That's all the fitting you need to do now!

You are ready to cut!!

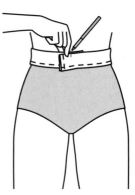

Summary of the Most Common Alterations

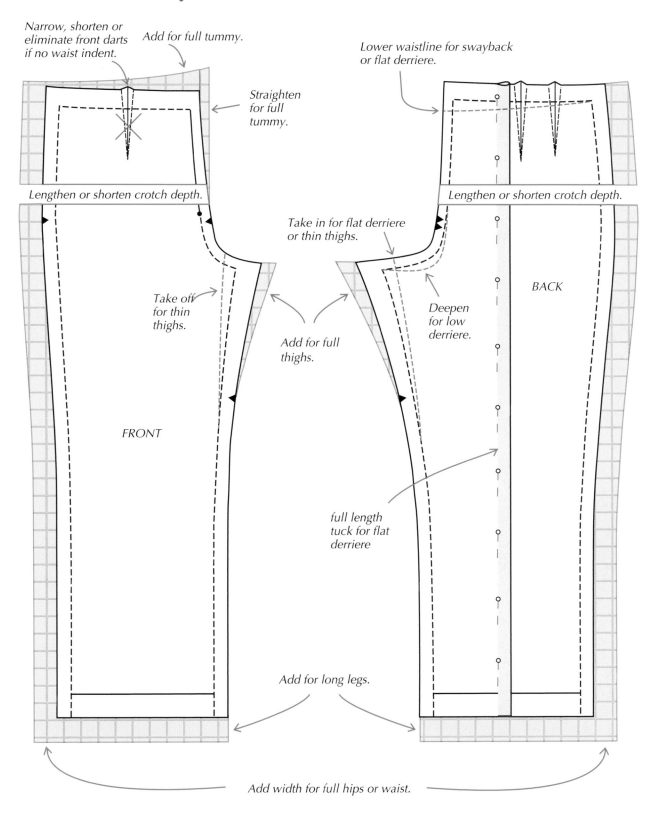

Narrow, shorten or eliminate front darts if no waist indent.

Add for full tummy.

Straighten for full tummy.

Lower waistline for swayback or flat derriere.

Lengthen or shorten crotch depth.

Lengthen or shorten crotch depth.

Take in for flat derriere or thin thighs.

BACK

Take off for thin thighs.

Add for full thighs.

Deepen for low derriere.

FRONT

full length tuck for flat derriere

Add for long legs.

Add width for full hips or waist.

NOTE TO TEACHERS: During the first tissue-fitting, use a pencil to circle on this page what your student needs to change with approximate amounts written as +3/4″ or -1/4″. You have our permission to make copies of this page to use in your classes.

CHAPTER 7

Fit-As-You-Sew

The Palmer/Pletsch **Fit-As-You-Sew** system will be one of the most important steps to a good fit, even if you are sewing with an already altered pattern. Why do we need to bother? Our weight fluctuates (for some on a daily basis!); we use fabrics of varying weights and drapability; and we don't **always** cut **perfectly** accurately. Fitting-as-you-sew allows you to deal with these variables and sew perfectly fitted pants.

Quick Tip We always sew pants in our underwear—then we are ready to try them on as many times as necessary (at least three times) without the dress/undress hassle.

- Cut out pants. See chapter 11 for cutting and marking tips.

- Sew the darts.

- Sew crotch seams starting 1½" from inseams to zipper opening.

- Insert zipper.

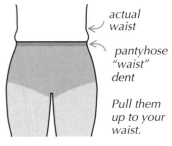

zipper opening

1½"

Get Ready to Pin-Fit the Fabric

Place pants on table and pin inseams and outside seams WRONG SIDES TOGETHER with pins in stitching lines, about 2" apart, and pointing down. There will be about a 1" hole in the crotch, which won't matter at this time.

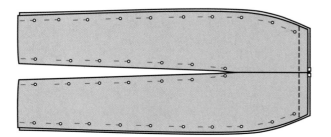

Try on pants right side out because your left and right sides may be different. Tie 1/4" elastic around your waist with the bottom of the elastic on the waistline seam. See pages 67 for when to use 1" elastic instead.

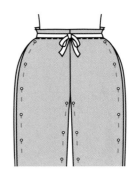

Now, Fit the Fabric

FIRST, is the elastic AT YOUR WAIST? That means if you are wearing pantyhose, they need to be at your waist also.

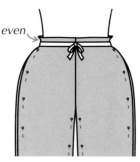

actual waist

pantyhose "waist" dent

Pull them up to your waist.

SECOND, is the bottom of the elastic on the seamline and even from the top edge of the fabric all the way around? **Get the elastic right before moving on.**

even

NOTE: You CAN fit yourself above fingertip level. You simply need two mirrors—a full length and a rear view—so you don't distort the fit by twisting to see your back.

Horizontal Wrinkles

This means the pants are tight in that area. Pin shallower side seams until wrinkles disappear.

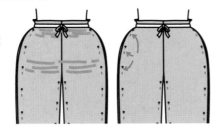

Vertical Wrinkles

This means the pants are too loose in that area. Pin deeper side seams until the wrinkles disappear.

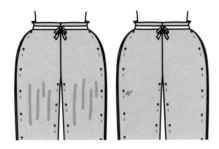

Uneven Hips

If one side is fuller and higher, pull down on the high side or up on the low side, depending on your crotch comfort.

The lower side will generally be flatter as well. If you see vertical wrinkles, pin a deeper seam on that side. (See Connie, page 55.)

Crotch Fullness

Often you will see excess fullness in the thigh area because the crotch in fabric is bias and can stretch. To remove this, start by pinning both front and back inseams deeper. One may need to be deeper than the other. For example, the back crotch is longer than the front and may need to be taken in more.

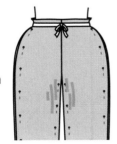 

Smiles

If you see smile wrinkles in the front and/or back, let out the inseam where you see the smiles.

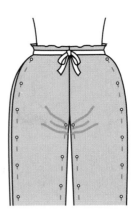

Crotch Depth

Technically, pants should hang down 3/4" to 1" from your body in woven fabrics and 1/4" to 1/2" in stretchy knits. It also depends on the style. Jeans fit more closely than trousers, and culottes hang down much lower. However, only YOU know how comfortable the crotch feels.

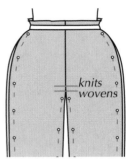

knits wovens

If too short, pull pants down EVENLY all the way around. (This is why we suggest a 1" waistline seam allowance.)

If too long, pull pants up EVENLY all the way around.

waistline

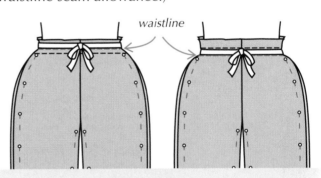

NOTE: (This adjustment can be done later, AFTER final sewing of crotch seam.) If only back crotch is tight, you are higher in the front with a low derriere. Sew back crotch lower, trim to 1/4" and try on. Repeat this process until the crotch is comfortable.

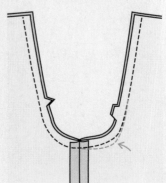

Baggy in the Back

If pants are baggy in the back, pull up at center back until wrinkles disappear. This often creates smiles in the front. If it does, let out front inseams.

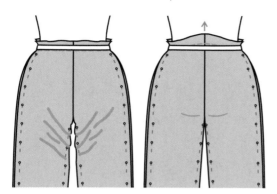

OUCH! Now you can't sit down. The pants have become too tight in the back crotch. If the front crotch seems long enough and only the back feels tight, sew

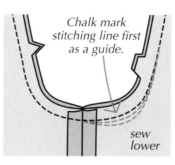

Chalk mark stitching line first as a guide.

sew lower

back crotch seam lower by 1/4" at a time. Trim seam allowance to 1/4" and try on. (See page 40.) The easiest way is to turn one leg inside out and put the other leg inside it; then stitch.

Sometimes, pulling pants up in the back to eliminate bagginess causes both front AND back to be tight. In that case, pull the pants down evenly all the way around until comfortable.

Full Tummy

The fabric is more sensitive than tissue so you may now see wrinkles pointing to the tummy. Pull pants down at center front until wrinkles disappear.

Pull down at center front

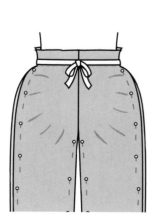
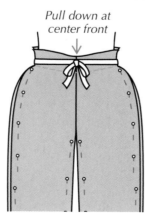

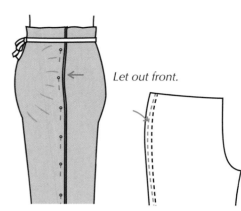

If the side seams pull toward the front, let out the front side seam only.

Let out front.

Darts

If darts pucker in front, make them narrower or eliminate them if your shape is straight in the front instead of curving in at the waist.

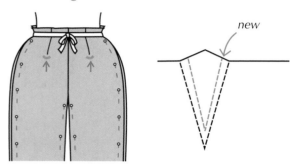

new

Back darts may need lengthening if you have a low derriere.

If there is a puddle of fabric below the front darts, or where the darts would have been, pull pants up in that area until puddle disappears. Mark your new stitching line at the bottom of the elastic. This is called "tweaking" the fit!

Pull up.

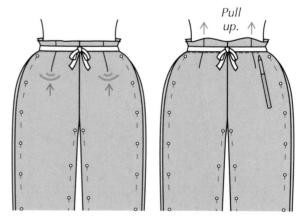

See pages 42-43 for "crotch oddities" that can be corrected in a finished garment.

See Chapter 12 for more dart fitting and fine-tuning tips.

Mark the Changes

chalk wheel

After you have the pants fitting well and all wrinkles gone, make sure you have pinned the side seams to your curves. The seams should come together gently along your body, not too tight or loose. As you pin, you can FEEL the body, so put pins next to it. Try to make your side seams smooth so they flow over lumps and bumps smoothly rather than pinning into your dimples.

Mark Waistline

Use a chalk wheel and mark just under the elastic. This chalk brushes off easily, so go to the sewing machine and baste along the chalk marks immediately after taking the pants off.

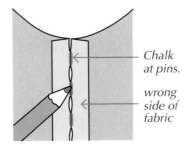

chalk waistline with chalk wheel

Mark Side Seams and Inseams

Take pants off, open seams at pins, and rub where pins go through the fabric with hard chalk. Now you will know where to sew.

Remove pins.

Chalk at pins.

wrong side of fabric

Back to Sewing

Before you started pin-fitting, you sewed the darts, sewed all but the bottom portion of the crotch seam, and inserted the zipper (if you were using one). Now it's time to finish sewing.

Sew Inseams

1. Working on a large flat surface, repin seams right sides together so they are ready to sew. Pin inseams beginning at hem. If they are uneven at top, check to see if:

   • Fabric layers are pinned unevenly.

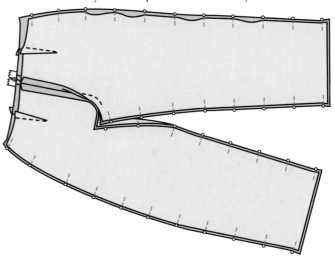

   • Or, if you let out or took in one inseam a lot more than the other, they will end up uneven. Trim them even at the top. (See page 34.)

(See page 34.)

Quick Tip

Keep a record of your changes for future sewing. Put your pattern back onto fabric and mark final stitching lines. Note the type of fabric used. Do this each time you sew this pant in different fabrics. This will teach you how to judge the way different fabrics fit.

wool crepe linen denim

If you have uneven hips, be sure to mark left and right waist stitching lines on your tissue with different color pens.

left
right

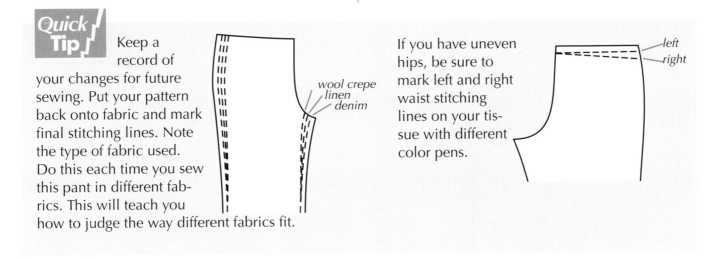

2. Sew inseams.

Quick Tip Use "taut sewing" to avoid puckering in long seams. Hold the fabric taut as if it were in an embroidery hoop while you sew. If one side of a leg seam is puckered, it was "eased" into the other layer. Taut sewing will help prevent this. Or, use a dual feed foot.

3. If seam allowances are too wide or uneven in width, trim them until narrower and even. Press open. Finish seam allowance edges.

Finish Sewing Crotch Seam

4. Pin inseams so they are matched at seamlines.

5. Sew the unsewn portion of the crotch seam.

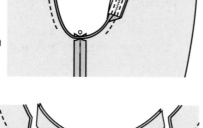

Reinforce by sewing again 1/4" from first row. Trim close to second row of stitching.

NOTE: Never clip or snip the lower crotch curve. It isn't necessary and will weaken it.

NOTE: Finish crotch so it will never rip out. Use the stretch overlock stitch if your machine has one.

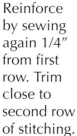

Sew Side Seams

Sew, trim to an even width, and press seams open. Finish seam allowances.

Trim waistline seam to an even 1" if using 1" waistband interfacing so you can match interfacing to top edge of fabric.

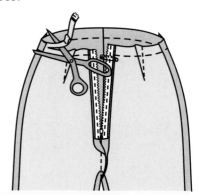

"Sanity" Tip: If you used a zipper longer than necessary in order to make topstitching easier, you will be cutting off the top stopper. Put a safety pin over the teeth to prevent the slider from coming off the top when you try on the pants.

Fit & Sew On the Waistband

Try on the pants and check to see if you need any "tweaking." If not, fit the waistband. (See page 111.)

Sew on waistband.

Check Fit

Before finishing waistband, try on the pants.

Wrinkles below band mean pants are too tight in the high hip area.

Let side seams out in this area on both sides.

These wrinkles mean you need to "unstitch" band ONLY in these areas, lower it, and restitch.

Pull up where wrinkled.

My Goodness, We Haven't Even Mentioned Ripping!!!!

If you really want perfect fitting pants, try them on 5-10 times while you sew to "fine-tune" the fit. Even letting out a seam 1/8-1/4" can make a major difference in fit...and that means **ripping!!!**

For example, letting out side seams only 1/8" can camouflage lumpy thighs, because you'll get an extra 1/4" in width on each side.

Let out here 1/8".

Cut stitches with a seam ripper every inch on one side of seam and pull thread on the other side. Pull out or brush off clipped threads.

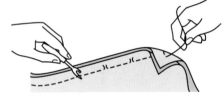

OR

Pull seam apart and then carefully cut stitches. Don't use this method on fine silks or knits.

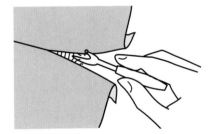

OR

Marta pulls bobbin thread until it breaks. Then she pulls the needle thread and then the bobbin thread again, Then there is no need to pick out short loose threads.

Make a Permanent Pattern

We don't recommend making a permanent pattern because you can't see through the tissue for refitting a year from now and you can't pull the pattern off of pins when marking fabric. However, some people want an indestructible pattern after they have done all of this fitting.

Fusing to Tissue

We would rather see you fuse to the tissue than to trace the pattern onto another paper. You won't be able to see how you vary from a standard size—unless you don't WANT to remember!!

To create a permanent pattern, attach fusible interfacing to the back of the tissue. To do this:

1. Place fusible interfacing on press board with fusible side up.

2. Place WRONG SIDE of pattern on fusible.

3. Press from the center of the pattern to the edges with a DRY iron on the wool setting. Avoid pressing over tape until you flip the pattern over.

4. Trim away excess fusible.

5. Using a press cloth, fuse again from the interfacing side.

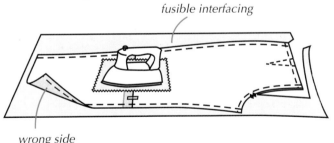

fusible interfacing

wrong side of pattern

Crotch Oddities

A new phrase? Yes! In the years we have been fitting people, we have seen it all and TRIED to find solutions. These things don't happen often, but rare doesn't mean nonexistent.

A Front Bubble

This means you need a straighter front seam. Pin a 1/8" deeper crotch seam in that area until the bubble disappears.

Two ways to get the same results:

Sew the seam deeper where you pinned. In essence you are straightening the crotch seam.

OR, if the seam is slightly slanted, let out the upper part of the seam, which also straightens it.

Pelvic Bone

If the pants are tight across your lower front, you may have an angular pelvic bone. Make the front seam more angular...allowing more room in front crotch length. Measure both stitching lines. The deeper one is longer.

If you are slanted in the pelvic area, shorten the seam by letting it out and making it less angular. Who would have guessed?? An oddity?? Yes!

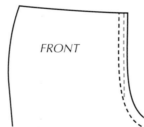

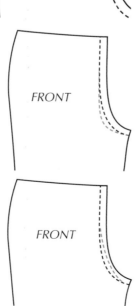

Very Flat in the Back

If you are very flat in the back, you might see a back bubble. Straighten the center back seam.

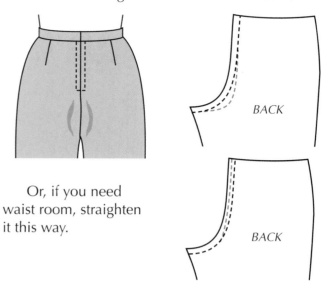

Or, if you need waist room, straighten it this way.

BACK

BACK

Low Flat Derriere and Full Tummy

For a flat back and full tummy, but small waist, your front crotch seam will curve in at the top or you can add curved darts. (See page 105 and Alicia, page 66.)

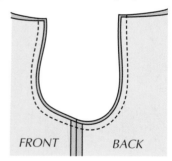

FRONT   *BACK*

High Front Low Back Oddity

If you are very high in the front and low in the back, this is what your crotch shape will look like.

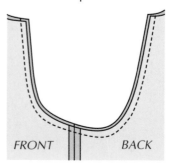

FRONT   *BACK*

Full Derriere

These changes usually work:

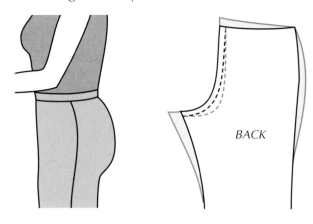

NOTE: If you add a lot to the front or back inseam when making these various fit adjustments, your crotch seam may become "peaked." Sew straight across and trim the peak away. An oddity? No comment.

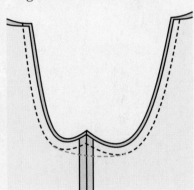

Concepts to Remember— More Oddities

By deepening or lowering the back crotch curve, you add length to it.

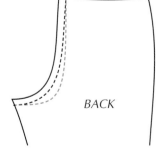

BACK

If you lower waist at top but let out the inseam, the crotch length may end up the same length as the original.

BACK

Thighs Pull When Walking

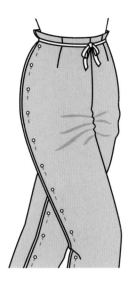

If your pants pull uncomfortably when walking and yet fit when standing, the solution is not easy. We teachers know!! First, make sure the crotch isn't too long. It may be caused by you having full front thighs, a protruding tummy, or a high front crotch.

Pull up the center front only, which moves the drape of the pants forward.

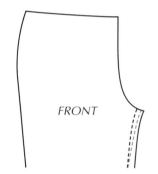

FRONT

Or, let out the front inseam for full front thighs

Or, pull up pants evenly all the way around for more movement. Lower the back crotch curve if necessary until comfortable. (See page 38.)

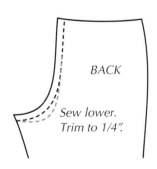

BACK

Sew lower. Trim to 1/4".

The oddity? Look at a set-in sleeve in a fitted garment. If the armhole is cut high, you can move your arm full circle. You are restricted in a low-cut armhole.

Similarly, a close-fitting crotch can give your legs more movement.

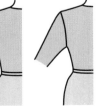

43

CHAPTER 8

Real People/Fitted Pants

Attending a Palmer/Pletsch workshop can be dangerous. We have found most of the REAL PEOPLE in this section by getting to know their bodies during Palmer/Pletsch Fit and Pant Fit Workshops. As you follow the steps each used to get her well-fitting pants, we hope you will begin to "see the light." We thank them profusely for being willing to help you learn by their example. They love fashion sewing as much as we do and we all want it to stay alive for future generations to enjoy!

Susie
IN A FITTED PANT

Susie is from the San Francisco Bay area and is a Palmer/Pletsch sewing instructor. She volunteered for the book photography while she attended a workshop in Portland. Susie told us that she'd love to participate, but she has full thighs. We told her that we wanted her full thighs to be in the book!

The key is to start out with a pattern that is as close to the right size as possible. (See chapter 4.)

The Front Before

There are a few wrinkles pointing to her inner thigh.

The Side Before

More width is needed at the upper side seam.

The Back Before

The tissue isn't coming up to her waistline at the center back. There are wrinkles pointing to the inseam.

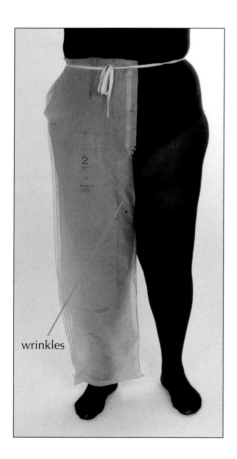

wrinkles

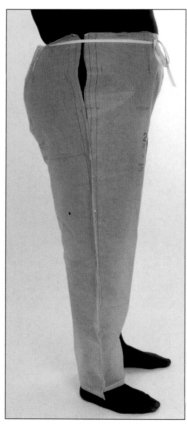

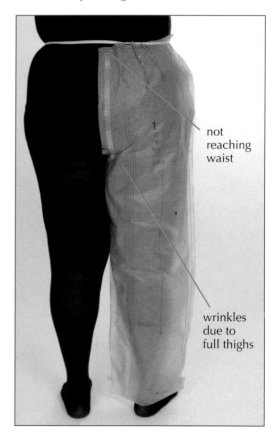

not reaching waist

wrinkles due to full thighs

When the tissue doesn't come up to the waist at the center back, the temptation is to add at the top of the center back. However, adding at the top won't remove the wrinkles at the inseam. If you let out the inseam (page 29), the wrinkles will go away AND the tissue will come up to the waist at the center back!

The Front After

Tissue has been added to side front and back and pinned to her shape. (See page 27.)

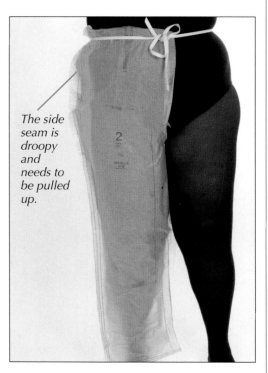

The side seam is droopy and needs to be pulled up.

The Back After

Since Susie had smiles in both the front and the back, we let out the inseams equally. This created enough length to get the tissue up to her waistline at the center back.

Susie needs a third dart at the waist near the side seam to curve the tissue into her waist.

We need to remove some of what we added from the back inseam as it is too full. More was needed for her fuller thighs in the front than in the back.

The Front After Adjustments

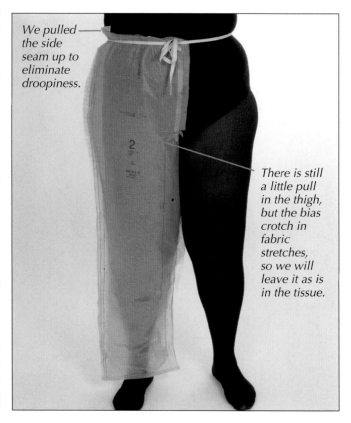

We pulled the side seam up to eliminate droopiness.

There is still a little pull in the thigh, but the bias crotch in fabric stretches, so we will leave it as is in the tissue.

The Side After

The side seam hangs straight. It is time to mark the bottom of the elastic.

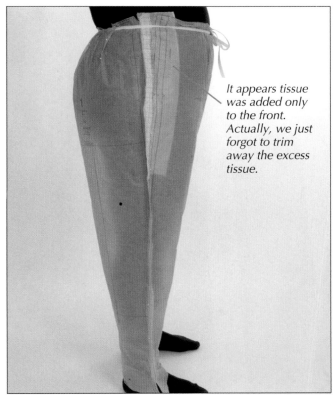

It appears tissue was added only to the front. Actually, we just forgot to trim away the excess tissue.

Pin-fitting in Fabric

The Front View

Everything looks good except that she is smaller on the left side.

The Back Before

The left side seam needs to be taken in and pulled down.

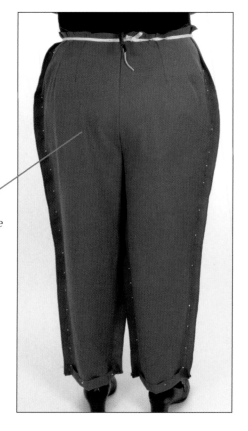

To eliminate wrinkles, take in seam and pull pants down.

The Side View

The pants hang perfectly.

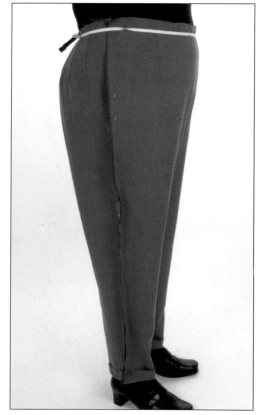

The Back After

We pinned the left side slightly deeper and pulled the pants down slightly over the middle dart to get rid of the wrinkles.

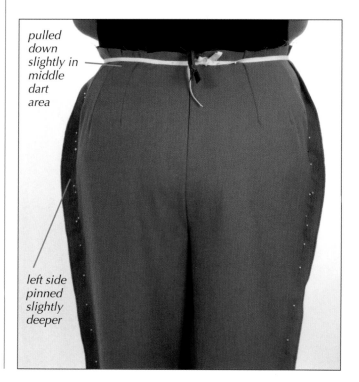

pulled down slightly in middle dart area

left side pinned slightly deeper

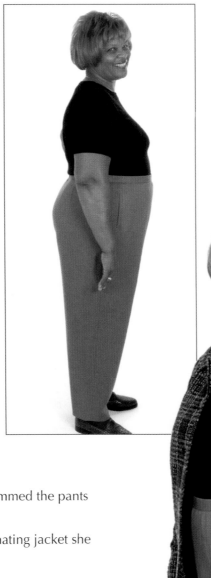

The Finished Pant

The finished pants look great. Susie hemmed the pants with a slight break on the shoe.

She completes the outfit with a coordinating jacket she sewed to go with her pants.

Melissa
IN A FITTED PANT

We chose Melissa, Pati Palmer's 17-year-old daughter, to show you how well commercial patterns **can** fit. She is taller than the standard height used by the pattern companies, so we added length. As she matures, she will have to see how she begins to vary from the standard and make alterations so pants will fit.

Melissa measures 37½" at the hip or a misses pattern size 12. (We told her it was only a number since she wears a size 6 in ready-made pants!) She is 5' 9½" tall, has a flat tummy and a rounded derriere (typical of a slender, youthful figure).

The Front

She is so flat in the tummy that she doesn't need the front dart. Or, we might just make it a little narrower. We could let out her front inseam just a little to remove the slight wrinkles pointing to it, but it is so minor we will do it in fabric.

We added 3" length to her legs, and allowed 1" seams at sides, inseams, and top, and 5/8" in crotch. Now she is ready to cut.

3" added using the gridded Perfect Pattern Paper (See page 28.)

The Side

The side seam hangs straight except for curving slightly toward the front thigh. Letting out the front inseam in fabric will take care of that.

If she wants the back to cup in more under her derriere, we could take in the back inseam.

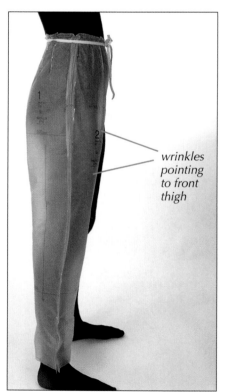

wrinkles pointing to front thigh

The Back

The back looks good. It is a little full in the back thigh area. Since it is minor, we will take in the back inseam in fabric rather than adjusting it now in tissue.

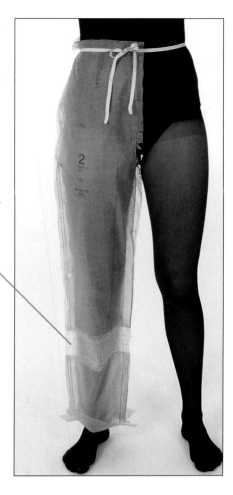

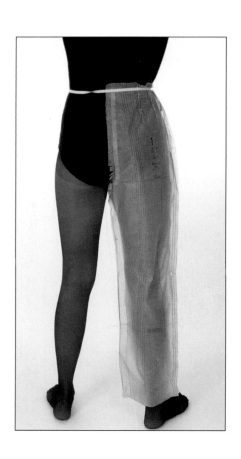

The Fabric Sides

The side seam is straight and there are no wrinkles. Yes, that is the zipper sticking out at the top in the back. We used an 18" zipper because we had one in red in our stash (the sewing on a Saturday night trick!). We will cut off the extra length after we sew on the waistband.

The Fabric Back

She would like the pants to fit more closely below the derriere.

Extra fullness can be removed by making back inseam deeper.

Melissa's Finished Pant

The Fabric Front

The fabric is a knitted suede cloth. The zipper and darts have been sewn in the back and the crotch seam was sewn to within $1\frac{1}{2}$" of the inseam. We pin the inseams and out-seams wrong sides together. Melissa tries the pants on right sides out with the bottom edge of the elastic on the waist seamline 1" from the top edge.

Marta
IN A FITTED PANT

You saw Melissa, 16. Now we have Marta, not quite 60. Marta says she used to be just like Melissa. Oh well, we dress for who we are NOW!

Front Silhouette

Marta is thick in the waist and has a common baby boomer figure. She is not knock kneed, but her upper inner legs are full.

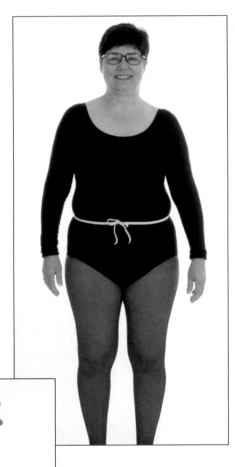

Side Silhouette

Marta is somewhat flat in the back for her size and full in the tummy. Her waistline is lower in the front than in the back.

Measure

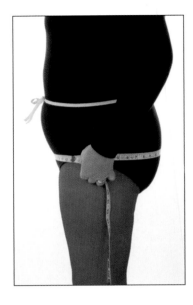

Marta measures 43" in her hips, which is between an 18 and a 20. Remember in "How to Buy the Right Size," we say that when you are between sizes, go to the smaller size unless you have a flat derriere. Marta used to go to a 20 and take a tuck in the back, but after l osing her thyroid, she got fuller in the front by quite a bit, compared to her back. Now she prefers to start with a size 22 to accommodate her front, taking a larger tuck in the back than on the size 20.

Experimentation is the key. She could make any size fit, but prefers to find the easiest one overall to work with.

The Front Before

Marta tries on the tissue. The tissue's center front is not reaching hers. There are also some wrinkles pointing to her tummy. The crotch is too long in the front. The dart points to a hollow and bubbles at the tip. Also, there are wrinkles pointing toward the front inseam.

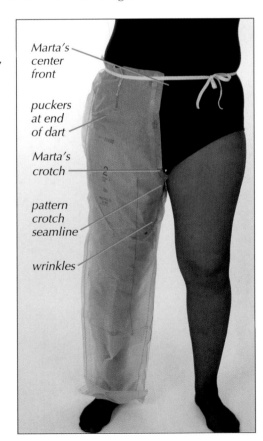

Marta's center front

puckers at end of dart

Marta's crotch

pattern crotch seamline

wrinkles

The Side Before

You can tell the front is too long by the way it pooches out and the drag lines from the side toward her knees. Marta's waist is higher in the back.

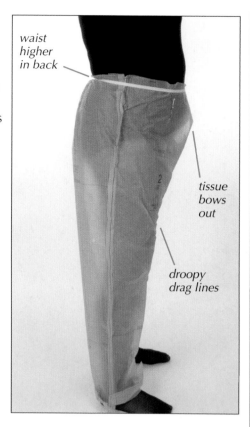

waist higher in back

tissue bows out

droopy drag lines

The Back Before

The back looks good. Vertical wrinkles mean there is a little excess width across the back.

Note that the waist-line seam on the tissue doesn't reach her waist on her fuller right side-back hip. We will check that later to see if we need to add tissue to the top.

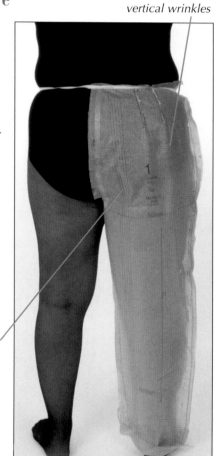

vertical wrinkles

excess tissue to be pinned out

The Front After

We pulled up the front tissue, and the pant front fits fine. Since she needed all of the length in the back and since this is a plain pant, pulling up the front is the easiest solution. (See page 30, low front waist.)

We unpinned the dart, which allowed the tissue to come to Marta's center front. The dart was in a flat area of the body, so it wasn't needed. (See page 27, darts.)

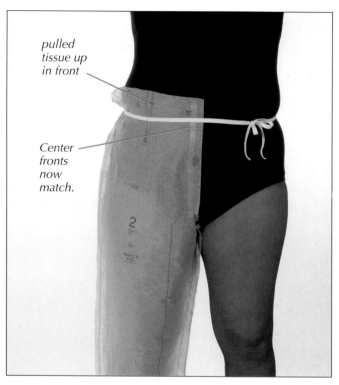

pulled tissue up in front

Center fronts now match.

The Back Adjusted

We pinched and pinned a tuck at the lowest part of the derriere to see how much width to remove.

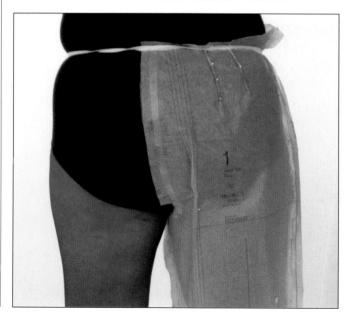

51

The Back After

Marta took off the pattern and taped in a full-length vertical tuck, removing 1" of width across the back. The back width now looks good.

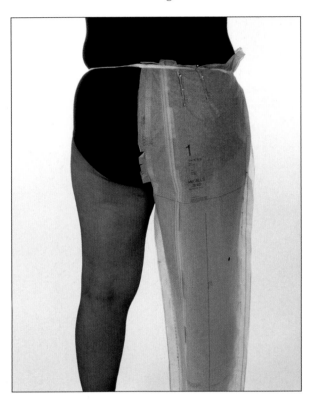

The Side Before

Because of the flat-derriere tuck in the back, she now needs to add to the waist at the side seam.

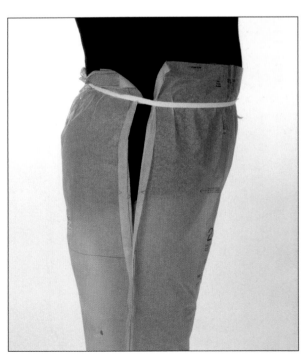

The Side After

She has added tissue to the front and back and repinned the side seam to fit her body. (See page 27.)

The front seems to droop a bit. We will pull up the front a little more.

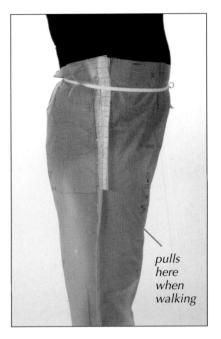

pulls here when walking

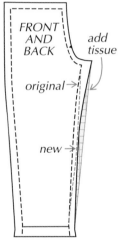

FRONT AND BACK

add tissue

original →

new →

Marta also felt the tissue pulling a little on her front thigh. She will let out the inseams from nothing at the top, coming straight down and back to the original seam below her knee. This gives more room for her full inner thighs. (See page 32, knock knees.)

We can now mark the bottom of the elastic so she will know where to sew on her waistband.

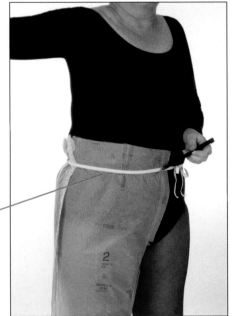

waistline seam marked

Marta is lower in the front than in the back. Once her waistline is marked, she leaves a 1" seam allowance above her waistline marking.

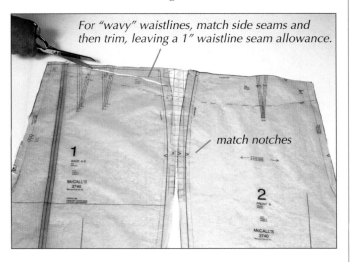

For "wavy" waistlines, match side seams and then trim, leaving a 1" waistline seam allowance.

match notches

The Fabric Front

They look great. The left side is a little full because it is smaller and we had tissue-fitted the right side.

excess fabric

The Fabric Side

The seam is straight and there are no wrinkles.

The Fabric Back

The excess fullness in the back inseam is caused by the bias crotch seam stretching. She also needs to pin the left side seam deeper and pull up the pants a little on that side. (See page 37, take in back inseam.)

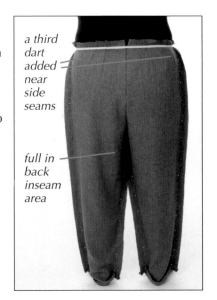

a third dart added near side seams

full in back inseam area

She took in the back inseams 3/4" and they look better. She added a third back dart toward the side for her high hip roundness. The dart is curved into her waistline (see page 105).

Place Welt Pockets Before Sewing Seams

For welt pocket placement she cut two 1/2" x 5½" strips of the gridded Perfect Pattern Paper (see page 139).

We taped them in place 1¾" from the waistline seam and 8" from the center front to the top of the welt and 9" from the center front to the bottom. Since one side is flatter, the pockets will be closer to the side and waistline seam on that side.

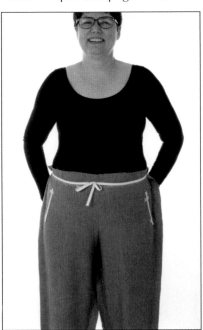

The pockets will be sewn before the side seams.

Chalk-Mark Stitching Lines

Marta chalk-marks the waistline. After taking off the pants, she will chalk the side seams and inseams where the pins are before removing them.

The Waistband

Marta wraps the waistband and interfacing around her waist, pinning it at the center back where snug but comfortable. She chalks center front and sides as well as darts for matching points when she pins the waistband to the pant. This will simplify adjusting the waistband for her two different sides.

The Finished Pants

They look good from the front, back, and side views. Marta hemmed them with a little drape on the front of the shoe so the pants will show less leg when she sits.

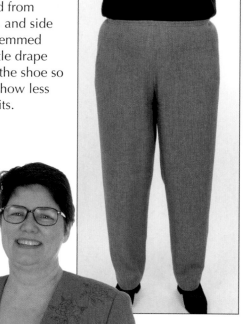

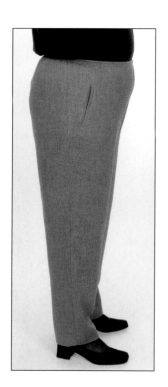

Marta is the creative one on our team. She is heavily into machine embroidery these days. She didn't just make a gray jacket to go with her pants, she embellished it. This tone-on-tone design is from a Martha Pullen redwork design. Redwork machine embroidery looks like outline stitching done by hand.

Connie
IN A FITTED PANT

Connie, a Palmer/Pletsch instructor from Indiana, not only volunteered to be in the book, but to edit it as well. She helped edit *Fit for Real People* and did a great job, so we asked her to help us with this one too! Thank you Connie!

Connie measures 40½" in the hip, which would be a size 16. She has some tummy fullness and a slightly flat derriere.

Connie also has a very high right hip. We will fit the high side in tissue and then take in the left side when we fit her in fabric.

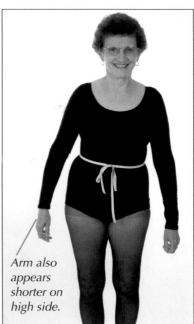

Arm also appears shorter on high side.

Front Before

This is a multisize pattern (14/16/18) with a finished hip width of 43", 45", or 47". We trimmed around the size 16. This gives her 4½" of ease, which is plenty even if we need to remove some width across the back for her flatter derriere. There are wrinkles pointing to the inseam in the front.

Front After

Since she needs more crotch depth for her high hip, we pulled the tissue down at the side. Most of the crotch smiles are gone. Letting out the inseam would have removed wrinkles also, but would have made the legs too wide for her thin thighs.

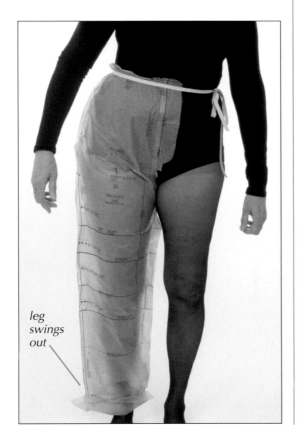

leg swings out

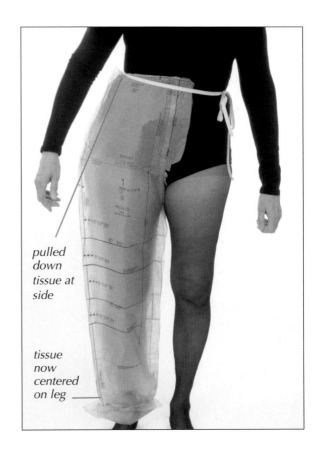

pulled down tissue at side

tissue now centered on leg

Back Before

We see the same thigh wrinkles in the back.

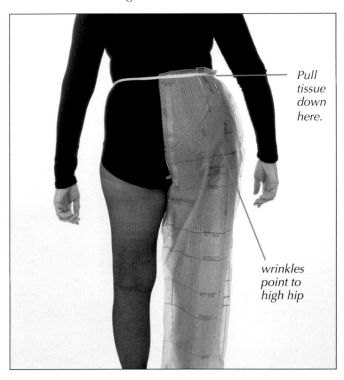

Pull tissue down here.

wrinkles point to high hip

Back After

After pulling the tissue down at the side, most of the wrinkles are gone. However, there is fullness across the back at the lowest part of the derriere.

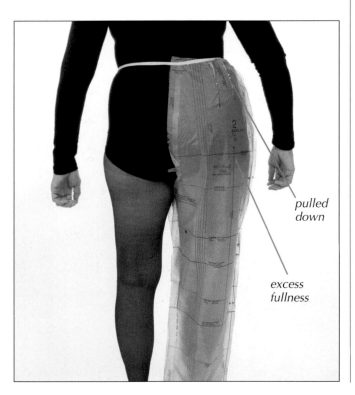

pulled down

excess fullness

We pinned a tuck to see how much needs to be removed. (See page 31, back tuck in tissue.)

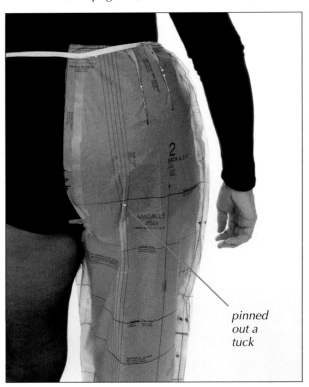

pinned out a tuck

We pinned out 1/2″ from waist to hem to remove the excess width. We also added tissue at the top to allow for a 1″ seam allowance for her full side.

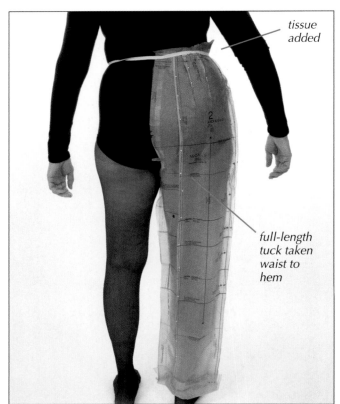

tissue added

full-length tuck taken waist to hem

Center Front

The center front of the pattern is not at Connie's center front. The pattern is slanted at the center front. By straightening it, we will get more width over the tummy.

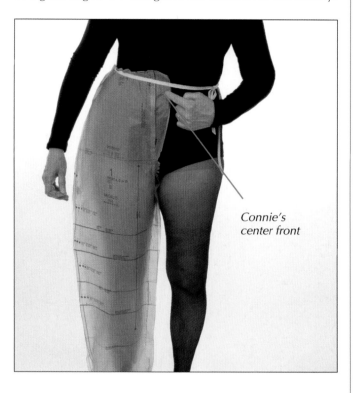

Connie's
center front

We have straightened the center front, making it parallel to the front grainline. This allowed the front to hang better over her tummy.

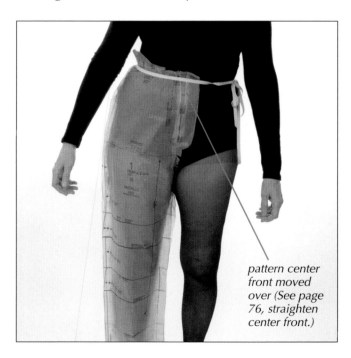

pattern center
front moved
over (See page
76, straighten
center front.)

(See page 76, straighten center front.)

We prefer to fit only one side of the body, the fuller side, and later pin-fit the smaller side to fit in fabric. However, if someone is very uneven and has a very wavy waistline and you want to see how they differ from side to side, you can buy two patterns, fit one side and then the other, then try both legs on as a whole pant. We try to avoid this. After gaining confidence, Connie now cuts both sides at once and then pin-fits the fabric to her smaller left side.

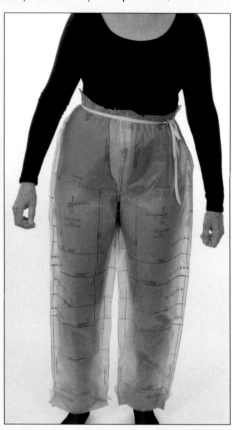

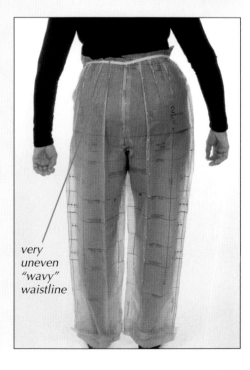

very
uneven
"wavy"
waistline

57

Pin-fitting in Fabric

Since we cut both sides from the pattern fitted to Connie's right side, we will need to adjust her smaller left side in fabric. You can see it is too large and too long for her left side. (See page 37, uneven hips.)

Adjust for smaller left side.

We pulled up the left side and pinned the left side seam deeper.

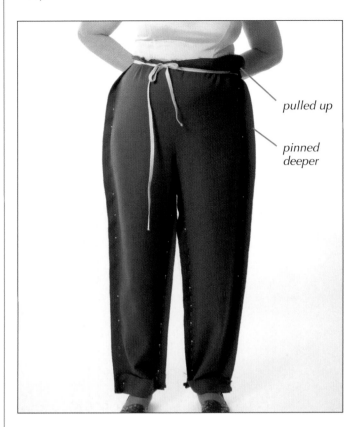

pulled up

pinned deeper

The left back is also too full and it droops. The back inseams look a little full as well. This is common as the back crotch is bias and can stretch, especially in this fine wool crepe.

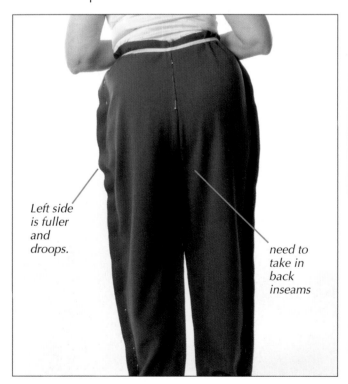

Left side is fuller and droops.

need to take in back inseams

The side seam on the left back needs to be taken in a little bit more. We could deepen the back inseams a little more as well.

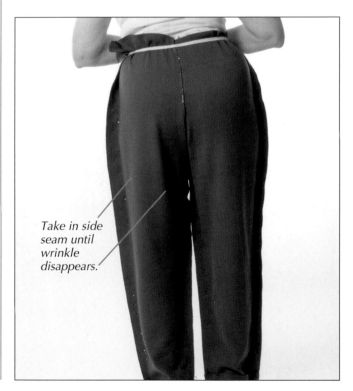

Take in side seam until wrinkle disappears.

The pants hang nice and straight viewed from the side.

Connie could let out the front inseam if she wants less emphasis on the tummy. However, she decided not to because the leg would be too wide. She'll wear a jacket to camouflage her tummy.

Connie marks her waistline at the bottom of the elastic with a chalk wheel.

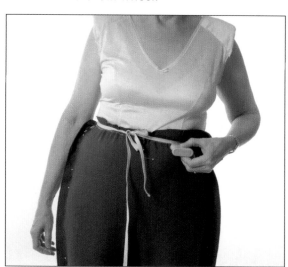

Her finished pants look great from the front...

...and from the side...

and from the back...

and are perfect with her creative jacket creation!

59

Melissa
LOW RISE ON A TALL TEEN

Melissa has an almost perfect figure. She wanted low rise pants with a flared leg. We will need to make sure the yoke fits her curvy shape. (See contour waistband, chapter 18.)

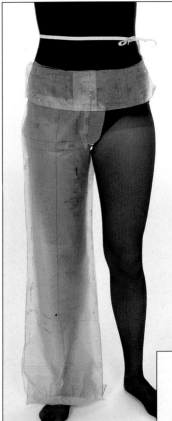

The Front Before

The front fits well.

The Back Before

The back looks good. We might take the back inseam in a little in fabric.

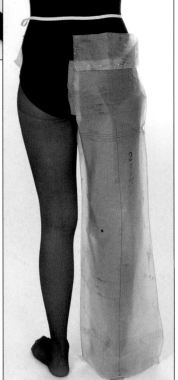

The Side Before

The side seam is straight. We need a little added to the yoke side seam.

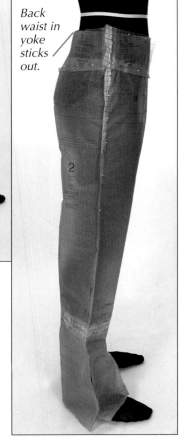

Back waist in yoke sticks out.

The Side After

We added Perfect Pattern Paper to the sides and repinned the pants to fit. The yoke is sticking out in the back.

We pinned a dart in the back yoke to eliminate the fullness. The dart goes to nothing at the bottom of the yoke, so it can be taped out before cutting.

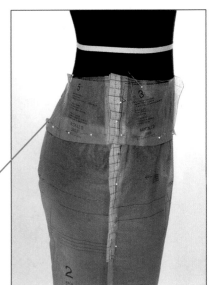

dart in yoke

The Pant in Fabric

Front

The pants are pinned with seams on the outside. We pinned deeper seams due to this stretchy wool/spandex fabric so Melissa could keep the pants up.

Side

The side seam falls straight.

Back

We will pin the back inseam deeper.

The Finished Pants.

Mom made a fleece hooded top to wear with them. The pants fabric is a fabulous quality wool and spandex. We did have to take the side and inseams in a little more in the finished pant due to the stretchiness of the fabric. Otherwise she wouldn't have been able to keep them on.

Alicia
IN A FITTED PANT

Alicia is a Palmer/Pletsch instructor living in Mississippi. She has a better figure than most of us, but her knock-knees cause a pant fitting challenge. Her hips measure 39″ which is a size 14. Since the pattern has 1″ side seam allowances, we should have enough width to take a flat derriere tuck if necessary.

The Front Before

The multisize pattern was trimmed to her size. It is a Palmer/Pletsch pant pattern with 1″ side and inseam allowances. Wrinkles are pointing to her knock knees.

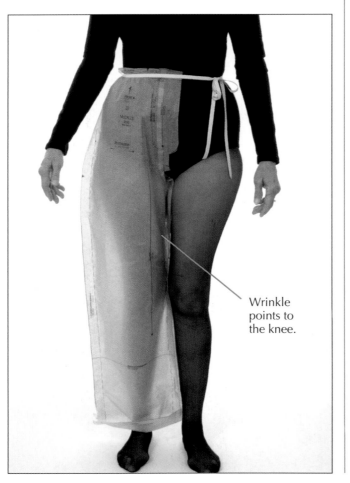

Wrinkle points to the knee.

The Back Before

The center back is not coming up to her waist. The wrinkles under her derriere mean that we need to deepen her back crotch seam which will add length and allow the tissue to come up under the elastic.

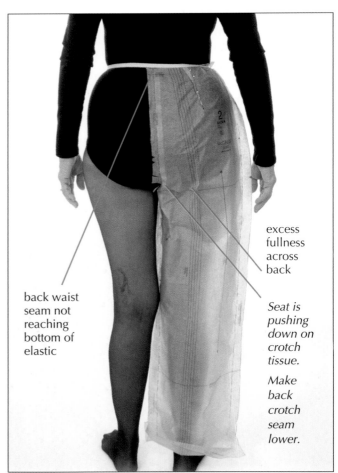

excess fullness across back

back waist seam not reaching bottom of elastic

Seat is pushing down on crotch tissue.

Make back crotch seam lower.

62

The Back After

We lowered the back crotch seam, making it longer and allowing the tissue to come up under the waist elastic. The full-length vertical tuck in the tissue removed 1" of width. (See page 31, back tuck.)

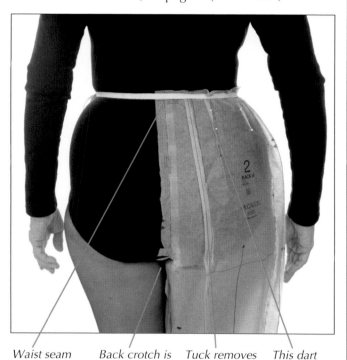

Waist seam now at bottom of elastic.

Back crotch is taped lower.

Tuck removes excess width.

This dart is pinned narrower.

The Front Before

The center front isn't coming to her center.

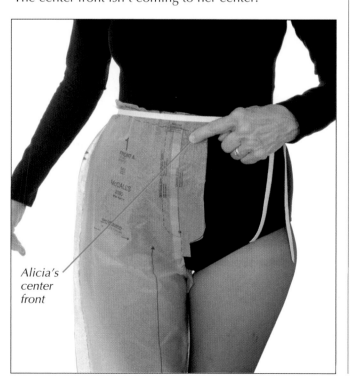

Alicia's center front

The Front After

We let out the side seam until the centers matched. We pulled the tissue down over her full tummy (page 30).

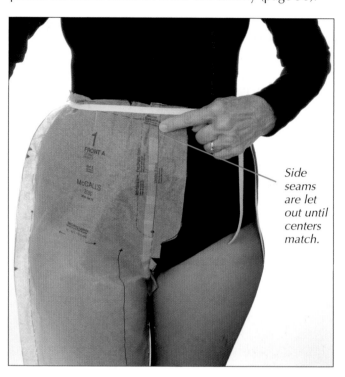

Side seams are let out until centers match.

We need to let the inseams out more in the knee area. See knock knees, page 32.

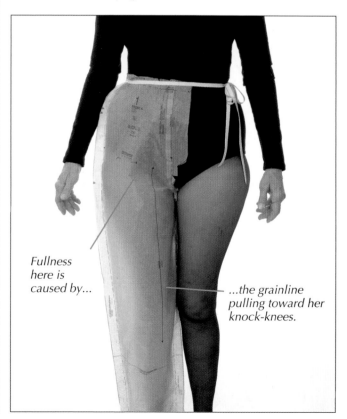

Fullness here is caused by...

...the grainline pulling toward her knock-knees.

63

The Front and Back After Additional Fitting

We let out the front inseam 1/2" and went straight down past the knee.

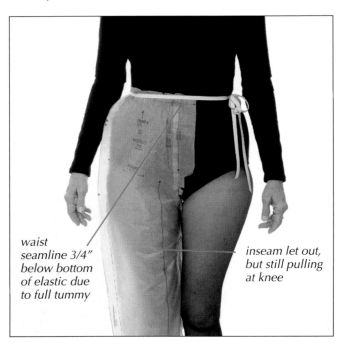

waist seamline 3/4" below bottom of elastic due to full tummy

inseam let out, but still pulling at knee

We let the front inseam out a little more until the leg tissue and grainline fall straight.

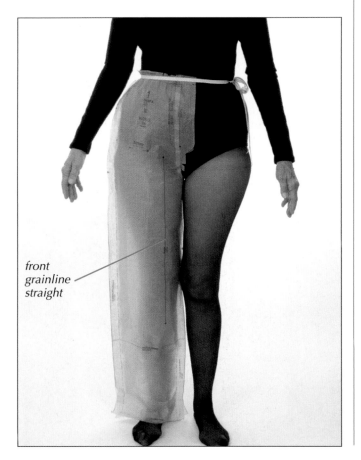

front grainline straight

By letting out the inseam past the knee, the back is hanging straighter also.

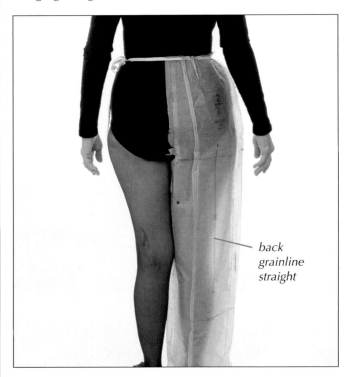

back grainline straight

Alicia marks her new waistline seam at the bottom of the elastic with a red pen. She will add tissue to maintain 1" seam allowances over her tummy.

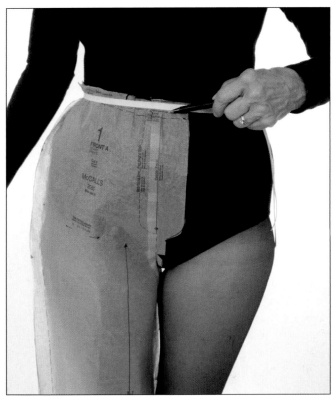

Fabric Front Before

Alicia cut the pants out of a beautiful wool crepe. Since her right side is slightly larger than her left, we need to adjust for the differences in fabric. It appears she could still use a little more room in the knee area as wrinkles are pointing to the knee.

Wrinkles point to knees.

Fabric Front After

We have pulled up the left side for her flatter hip and pinned the side seam deeper. We let out the inseam in the upper thigh and knee area.

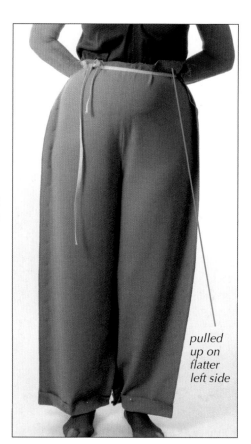

pulled up on flatter left side

Fabric Back Before

The back looks good, but we will need to take in the left side and pull down the right back until the wrinkles disappear. She is fuller on the right back hip than the left.

NOTE: We decided to sew a back lapped zipper instead of a fly front.

Take in left side seam to remove this.

Wrinkles point to full right back hip. We need to pull fabric down here.

Fabric Back After

Here the right back was pulled down at the waist, which removed the wrinkles. We've pinned the back inseam deeper at the top and let it out in the knee area.

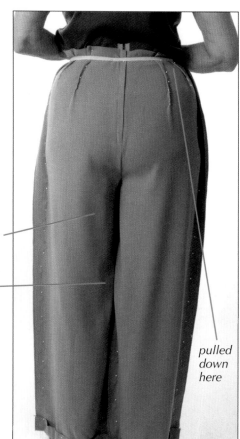

pulled down here

The Side View

The side seam hangs straight. If she wanted less tummy emphasis, she could let out the front inseams, but the legs would be wider, so she decided not to. We curved in the top of the center front seam for her small waist (see pages 42 and 105).

(see pages 42 and 105)

Let out front inseam for less tummy emphasis if desired.

We are marking her waistline seam at the bottom of the elastic with a chalk wheel.

Alicia's Finished Pants

Ease replaces darts across front to bring fabric into her waist.

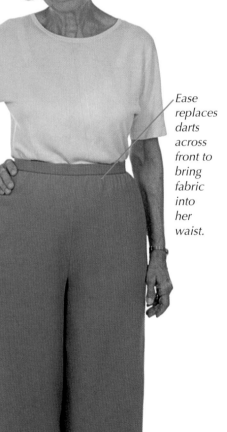

Verna
A NEW WAIST FIT CONCEPT

Verna has been to our pant workshop three times. She prefers a fitted pant. Her waist is at an angle. We first fit her using 1/4" elastic. After attaching the waistband, the pants kept drooping in front. This time we used 1" elastic and Verna put it where her waistband would be. We marked the bottom of the elastic and FINALLY got her band in the right spot!!

The Side

final altered tissue

1" elastic is placed where band will be.

The Front Before

Verna is 3" lower in the front than the pattern.

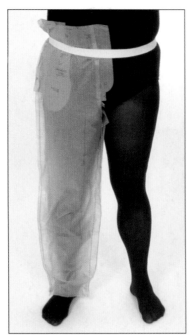

The Front After

So that the pocket opening would stay the same length, we tucked the front below the zipper. We still needed to lower the elastic at the top. She ended up with a 5" zipper.

horizontal tuck across front only

lowered elastic across front even more

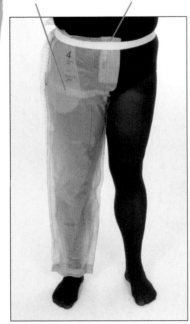

The Back Before

We pull tissue up at the sides because she is so straight. Also, the back is too wide.

fullness and a little bagginess

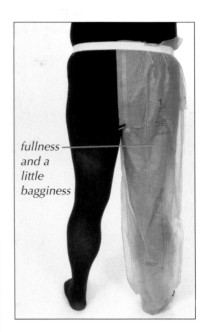

The Back After

To eliminate the bagginess in the back, we had to lower the back crotch seam 1". Verna is VERY LOW in the back crotch, but high in the back waist and low in the front waist.

pulled up until bagginess is gone

width added

vertical tuck

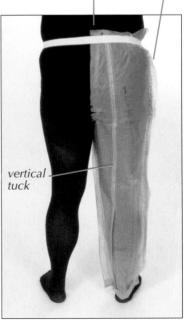

Sue
IN A PAIR OF JEANS

Sue Neall, one of our editors, is also the Palmer/Pletsch education director in Australia. While she was here editing the first draft of the book, she sewed a pair of jeans. Jeans are easier to sew if you tissue-fit them first so you can see how all of the pieces go together.

The Front Before

The center front on the tissue doesn't come to Sue's center front, which is why there is a major wrinkle pointing toward the thigh.

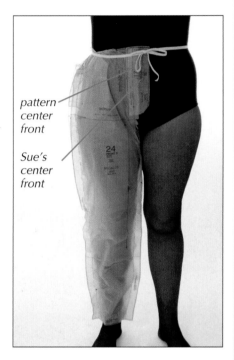

pattern center front

Sue's center front

The Front After

We unpinned the side seam to get the pattern centered. Now there are fewer wrinkles pointing to the inseam.

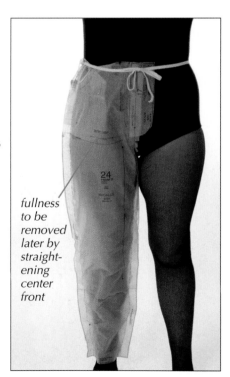

fullness to be removed later by straightening center front

The Back Before

The tissue doesn't come up to her waist at the center back. Also, there are smile wrinkles pointing to the inseam.

Center back is not up to waistline.

Let out inseam to get waist seamline up higher.

waist seam

smiles

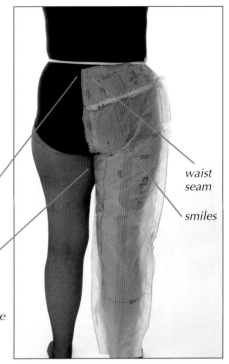

The Back After

After letting out the inseams, the back comes up to the waistline and the wrinkles are gone.

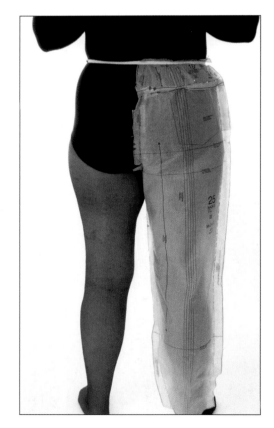

There is a little fullness at the lowest part of the derriere. We also need to lower the back sitting room another 3/8" (page 38).

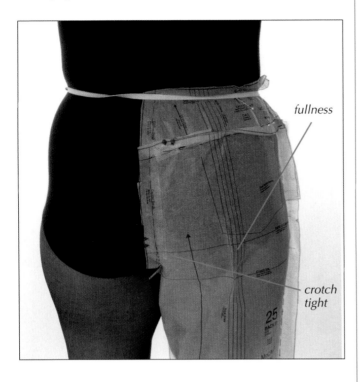

fullness

crotch
tight

We taped a vertical tuck through the yoke and pants back to eliminate 1" of excess width.

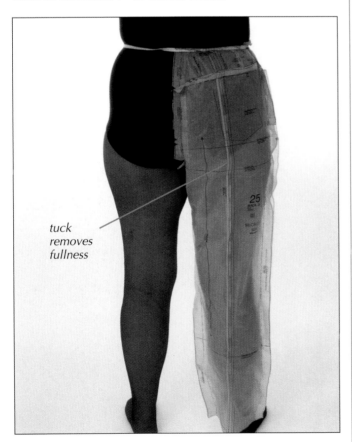

tuck
removes
fullness

Extended Calf

There are wrinkles in the front leg and the side seam bows to the back in the calf area.

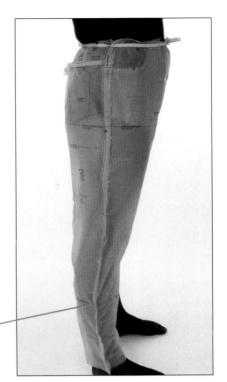

extended calf
pulls seams
toward back

From the knee down we let out the back inseam and side seam to create more room for her fuller calf in this slim pant.

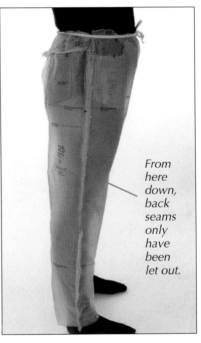

From
here
down,
back
seams
only
have
been
let out.

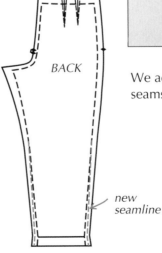

BACK

new
seamline

We added to back seams only.

Additional Front Changes

Front fullness is eliminated by straightening the center front, which was on a slant, common in fitted pants. This also gave Sue a little more room across her tummy. We pulled the tissue down at the center front for more length over her slightly fuller tummy. See page 27, straighten center front.

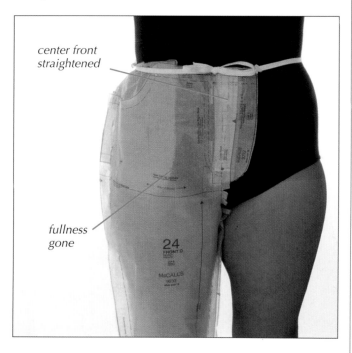

center front straightened

fullness gone

24
FRONT D
McCALL'S

Sue marks her new waistline seam at the bottom of the elastic. The new waistline is 3/4" higher in the center front and about 1/4" higher than the pattern waistline everywhere else.

mark new waist seam line

24
FRONT D

Pin Fitting in Fabric

Sue cut out the pants and sewed the pockets, zipper, and yoke. She then pinned the inseams and side seams wrong sides together.

The side hangs perfectly straight.

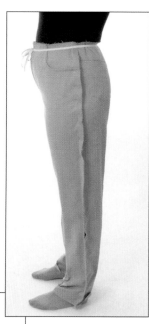

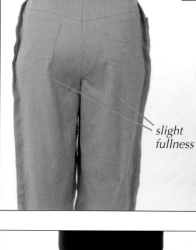

slight fullness

The back is slightly full.

Take in crotch seam and inseams.

A quick way to solve this in fabric is to deepen the crotch seam. This also straightens it a bit which works well if you have a flat derriere. We have also pinched out a little of the back inseams. We will take them in See page 42.)

Even though we fitted the yoke, in fabric there is too much width at the waistline at the side back.

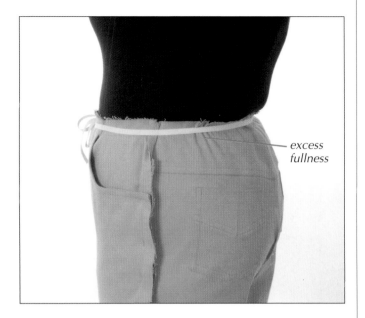

excess fullness

We first took in the sides seams and got pulls.

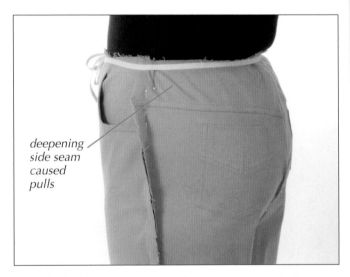

deepening side seam caused pulls

We tried taking in the center back and got pulls the other way.

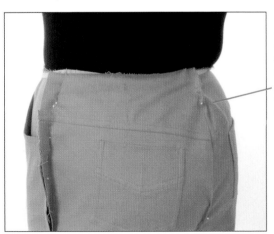

took in center back and pulls change direction

We then pinned out the fullness into a dart right where it wanted to be. Sue didn't want a dart, so she re-cut the yoke with the same size dart dart pinned out of the yoke tissue.

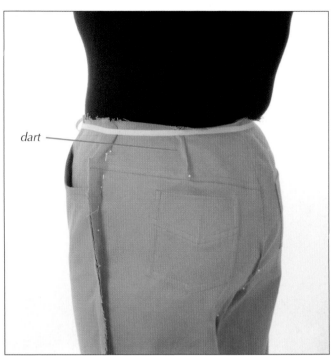

dart

The Waistband

Sue fits and marks the waistband with chalk.

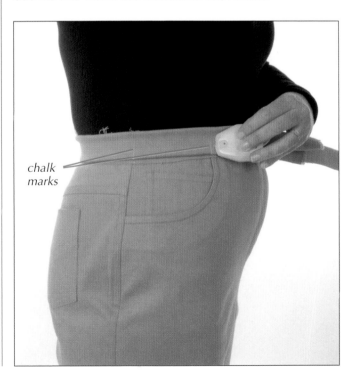

chalk marks

The Finished Jeans

Sue made a suede jacket to accessorize her finished jeans.

A Word About Fabric

Sue's fabric is a stretch cotton that has a lot of body. To make the jeans fit snugly, we got a "pull" across the front, even though the fit is good.

When Nancy, a Palmer/Pletsch instructor from Sammamish, WA, and one of our cover models, made her jeans, she chose an all-cotton non-stretch denim that felt slick and stiff until it was washed. After washing it three times, recommended for denim, it became very soft with a brushed surface.

Nancy's jeans fit snugly, but without all of the pulls you see in the stretch cotton fabric Sue used.

This only proves that every fabric will fit differently, so get used to it!! If you want BULLET-PROOF FIT, use wool crepe. It molds to the body.

Nancy topstitched the seams with top-stitching thread.

CHAPTER 9

Terrific Pleated Trousers

Trousers Are Easy

Do you realize that trousers are the most flattering pant style we can wear? This is because the details and the extra fullness in the front camouflage lumps and bumps.

Topstitch pleats and top of pockets to inset to give a flat look over the tummy.

Eye follows pocket slant to give illusion of a smaller waist.

Fly front creates a slim vertical line.

Fuller here camouflages full tummy and thighs.

Pleat becomes crease – gives a full-length vertical line.

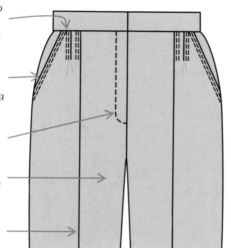

Anyone can wear trousers and look good in them IF they fit and IF the details are well done. However, because of all the details, we don't recommend that you sew your first pair of pants using a trouser-style pattern. First, learn more about your body using a simple basic style. Then, concentrate on sewing flattering trousers.

An Illusion Trick

This will happen if your trousers are too tight.

For less tummy emphasis, add to the front inseam.

Trousers will hang straight down from your tummy because of the extra fullness in the front.

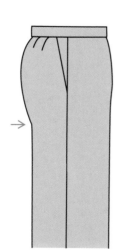

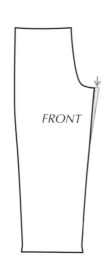

FRONT

74

Tissue-Fitting Trousers

Get the Tissue Ready

Tape front and back crotch next to the seamline. If the pattern has lower back crotch stitching lines, tape below the lowest line. See page 26. Use short pieces of tape in curved areas, lapping them at least 1/2".

Clip curves to tape. Pull on curves to make sure tape won't tear.

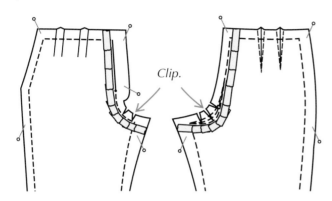

Clip.

Place pant front on top of side panel, matching circles to seam intersections, and pin in place.

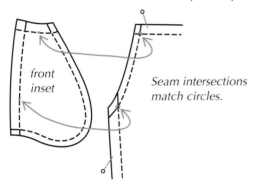

front inset

Seam intersections match circles.

NOTE: When cutting lining front for a trouser, lap the inset pattern piece under the front just like this in order to eliminate a pocket in the lining.

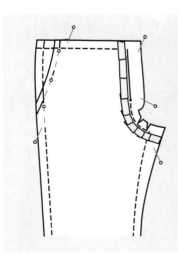

NOTE: Straight vs. Curvy Bodies

Some trouser patterns have "play" in the pocket to make room for hands. If you curve in a lot from your upper hip to your waist, leave the play. If you are straight, the pocket will gap so remove it.

To remove the "play" in the pocket, match the side seam on the front to the lower circle on the side inset. To ADD play, do the opposite.

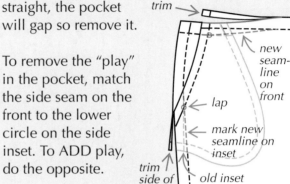

"play" in pocket

FRONT

trim

new seamline on front

lap

mark new seamline on inset

trim side of inset

old inset seamline

Smooth front until front waist seam intersection is directly above the circle. Re-mark the waist seamline on the front. Trim excess tissue off top of the front and lower side seam of the inset.

Pin pleats as they will be sewn. (From WRONG side, match pleat stitching lines, and from RIGHT side, fold pleat in direction of arrows printed on the pattern.)

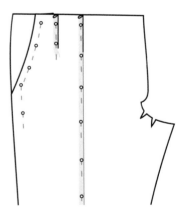

Crease the pattern on the crease line up to the pleat. Flatten the pleat to the thigh area and pin through all layers. This will keep you from using the pleat ease while fitting.

Pin back darts on the outside. Place front and back legs WRONG SIDES TOGETHER. Pin in seamlines, with pins pointing down so they won't fall out when fitting. Don't put any pins above waistline seam. (OUCH!)

Now try on trouser tissue.

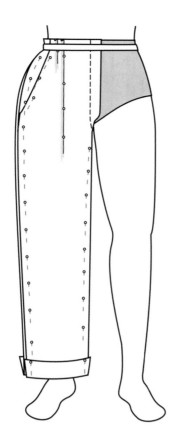

Follow the same tissue-fitting procedures as in Chapter 6, page 21, with these additions:

Waist Width

If you need waist width only, add to the back side seam and to the side seam on the front inset only. Do NOT make front pleats narrower.

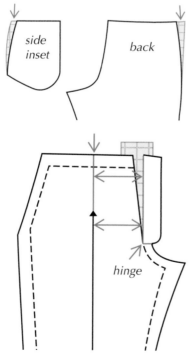

If the pattern center front is slanted, you can straighten it. This works well if you have a full tummy. Cut on center front to bottom of zipper opening. Cut from outside edge to first cut, leaving a "hinge" of tissue.

Straighten center front until it is parallel to the grainline. Insert tissue.

Waist and Hip Width

Add as shown.

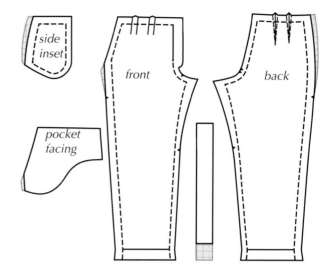

Lap front and back pattern pieces to make sure the amount and shape added is the same on the front and back at the side seams.

Pleat Length

You don't want pleat stitching to stop above the fullest part of your tummy, especially if you curve in above the tummy.

Sew pleats down further, stopping at the fullest part of the tummy.

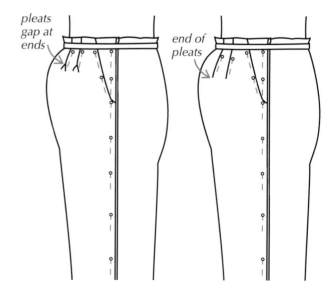

Crotch Depth

Draw a line on the front at the bottom of the fly, but ABOVE the crotch curve, and another line anywhere above the crotch curve on the back.

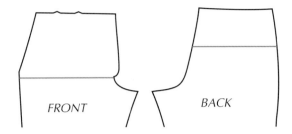

If you need to shorten or lengthen the crotch a lot (1½″ - 4″), you may need a second lengthen-and-shorten line on the front to change the zipper and pocket length as well. In this case, add a line to the side INSET and pocket stay or facing, too.

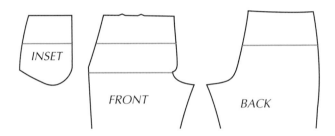

Very Uneven Crotch Depth

We have had a few women in our classes who are very low in the front and high in the back. It's where they wear their pants and YES, the pants do stay up. These women need a shorter front crotch, zipper opening, and pocket opening. If you are really high in the back, you may even need to add tissue to the top of the back. Make one or two tucks across the front and none on the back. Mark waistline below elastic. See Verna, page 67.

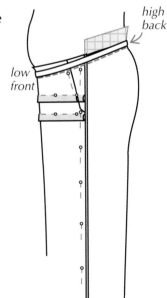

high back

low front

Finalize the Tissue

- Mark waistline at the bottom of the elastic and pin positions as described on page 34.

- After making all of your alterations, trim all seams except crotch to an even 1″. Since the tissue is touching your body, the larger seam allowances will allow for fabric variations.

- Trim crotch to an even 5/8″.

- Make the same adjustment on the pocket lining/stay piece that you made on the front.

- Press the tissue from the wrong side to avoid the tape.

Repin Tissue to Check for Accuracy

Place front and back legs WRONG SIDES TOGETHER on a cardboard surface. Start by matching HEMS FIRST. Pin into cardboard through hemlines.

Smooth tissue to top and pin into cardboard, matching seamlines along the way.

If inseams and side seams don't match at top, trim them until even. (If you have made major changes in crotch length, the inseams often will change in length. The only reason the outseams might not be the same length is because of how the inset is pinned.)

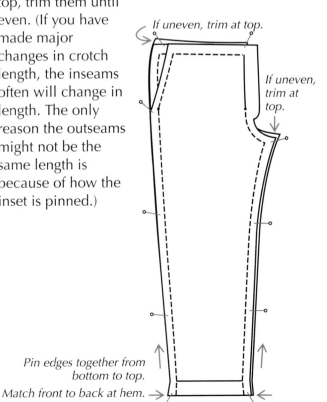

If uneven, trim at top.

If uneven, trim at top.

Pin edges together from bottom to top.

Match front to back at hem. →

Cutting & Marking Trouser Fabric

PRO Tip There are up to 14 chances to make mistakes (seam allowances, darts, pleats, and lapping points such as pockets and fly zipper). To prevent a disaster, we urge very careful marking.

- Be sure you have 1" seam allowances at side, waist, and inseams.

- Mark pleat stitching lines and circles with tracing paper or tailor tacks.

- We like putting a few tailor tacks along the front crease as well. This will help get the pant crease in the right place.

Also, tailor tack the circle to mark where you stop stitching the crotch seam at the bottom of the zipper opening. Make a big loop at the circle. Snip loop to remove pattern. There is no need to separate the fabric, however, as the crotch is ready to sew (if you cut right sides together).

To tailor tack:

1. Use a long double strand of thread. Sew a running stitch through tissue and both layers of fabric along crease line.

2. Snip the middle of each stitch so you can lift off the pattern.

3. Gently pull the layers apart and snip threads between so some thread remains in each layer.

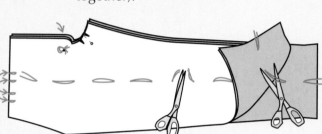

Quick Tip

Snip-marking helps with speed and accuracy. Snip 1/4" into cut edge at the following places:

Snip circles so you'll know circle is 1"from snip.

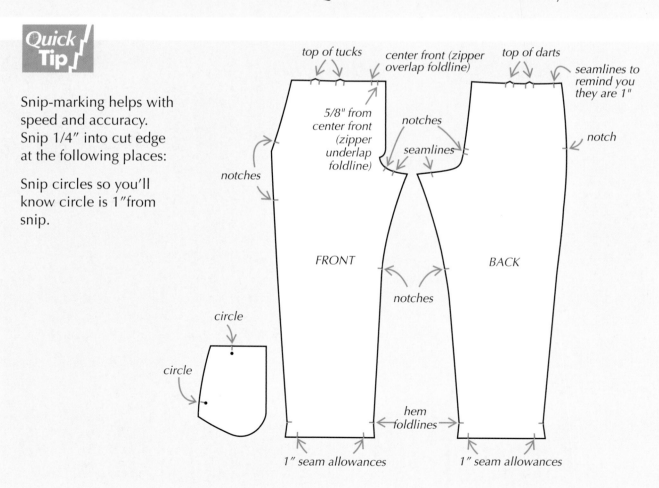

top of tucks

center front (zipper overlap foldline)

top of darts

seamlines to remind you they are 1"

5/8" from center front (zipper underlap foldline)

notches

seamlines

notch

notches

notch

FRONT

BACK

notches

circle

circle

hem foldlines

1" seam allowances

1" seam allowances

Sewing Order at a Glance

1. Sew front crotch seam starting 1½" from inseam to zipper opening circle. Backstitch.

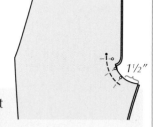

NOTE: Since you cut right sides together, you might as well pin and sew the crotch seam at this time. However, some people prefer to finish each front separately, then sew crotch seam.

2. Sew back crotch seam beginning 1½" from inseam up to waist. Clip above curve.

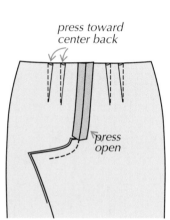

press toward center back

press open

3. Press crotch seam open above clip.

4. Sew back darts. Press toward center back.

5. Stitch pleats, backstitching at circle.

6. Press the pleats in the direction your pattern indicates.

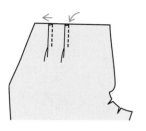

DON'T CHANGE THE DIRECTION OF THE PLEATS UNLESS YOU RE-MARK THE PLEATS.

The crease is designed to go into the fold of one of the pleats.

If you press them in the opposite direction, the crease will go off grain to meet the new fold.

Re-mark pleat lines as shown.

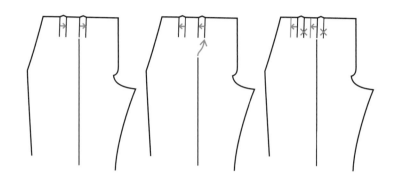

TIP: For a sporty look, topstitch tucks flat in a "U" shape to 1½" below waist SEAMLINE. Stitch next to fold, pivot and stitch across the bottom, pivot and stitch 1/4" from fold to top.

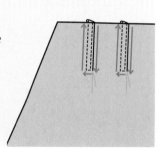

![PRO Tip] **Which Direction Is Best for Pleats?**

There isn't one as long as your trousers are sewn and pressed properly and they fit well. It is done both ways in ready-to-wear. We used to prefer pleats pressed toward the side, but have since lightened up!! Try patterns designed both ways and you be the judge.

Pleats pressed toward side (from inside). You look into pleat from center.

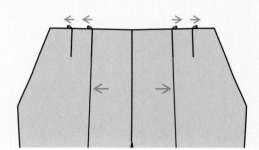

Pleats pressed toward center (from inside). You look into pleat from side.

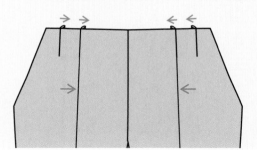

Crease Front Legs Before Continuing to Sew

(For general creasing tips see page 102.)

6. Place pant FRONT on a flat ironing surface. Fold along tailor tacks. Pin straight into ironing surface. Put pin in stitching line of pleat closest to center front.

   Crease each leg with an up and down motion of the iron. Let cool before moving.

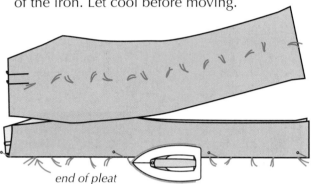

end of pleat

7. Remove tailor tacks. Lay the front flat on a pressing surface and top press the stitched pleat. Below the pleat, let the fabric fold under to the width of the pleat. Continue pressing down to the thigh area, creating an unsewn pleat that lies flat. It should slightly taper in width as it goes down the leg.

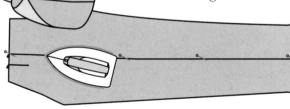

Let cool before moving.

8. Sew pockets. (See chapter 20.)

9. Sew fly-front zipper. (See page 107.)

Quick Tip

It is always easier to sew these details with the front flat and unattached to the back. Flat first is always faster!

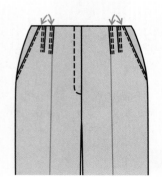

10. Pin inseams and side seams WRONG SIDES together with pins pointing down and none above waist seam.

11. Fine-tune the fit. (See Chapter 7.)

12. Mark waistline seam if changed. Take pants off.

13. Mark seamline changes on wrong side of fabric.

14. Pin RIGHT SIDES TOGETHER and sew seams. Press open. Finish sewing the crotch seam. (See page 40.)

15. Apply waistband. (See chapter 14.)

16. Hem pants. (See chapter 22.)

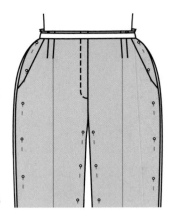

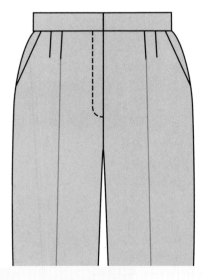

FIT Tip During fabric fitting, if you pull pants up more than 1" in the waist, go back to your pattern and make a tuck in it to shorten crotch depth. Then next time you won't have to lengthen pleats or lose some of your pocket and zipper opening length. See shortening crotch depth page 29.

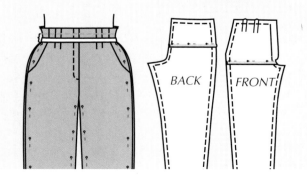

BACK *FRONT*

CHAPTER 10

Real People/Trousers

Sue
IN TROUSERS

Pati and Marta scrambled to complete the rough manuscript of this book in time for Sue Neall, the director of education for Palmer/Pletsch in Australia, to begin editing. In October 2002, Sue came to the United States and stayed with Pati. Since Sue sews beautifully and represents a common baby boomer body shape, Pati decided she would be the perfect person to be featured in the book!

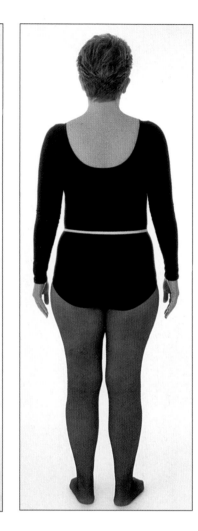

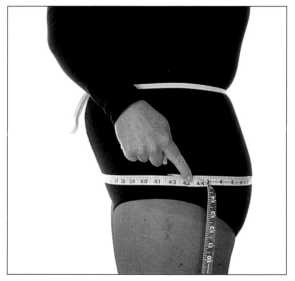

To find Sue's best pattern size, we measured her hips. She measures 41½", which is between a size 16 and 18. If you are between sizes, use the smaller size unless you have a flat derriere. Since Sue is flat in the back, we chose a size 18 which will allow us to take a tuck down the back and keep the side seam at Sue's side.

The Pattern

Sue chose a McCall's Palmer/Pletsch pant pattern with special tissue markings and 1" side, inseam, and waist seam allowances to allow for different weights of fabric. Also, alteration lines are printed on the tissue, such as tuck lines for flat derriere and lower back-crotch stitching lines for the over-40 crowd.

The Front Before

We pinned the pleats as they will be sewn and then pinned the larger pleat flat through all layers in the thigh area to prevent the pleat from giving extra width when pinning the side seams to fit.

Sue's waist is larger than the pattern (which may have fitted her when she was 18 years old and before three children!). Since the center front doesn't come to her center front, we will need to expand the waist. The smiles in the crotch area need not be addressed until we fix the waist.

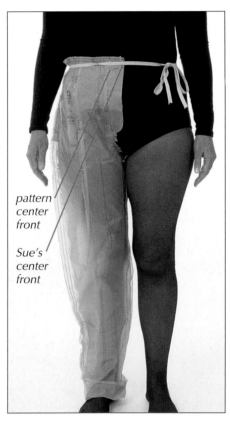

pattern center front

Sue's center front

We unpin the side seam down to the upper thigh.

Sue is so straight at the sides, the pattern has too much length and is bowing out. Later we will pull the tissue up at the sides.

We won't fill in the sides with tissue until we have done all other alterations, as the amount needed may change.

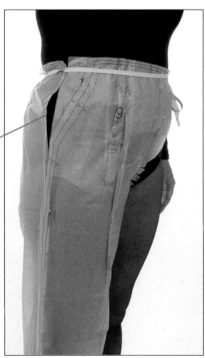

The Front After

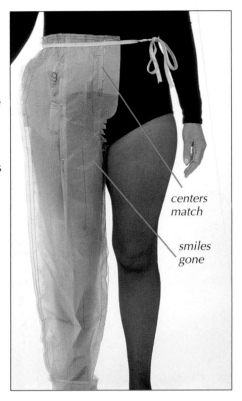

Now the center front comes to her center. Note that the smiles in the crotch disappear once the tissue comes to her center front.

centers match

smiles gone

The Back Before

The back looks a little baggy. Note the wrinkles from the sides to the inseams.

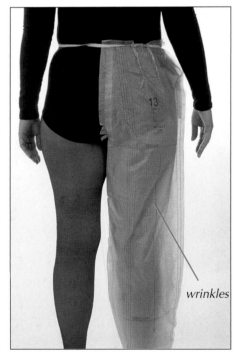

wrinkles

The Back After

We pull up the tissue at the center back until the bagginess disappears. However, it seems a little full across the back.

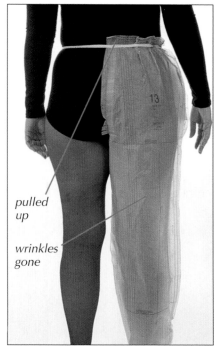

pulled up

wrinkles gone

We pin a small tuck at the lowest area of her derriere to see how much width we need to remove. (See page 31, back bagginess.

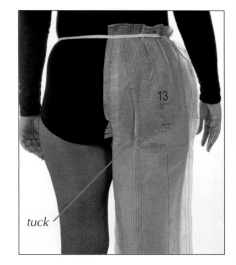

tuck

After taping the tuck in place, Sue again tries on the tissue. The back is still a little full in the thigh areas, so we will take in the inseam.

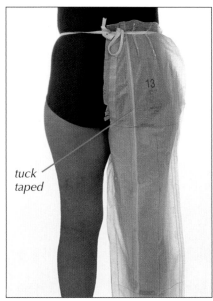

tuck taped

The Front, After Back Adjustment

But first, let's look at the front. Pulling up the back has caused smiles in the front crotch. We need to let out the front inseam.

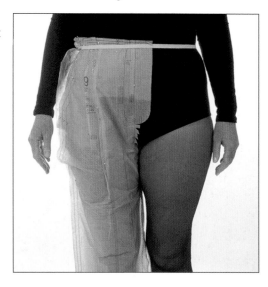

We drop the tissue to shift the inseams. We pin the back inseam a little deeper and let out the front inseam.

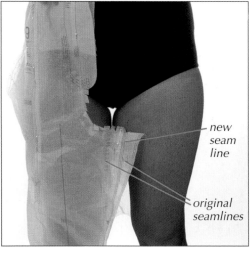

new seam line

original seamlines

Now, the front looks good, but the sides still bow out due to her straight, rather than curved, hips. Also, this extra side length in the tissue is causing the front crease to veer toward the inseam.

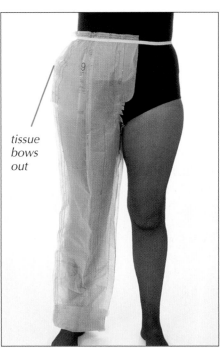

tissue bows out

83

Adjusting the Sides

The gap at the sides will narrow when we pull up the tissue.

We pull the tissue up at the sides until it is flat against her body.

We pin the tissue up against her body. Then we add tissue to make even 1" seam allowances.

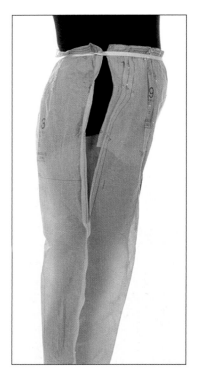

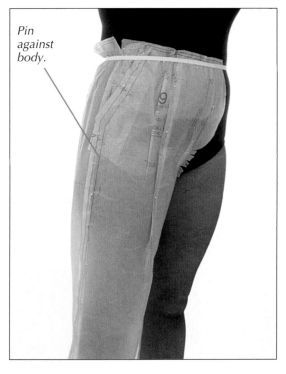

pulled up

Pin against body.

Front After

From the front, the tissue looks good. We turn up the hem of the tissue until it drapes a little on the front of her foot, which should allow enough length for a flat shoe. If she wants to wear heels, Sue would need to test the length with those shoes.

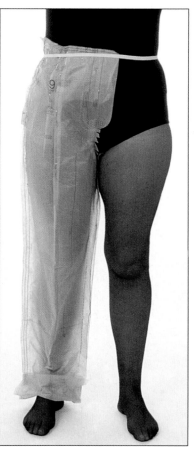

Back After

The back looks good. When Sue made her jeans, she did an extended calf alteration on the back leg. Because the trouser is fuller, she doesn't need to do this.

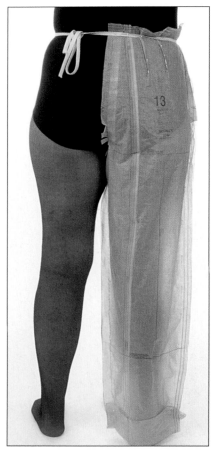

Sue marks the bottom of the elastic all the way around. After taking the tissue off, she will mark the pin locations at the sides and inseams with a pen that will go through both layers.

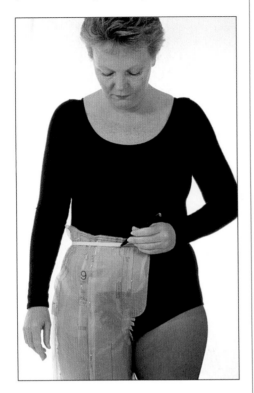

Fitting in Fabric

Sue has sewn the pockets, pleats, and zipper. She marked the crease with tailor tacks after cutting out the trousers. She has pinned the side seams and inseams wrong sides together and puts on the pants with elastic tied around her waist. It is important to fit with the pants right sides out because your left and right hips may vary in size.

The Side

The side is perfect. The pants hang great. The side seam is perpendicular to the floor.

The Front

They look fabulous in the front. The only thing we see is a little drooping in the center of each leg.

We pull up the pants in the pleat area to remove the droop. Sewing the waistband lower in this area will anchor it. It is OK to have a wavy waistline.

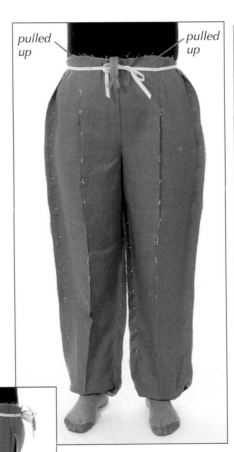

pulled up

pulled up

The Back

The back, below, looks good. However, there is a little extra fullness in the back inseam. This happens in fabric, depending on how much the bias crotch seam stretches in different fabrics.

droopy

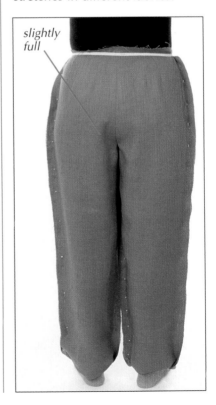

slightly full

The Back After

We pin a small tuck to help us decide how much to take off the back inseam. We decide to make the back inseam 3/4" deeper.

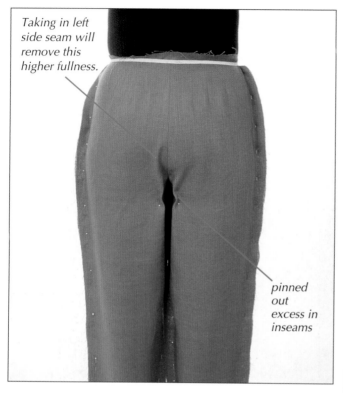

Taking in left side seam will remove this higher fullness.

pinned out excess in inseams

Sue took off the pants and repinned the back inseams 3/4" deeper. Voila! It looks great!

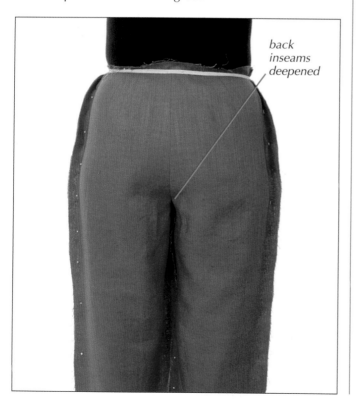

back inseams deepened

She now marks with a chalk wheel along the bottom of the elastic so that she will know where to sew on her waistband.

The Waistband

After sewing and pressing all of the seams, she tries the pant on again.

Sue has sewn her 1" non-roll interfacing to the waistband and wraps it around her waist just as it will be stitched on. She pins the center front so the band is comfortable and then smooths the pant waist ease underneath the band. What you see is what you will get! Now she marks all of the matching points with chalk so when she pins the band to the pant, she can match the marks and get a perfect fit even if her left and right sides are different. (See page 111, waistband.)

The Finished Trousers

The finished pant, front, side, and back. Sue likes the hem to break on her shoe so that when she sits, less leg shows.

If you sew pants in a colored fabric like this beautiful linen, make a jacket to match so you will have a complete outfit. Here is Sue in her accessorized completed outfit.

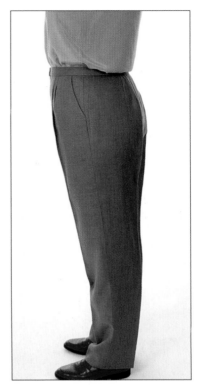

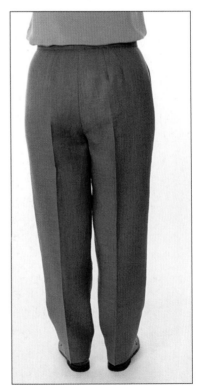

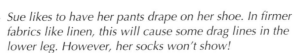

Sue likes to have her pants drape on her shoe. In firmer fabrics like linen, this will cause some drag lines in the lower leg. However, her socks won't show!

Jean
IN TROUSERS

Jean Baxter is a Palmer/Pletsch Certified Sewing Instructor from Granite Bay, California. She is a about 5'5" tall. Her shoulder and hip width are the same and she has a definite waistline, making her an hourglass figure type. From the side you see she has back waist indentation, but not front.

From the back Jean has the same hourglass silhouette as from the front. This means showing her waist in pants will be more flattering than wearing an overblouse.

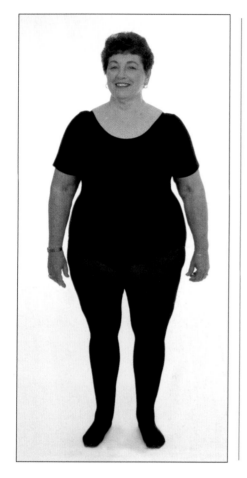
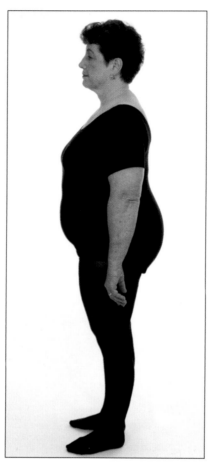
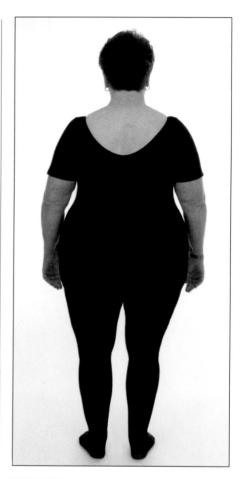

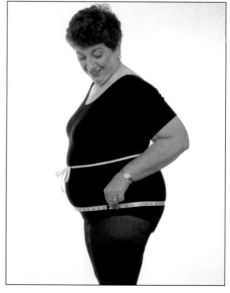

Jean has tied 1/4" elastic around her waist. She measures 54½" in the hips, which would put her in a size 30W. Jean took our pant workshop before there were sizes larger than a 24, so we used a size 24. We found we liked it because the leg width was narrower.

Remember, you can make any size fit, but sometimes you need to experiment. This trouser is roomy. Jean might go to a larger size in a fitted pant.

The Front Before

She tries on the tissue. The center front isn't coming to her center front. Also, the front crotch is long.

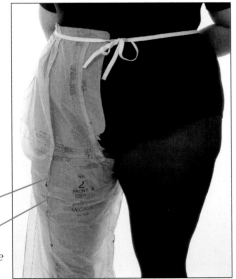

Jean's crotch

tissue crotch seam line

The Front After

We let out the side seam until the center front came to Jean's center front. Note the smiles in the front crotch.

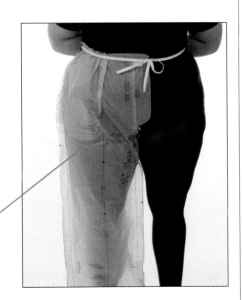

wrinkles point to front inseam

The Back Before

The tissue doesn't reach her waist at the center back.

There is also a slight pull on the grainline toward the inseam.

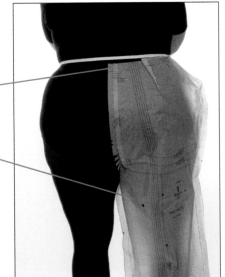

Inseam Adjustment

Due to smiles in the front and needing length in the back to get the tissue up under the elastic, we drop the tissue and let out the inseams an even 1″.

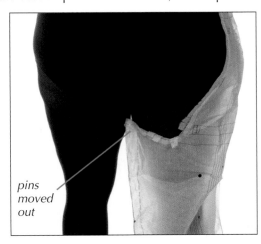

pins moved out

The Back After

Now the back comes up to the waist and the back grainline hangs straight. There is, however, extra fullness across the back at the lowest point on the derriere.

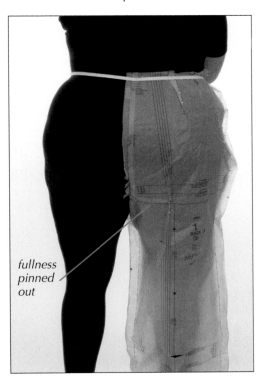

fullness pinned out

The Waistline

We pull up the tissue until the front crotch touches her body. It will hang down at least 1/2″ in fabric as the bias crotch seam will stretch a little.

The bottom of the elastic indicates the new waistline. The stitching lines for the front pleats will need to be lengthened. Note also that the front smiles are gone.

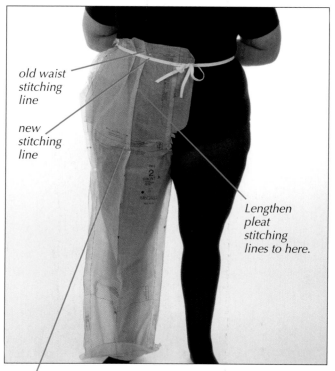

old waist stitching line

new stitching line

Lengthen pleat stitching lines to here.

To make sure we don't use the pleats for extra width when fitting the side seams, we pin the pleat closed in the thigh area.

Adjusting the Sides

We took a vertical tuck in the back tissue to remove the excess width. Note the tissue is more rounded at the side than Jean is.

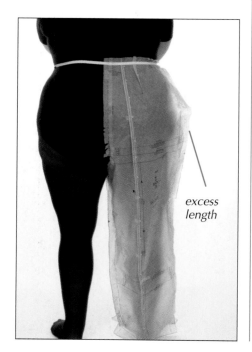

excess length

Now we see that the side seams don't meet after taking the tuck. Also, they bow out.

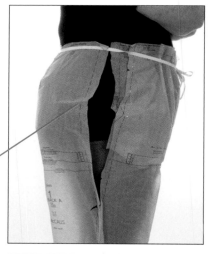

seams bow out

First, we pull the tissue up at the sides to eliminate the bow. Her new waistline seam is at the bottom of the elastic.

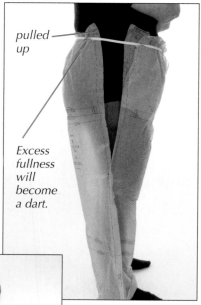

pulled up

Excess fullness will become a dart.

We add tissue to the sides and pin the tissue to skim along her body. We then add tissue where necessary to make even 1″ seam allowances. The 1″ seam allowances are necessary for fabric variations.

We mark the tissue at the bottom of the elastic for her new waist seamline. She will trim the waist seam allowance to an even 1".

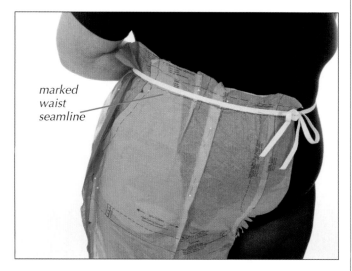

marked waist seamline

The back looks good.

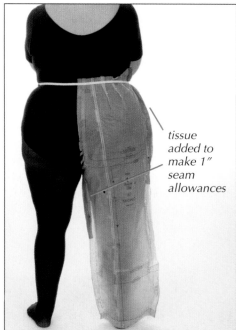

tissue added to make 1" seam allowances

Note that we have added a third dart near the side seam to eliminate the excess fullness created after we pulled the tissue up at the sides.

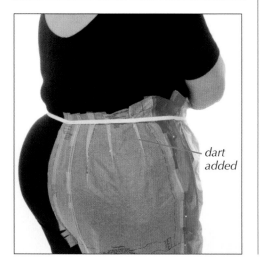

dart added

The Front in Fabric

Jean cut out her trousers, sewed the pleats, pockets, and zipper. She pinned her front to her back wrong sides together to make "tweaking" the ease simpler. You must try on pants right side out since your sides might be different.

She tucked in her cotton shirt for the fitting. If her shirt had been silk, fitting the pants with it tucked in wouldn't have been necessary.

The Back in Fabric

They look good, but there is excess fullness in the back, typical because the bias crotch stretches in fabric. The back crotch curve is longer and more sloping than the front, so it stretches more.

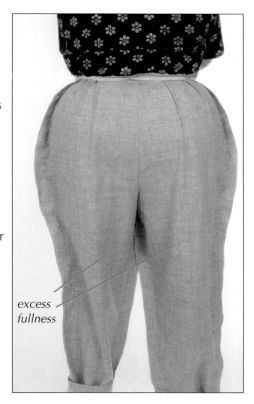

excess fullness

NOTE: To make sure we don't pull the pleat open, we pin it flat to the thigh area.

Pin pleat through all layers here.

A Little "Creative" Fitting

By taking in the back side seam only, we are able to reduce some of the excess fullness in the back in this area without affecting pocket placement.

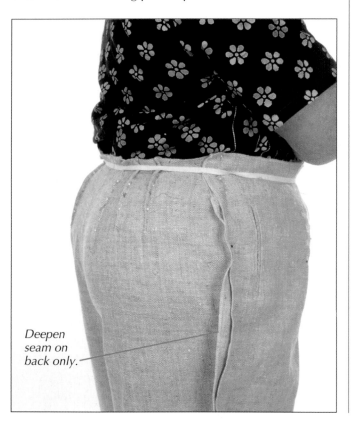

Deepen seam on back only.

We also deepen the back inseam to remove fullness between the legs.

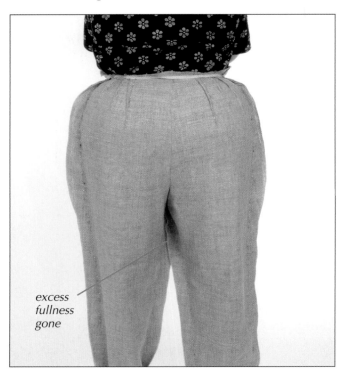

excess fullness gone

The Waistline

Jean is small in the waist compared to her upper hip. We deepen the darts at the top, curving them into her waist. You can also see in the photo above that her right hip is slightly fuller at the upper back. Marta fine-tunes Jean's darts by pinning them exactly to her shape on each side.

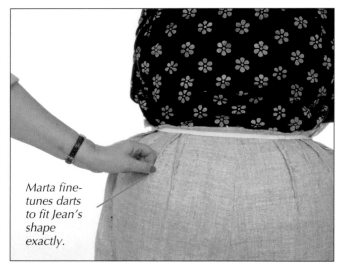

Marta fine-tunes darts to fit Jean's shape exactly.

Once you perfect the darts, mark on wrong side where the pins are positioned. Unpin. Place tissue on pants and trace new left and right back darts with different color pens. Darts may vary in size on the left and right.

Tweaking (Nit-picking) the Fit

Jean has sewn her side and inseams and machine-basted along the waistline seam. There is a little excess fullness on the right side below the high hip. We pin the seam slightly deeper—only 1/8″.

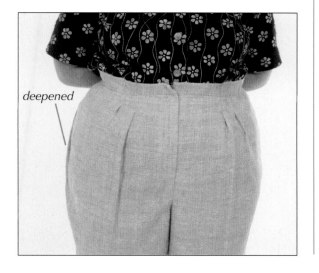

deepened

Jean sewed a jacket out of the same linen fabric and here wears her completed outfit with a silk blouse.

Mark the Waistband

We sewed the interfacing to the waistband and wrapped it around the pants. It is pinned comfortably snug at the center front. The pants are smoothed out under the waistband. Using chalk, we marked where the waistband meets pleats, pockets, side and crotch seam in back, and darts. Now she can pin the band on and it will fit the right and left sides perfectly.

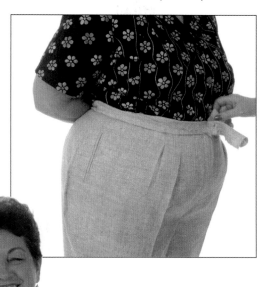

...the side seam falls straight. Now, let's pin up the hem for the shoes she will wear with her pants.

Now the back looks good.

The front fits nicely and...

93

Marta
IN TROUSERS

The Front Before

Marta tries on the tissue. The tissue is not meeting her center front and there are wrinkles pointing to the inseam.

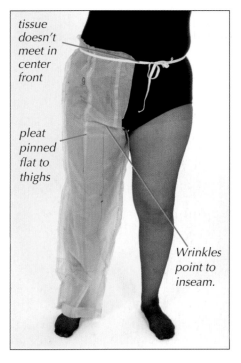

tissue doesn't meet in center front

pleat pinned flat to thighs

Wrinkles point to inseam.

The Side Before

The front tissue droops.

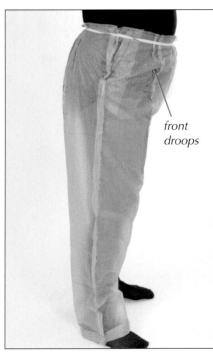

front droops

The Back Before

The waist seamline at the center back is not reaching Marta's. Also, there is extra vertical width across the derriere.

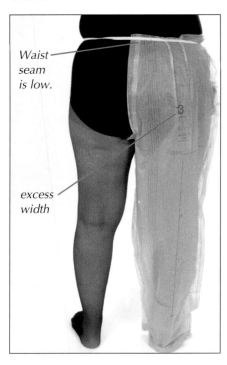

Waist seam is low.

excess width

We pull up the front to see how much to shorten it. We let out the waist at the side seam until the center fronts match.

We pinch a tuck at the lowest part of the derriere to see how much width needs to be removed.

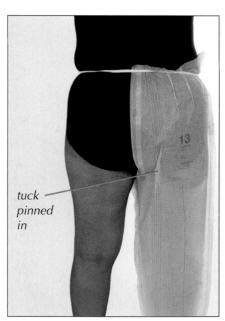

tuck pinned in

Marta took off the tissue and shortened the crotch depth by 1 1/2" with a horizontal tuck across the front and the back.

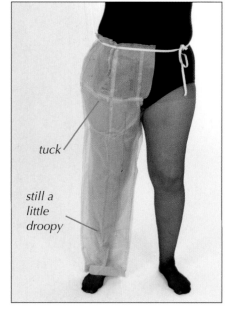

tuck

still a little droopy

Walking Ease

The tissue grabs her front thigh when she walks. You can see her knee is almost as full as the top of her inner thigh.

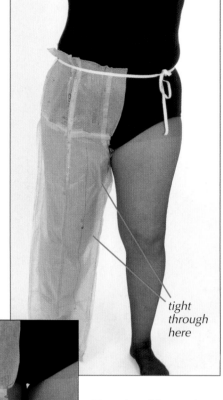

tight through here

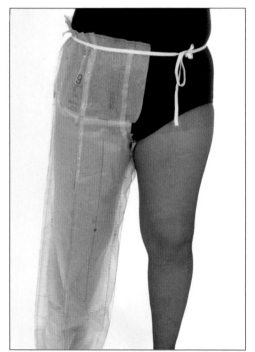

To solve this, we let out the inseam from just below the knee, tapering to original seamline at the crotch.

let out

Now Marta can walk without the tissue pulling.

The Back After

The full-length vertical tuck is pinned. Tissue is added to top of back. (If we had not shortened both back and front crotch depth, we would have needed to true the waistline seam at the side when finished altering.)

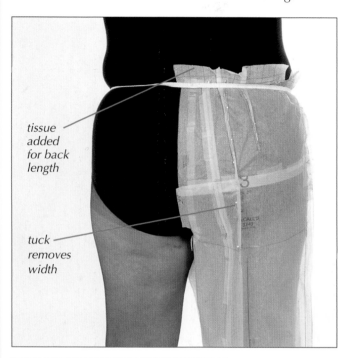

tissue added for back length

tuck removes width

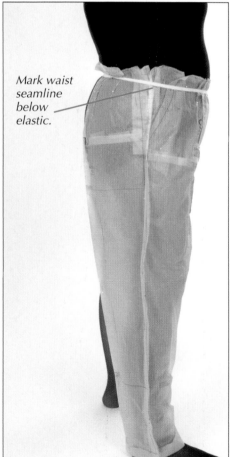

Mark waist seamline below elastic.

You can see Marta's waist drops down in the front. We mark her waistline below the elastic. She really has a wavy waistline.

Fitting in Fabric

The fabric is pinned wrong sides together and the deepest pleats are pinned flat to the thighs.

droopy

To remove the droop at the knees, we pulled the pants up straight above the pleats. The droop is gone.

Pull up here.

From the side, everything hangs well. It's time to finish the pants.

The back looks good except for the little excess fabric. Her left side is flatter so the excess is greater there.

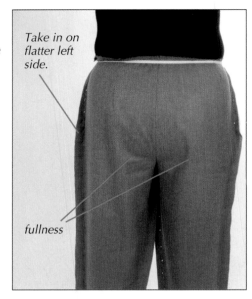

Take in on flatter left side.

fullness

We pin her left side seam a little deeper. We pin the rest of the excess out in center back seam which in essence straightens (deepens) the crotch seam. (See page 43.)

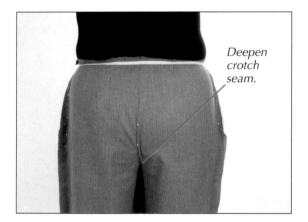

Deepen crotch seam.

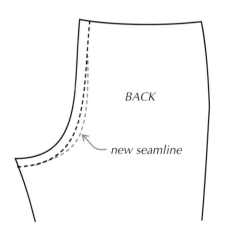

BACK

new seamline

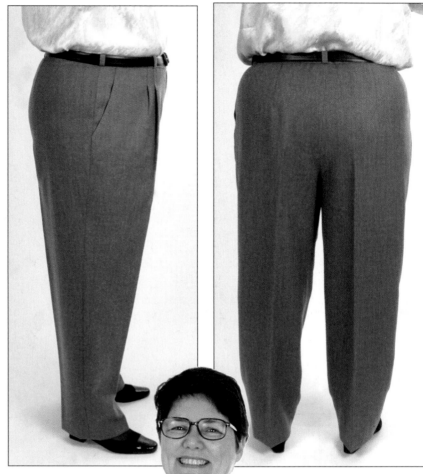

The Finished Trousers

Marta models her finished trousers.

She teaches our tailoring workshops and her beautiful jacket shows off her skills.

Cut, Mark, Sew, and Press

- Once you learn to fit yourself, make five pairs of pants in one month! Concentrated practice will make sewing and fitting pants easier.

- Use a pattern more than once. It gets faster each time.

- You should be able to sew one pair in three hours and two pairs in four hours. Sewing two pairs at one time adds only one hour to the total sewing time. That's because repetition turns your sewing room into a mini-factory. Press a seam and while it cools, sew a seam on the other pair.

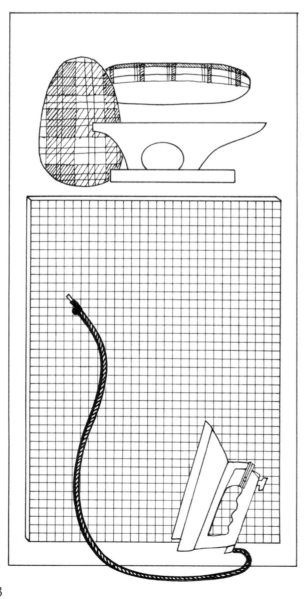

Quick Tips...Cutting

1. Fold fabric right sides together so the crotch seams will be in a ready-to-sew position. Can't tell right from wrong side? Pick one and use consistently. Most fabrics come folded right sides together. An exception is quilting cottons.

2. Make sure pattern and fabric do not have wrinkles.

3. Placing pattern pieces in one direction eliminates the possibility of shading differences or the "nap" effect of some fabrics.

grainline parallel to edge of fabric

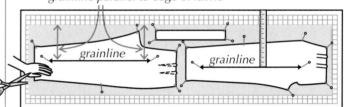

4. Use a gridded cardboard cutting board so you can line the selvage along printed lines and place pins vertically into the board in every corner of the fabric.

5. Use a see-through ruler for placing pattern on fabric. Measure from each end of the grainline to the edge of the fabric. Grainline should be parallel to the selvage or folded edge of the fabric.

6. Use only eight pins. The first two go at each end of the grainline. Pin into the cutting board with pin heads angling outward from the center to keep the pattern from shifting.

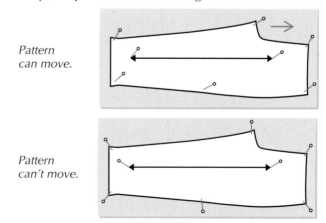

Pattern can move.

Pattern can't move.

7. Your hands can be extra pins. Keep one hand on the pattern edges while cutting. Practice by cutting slowly at first, but soon this will become a real time-saver!

8. Allow 1" IN-CASE seam allowances at waistline, inseams, and side seams. It's like having an "in-case" dinner in the freezer. Do this when you are not quite sure how a design will fit or you are using a heavy fabric that might require more room.

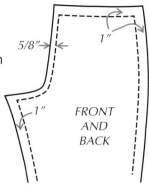

9. Cut the waistband on the selvage to eliminate the need to finish the inside edge.

10. If you are using an expensive fabric and can't quite fit the pattern onto its width, piece the crotch. It won't show. Remember to add seam allowances!

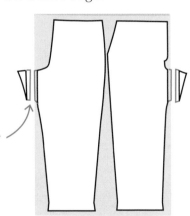

Quick Tips....Marking

1. Snip-mark edges: Cut off notches and snip only 1/4" into edge. Snip-mark the following:

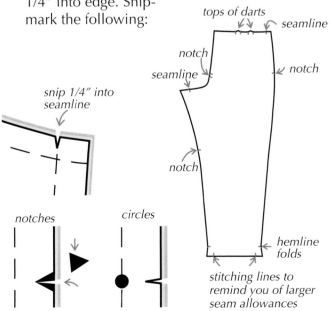

2. For interior ends of pleats and darts, use pins. Put pins through all layers at pattern markings. Using chalk or a water soluble marker, mark wrong side of fabric where pins go through. Or, tailor tack through circles.

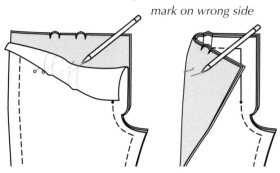

mark on wrong side

3. To pin pleats and darts, match snips at top and pin. At other end, pin so you will know where to stop sewing.

4. Use tracing paper where accuracy is essential. Put a layer under and on top of your fabric so it marks on the wrong side of both layers of fabric. A plastic baggie will keep your pattern from tearing. Use a smooth tracing wheel; a serrated one can cut both your pattern and some fabrics.

Tip: Test tracing paper to make sure you won't see it on right side and that it washes out or steams away.

Speed Up Your Cutting and Pressing

Make a "cut 'n press" board and get all of these benefits:

- You can pin into its padded surface...more accurate than lifting the fabric to pin through the layers.

- Place it on top of a chest for a back-saving cutting and pressing surface.

- The large surface makes it easier to fuse interfacing to large pieces or several smaller pieces at once. Also, it is nice for creasing pants.

- It is a space saver—a dual-purpose cutting and pressing surface you can leave out all the time.

Materials

- 1/2"- or 5/8"-thick particle board (plywood will warp more quickly). It should be long enough to cut out a pant leg and wide enough for 60" fabric folded in half. (Pati's is 32" x 48"—a third of a 4' x 8' sheet of particle board. Marta's is 36" x 48" and her next one is going to be 36" x 60".)

- 1/2"-thick layer of absorbent padding such as wool or firm cotton felt. Wool army blankets work well. Cotton and wool batting found in quilt shops also works well. (Old wool from your stash can work too—a few moth holes won't hurt!) Don't use polyester batting.

- Smooth muslin to cover the padding, or a medium-colored gingham-check fabric.

- A staple gun to attach the cover to the underside of the board.

- Masking tape to cover the staples.

See our book *Dream Sewing Spaces* for more sewing room tips.

Quick Tips...Sewing

- Use "taut sewing" to prevent puckering of seams. Pull equally on the fabric in front and back of needle as you stitch. Do not stretch, just pull taut as if you were sewing with your fabric in an embroidery hoop. Let the fabric feed through the machine on its own. For knits, stretch the seams a little or you will get puckering on the lower legs because the knit fabric will have more give than the thread.

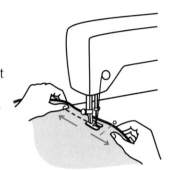

- Prevent "scooting." The upper layer often scoots forward when sewing. The long length of the leg seams multiplies the effect. Prevent it by using lots of pins. If you begin to see a bubble, lift the take-up lever to raise the presser foot just a hair. Place fingers of your right hand on the sides of the presser foot to help excess fabric feed into the seam. Using a lighter presser foot pressure lessens scooting as well. If you have a dual-feed foot or walking foot, use it.

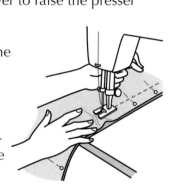

- Backstitch 5/8" into the seam at seam intersection points instead of at the edge. When you trim a seam, you trim off backstitching if it is done at the edge. Or, use a stitch length of 1mm for the first inch of the seam, especially on fine fabrics, for less bulk than backstitching.

backstitch 5/8" down from top

Easy Seam Finishes

- **None**—a seam finish may not be necessary when you plan to dry-clean a fabric that doesn't ravel easily, like many wool flannels, especially if you line the pants.

- **Serging**—the serger or overlock machine trims and overcasts the edge in one step. Use a 2-thread finish for the least bulk.

- **Pinking**—is best for lined pants out of moderately ravelly fabrics. When pinking, hold the blades loosely, because squeezing them will chew your fabric.

- **Zigzagging**—a fast, durable machine finish for medium and heavyweight fabrics. Use a stitch length of 2mm and width of 3mm.

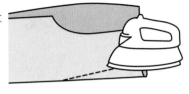

- **Triple zigzag or serpentine stitch**—excellent for lightweight silky fabrics. Used with taut sewing to prevent the edges from puckering.

- **Precut strips of nylon tricot such as Seams Great®**—Wrap this 1/2" strip around a seam allowance and start sewing. Then as you slightly pull on it, it continues to wrap the edge as you stitch. It is excellent for VERY ravelly fabrics. Avoid a hot iron when pressing seams.

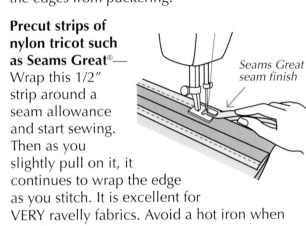

Seams Great seam finish

- **Double-stitched narrow seam**—perfect for loosely fitted pants of velours, sweatshirt fabrics, or lightweight knits. After sewing seam, stitch seam allowances together 1/4" from first stitching. Trim to stitching.

1/4"

- **Stretch overlock (or double overlock) stitch**—stitches a seam and overcasts in one step. It is the most durable stitch you can use for the curve of a crotch seam.

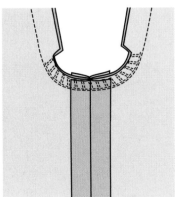

Press As You Sew

Pressing is second only to fitting in importance for the quality look of a finished garment.

Pressing Darts

1. Press darts flat first to flatten fold line and to eliminate any puckered stitching.

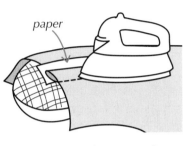

2. Press darts toward center over a curve on a pressing ham that matches the curve of the dart (and your body!). Tuck paper under the fold if necessary to prevent an indentation from showing on the right side.

paper

3. Flatten dart, especially point area, with a pounding block/clapper. Hold down firmly until fabric cools.

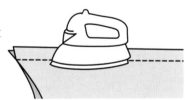

Pressing Seams

1. Press seam flat just as it was stitched to remove any puckers.

2. Press seams open over a seam roll or Seam Stick® to prevent seam imprints from showing on the right side. Use a ham if seam is curved.

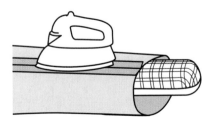

NOTE: The Seam Stick is a half dowel long enough to press open an entire leg seam.

3. While the seam is still moist and warm, apply pressure using the pounding block. Leave it in place for five seconds. As the fabric cools under the pressure and the wood absorbs the heat and steam, the seam gains a "memory."

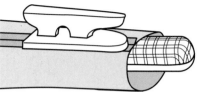

4. Do not move pants until fabric is cool or else what you have pressed in will fall out. Fabrics don't have a memory until they are cool.

Creasing Pants

A pant crease is a vertical line that can make any figure appear taller and more slender. Some fabrics crease beautifully; others won't hold a crease. Test a scrap before deciding to crease. Some styles lend themselves to creasing and others don't.

When we might NOT crease a pant:
It is a soft fabric.
It is a knit.
It is a fitted or sporty style.
It is a very full pant.
It is a jean style.

The FRONT crease goes to mid-hip. The BACK crease stops at the crotch line.

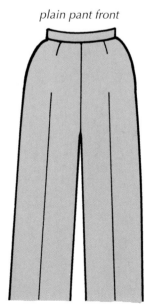

plain pant front

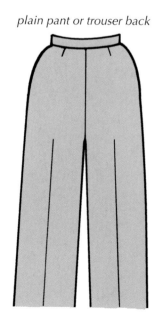

plain pant or trouser back

In trousers, the front crease should meet the edge of one of the pleats, generally the one closer to the center front. This gives a slimming vertical line from waist to toe. (See page 80 for details on pressing the front crease in a trouser while sewing.)

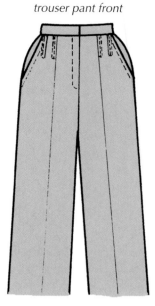

trouser pant front

Place pants on a pressing board (page 100). Match inseams and outseams up to the knee area. (Pin them together.) Make sure creases are smooth and appear to be on straight of grain above knee area.

Use a press cloth if the fabric shines.

Press with an up and down motion instead of a sliding motion. Then use a pounding block to get a crisp edge. Let cool before moving.

Press under leg first and then upper leg while it is on top. Then flip pant over and repeat.

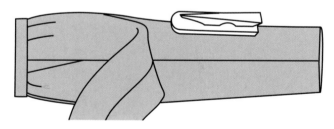

Pressing Trouser Creases

Press trouser creases in the same way, except the front crease goes all the way to the pleat, usually the one closer to the center front.

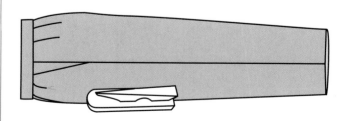

When you press a crease into a pleat, it is less awkward if the pleat is next to the press board so you can press up INTO it.

1. Press the pleat in the direction pattern indicates.

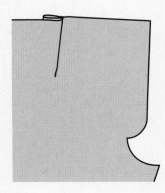

2. Place pant front right side down on the pressing surface. Fold front of pant over the pleat stitching to expose crease fold

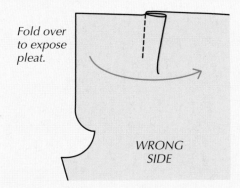

Fold over to expose pleat.

WRONG SIDE

3. Press crease.

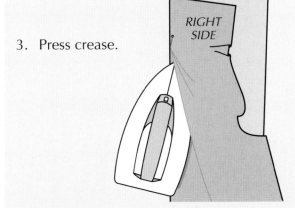

RIGHT SIDE

See page 80 for pressing the crease BEFORE sewing the pant front.

Usually one pleat is deep and the other more shallow. Both get slightly narrower at the bottom, especially the more shallow one.

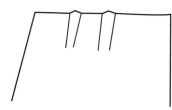

To make trouser pleats more flattering, slip a seam roll or sleeve board under the front pleat. Pin into the surface to hold the pleat in place.

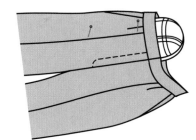

Use a press cloth if the fabric shines. Top press the deeper pleat flat from the waist to the thigh. It can get a little narrower at the thigh. Use a pounding block to flatten. Let cool before moving.

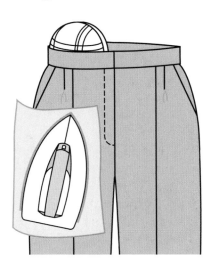

If pants with pleats were shorts, the hem would look like a pleated skirt.

The narrower pleat can be lightly pressed into a dart shape.

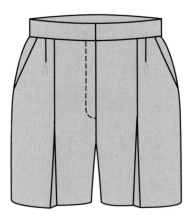

CHAPTER 12
All About Darts

Fitting Darts

Darts are only markings placed on patterns by the pattern companies. They are used to make the waistline the measurement on the size chart. They also shape flat fabric to the curves of the body. Curvy bodies need more or deeper darts than straight bodies.

Slanted crotch seams can replace some dart width. Curved side seams can also replace some dart width. All need to be taken into account.

Depending on your shape, you may need no darts or more darts than are printed on the pattern.

No Darts   **One Dart**

Two Darts   **Three Darts**

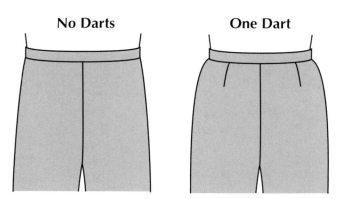

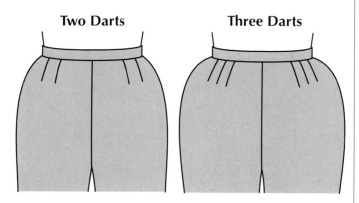

You can fit darts while you are tissue-fitting and then fine-tune them on your body in fabric.

Excess fullness where the darts end indicates the darts are not stopping at body bumps. The darts may be too long, too deep, or not needed.

Most women have a rounded tummy, and the area on both sides of it is hollow. But too often, the darts point toward the hollow area rather than to a bump, creating too much fullness below!

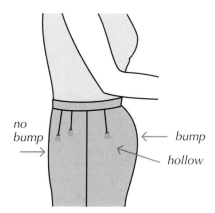

no bump   *bump*   *hollow*

Slanting the darts to point toward the tummy would solve this problem, but it wouldn't look good. Instead, you could move the darts closer to the side seam where they would point to the hipbone.

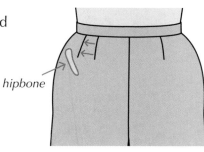

hipbone

Or, sew them: narrower,   shorter, or,   narrower and shorter.

Pulls mean the dart needs to be moved over.   Fullness at the waistline means the darts need to be curved.

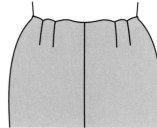

If you sew curved darts, start the curve at the waistline seam.

If you start the curve at the top edge, the waist will be too small.

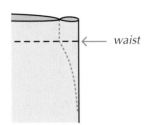 

← *waist*

Many of us have a "pillow" near the side back. You may need three back darts. While fabric fitting, pin the darts on the outside to fit your shape. Chalk-mark where the pins go through the fabric so you will know where to sew. First, transfer the marks to your pattern so you won't have to do this again.

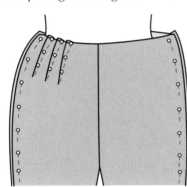

You may also need to curve the side seams just below the waist.

Do it like this,   not like this.

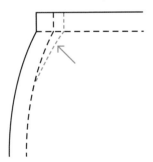 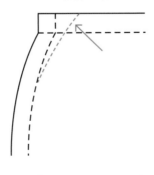

Some people will choose to ease the front waistline to the waistband instead of sewing darts. If your fabric will ease well, this is a good choice.

Sewing Pucker-free Darts

For a perfect dart without tying threads, stitch toward the point, change to a short stitch length for the last 1/2"-3/4". The last five stitches should just catch a fiber of fabric along the fold. Stitch off the edge. Lift the presser foot and pull dart toward you and stitch in the dart fold to anchor the threads.

Special Tips for Dart and Center Seam Fit

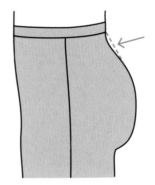

You could curve darts into your body, but if you don't want to emphasize the hollow, let the dart skim over it.

If you curve into your waist a lot, you may need to sew a curve at the top of the center front seam.

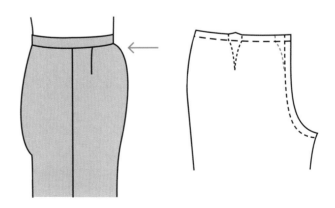

Also see page 42, as well as Alicia, page 66.

Zippers Made Easier

Zipper Length

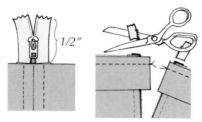

Buy a zipper 1"-2" longer than you need! The slider won't get in your way and cause crooked topstitching. Sew in, then unzip zipper, sew band over top and cut off excess.

> NOTE: Today's synthetic coil zippers are self-locking. They don't need to be zipped to the top to stay up. This means they are now shortened from the top, not the bottom.

Use a zipper that's long enough for you. A 9" zipper works for most people and will end up with enough length for the slider to be off the top edge of the fabric. Use a shorter one if you are short in the crotch and a longer one if you are long in the crotch. If your waist is small and your hips large, you'll need a longer zipper.

Put zippers in center front or back even if the pattern calls for a side seam zipper, so you can alter side seams without restitching the zipper.

Timesaving Tapes:

- Basting tape, a 1/8" tape that's sticky on both sides, is used to eliminate hand basting. It comes on a reel covered with protective paper. Stick it to edges of zipper, peel away paper, and stick zipper to fabric. Stitch next to tape, not through it.

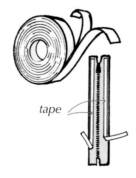

tape

- 1/2" Scotch® Magic™ Tape, used as a straight topstitching guideline for both lapped and centered zippers.

Centered Zipper

For beginners, this is easiest method, and it is the one shown in pattern instructions. Using a longer zipper will make it much easier to do a neat job.

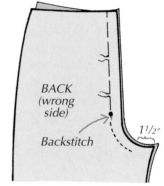

BACK (wrong side)

Backstitch

1½"

1. Permanently stitch crotch seam beginning 1½" from inseam and backstitching at zipper opening. Machine baste seam closed. Snip basting every 1-1½" on one side.

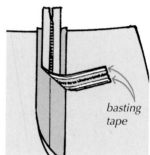

basting tape

2. Press seam open. Place basting tape on right side of zipper edges. Center zipper coil over seam and stick in place.

Scotch tape

3. Center 1/2" tape over seam and topstitch along each side using zipper foot.

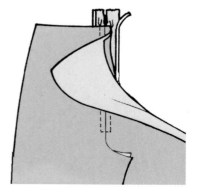

4. Remove tapes and machine basting.

Lapped Zipper

We prefer this method over the centered for a more professional look, but for a beginner, the centered is easier.

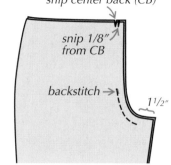

1. Snip-mark for zipper placement as shown. Permanently stitch crotch seam beginning 1½" from inseam, backstitching at zipper opening.

   snip center back (CB)
   snip 1/8" from CB
   backstitch →
   1½"

2. Press under 5/8" on the left back to create the overlap and 1/2" on the right back to create the underlap. Press the underlap to 1" below zipper opening.

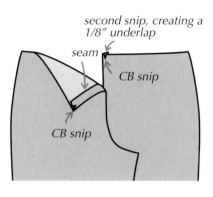

   second snip, creating a 1/8" underlap
   seam
   CB snip
   CB snip

3. Place basting tape on right edge of zipper tape and stick underlap fold next to zipper coil. Stitch close to fold with zipper foot to about 1" below zipper opening.

   basting tape

4. Place basting tape on overlap fold.

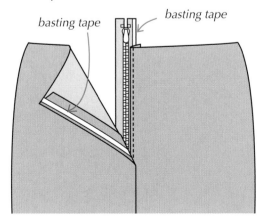

   basting tape
   basting tape

5. Stick overlap over zipper matching center back snips. Stick 1/2" Scotch Magic Tape next to fold. Pin through all layers to prevent scooting and topstitch with a zipper foot next to tape. Remove basting tape and Scotch tape.

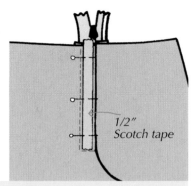

   1/2" Scotch tape

TIP: On lightweight or slippery fabrics, fuse a 1" strip of lightweight fusible interfacing in zipper area before sewing zipper. PerfectFuse Sheer works well; it won't pucker after washing.

Fly Front Zipper for Women

A fly front zipper is like a lapped zipper. There is an overlap and an underlap. A woman's fly laps right over left generally. Some manufacturers of ready-made pants use the men's lapping direction, left over right. The fold line on the overlap side is the center front (CF).

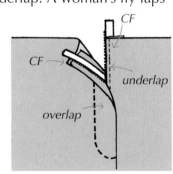

   CF
   CF
   underlap
   overlap

Check your pattern before cutting. The fly front extension should measure at least 1½" wide so it will be caught in topstitching.

If the fly front is not 1½" wide, add width when cutting.

Add a fly front extension to ANY pant or skirt pattern. Just add 1½" from CF and make it 7"-8" long.

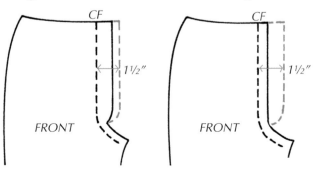

   CF
   1½"
   FRONT
   CF
   1½"
   FRONT

1. Snip-mark fold lines for the overlap and underlap. The overlap fold is the center front (CF). The underlap fold is 5/8" toward the cut edge from CF.

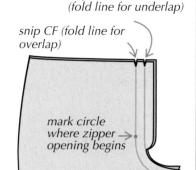

snip 5/8" from CF (fold line for underlap)

snip CF (fold line for overlap)

mark circle where zipper opening begins

FRONT

NOTE: With the 5/8"-deep underlap, your zipper will never show, so color matching isn't necessary. We've used red zippers in purple pants to prove the point!

Also mark the circle where the zipper opening begins. Pin the crotch seam together at that circle.

2. Stitch crotch seam, beginning 1½" from inseam up to zipper opening. Backstitch at the circle.

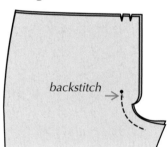

backstitch

3. Fold right front (overlap) under from crotch seam to CF snip. Press.

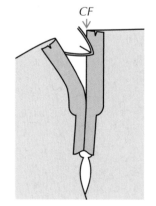

CF

4. Fold left front (underlap) under from crotch seam allowance edge to underlap snip. Center front snips will also match.

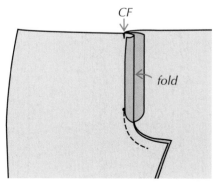

CF

fold

PRO Tip To prevent knits from stretching, fuse interfacing such as PerfectFuse Sheer to wrong side of fly extensions from fold to cut edge.

5. Place basting tape on underlap side of zipper. Peel away protective paper and stick to underlap. Stitch next to fold using a zipper foot.

6. Place basting tape on edge of overlap. Peel away protective paper.

7. Line up CF snips and stick overlap in place.

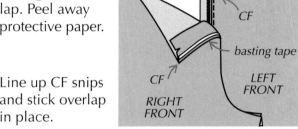

basting tape

CF

basting tape

CF

RIGHT FRONT

LEFT FRONT

OPTIONAL: With our instructions it is not necessary to flip the overlap out of the way and stitch the zipper to the extension before topstitching UNLESS you want extra strength or wider topstitching.

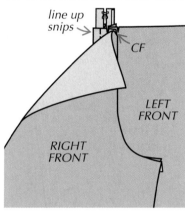

line up snips

CF

LEFT FRONT

RIGHT FRONT

8. Lay fronts on a flat surface and pin horizontally through all layers to prevent scooting of top layer while stitching. Place the last pin just below the zipper stop so you can stitch just below it.

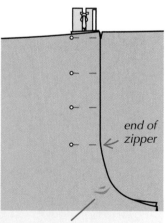

end of zipper

PRO Tip If you see a bubble here after pinning, unpin and run your hand from the zipper opening on the overlap side up to the top. This will smooth the bubble out by scooting some of the fabric to the top. Repin. Use 505 Temporary Spray between the layers to prevent scooting.

9. Topstitch 1" from center front using one of these methods to help you stitch straight:

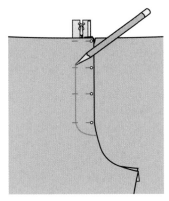

- Draw stitching line with chalk or water soluble marker.

- Stick pins into fabric 1" from fold. Place Scotch Magic Tape next to the pins. (Do not use tape on napped fabrics.) Or, use two rows of 1/2" tape, one next to the fold and one next to it to create the 1" guideline.

1" wide

Stitch next to the tape. When you get to the curve, step on the accelerator and go! It's easier to make a nice curve when you stitch fast. Remove tape.

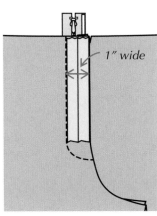

template

- Make a template using the stitching line from the pattern. Place it on the fabric and trace around it with chalk. Tuck template back into pattern envelope to use again!

stitch

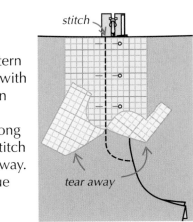

tear away

- Use Perfect Pattern Paper, a tissue with a 1" grid. Pin in place with the dark 1" line along overlap fold. Stitch along line 1" away. Tear away tissue paper.

Bartacking

In some sporty pants or pants that will get heavy wear, a reinforcing bartack is done through all layers at bottom of zipper opening.

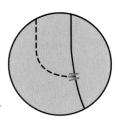

Fly Protector

We do not feel one is necessary on women's pants unless you use a scratchy metal zipper rather than a smooth synthetic coil zipper. It just adds bulk. For information on sewing a fly protector, see men's fly front zipper, page 165.

Invisible Zippers Are Back

The invisible zipper of the '70s was bulky. Today's has a fine coil. You can buy the special foot that opens the coil as you sew or use a zipper foot as follows:

NOTE: Sew the zipper to the pants before sewing the crotch seam.

1. Open zipper. From the wrong side press the teeth flat so you can sew close to them.

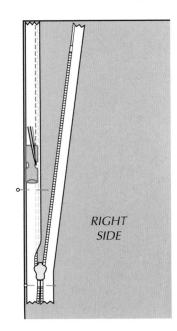

2. Place open zipper right side down onto right side of fabric. To prevent stretch, you may use basting tape to hold zipper in place. For lightweight fabrics fuse interfacing to WRONG side in zipper area.

3. The top edge of the zipper tape should match, the top of the pant, and the long edge should match the edge of the fabric. Sew next to teeth until front of foot hits the slider. (Take out pins as you sew.)

RIGHT SIDE

4. Close the zipper and flip it to the right side.

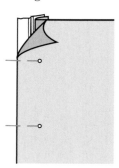

5. Place other garment section right sides together and pin zipper to fabric edge as shown. Or, use basting tape to hold in place.

NOTE: Be sure the top edge of zipper matches top of fabric and long edge matches edge of fabric. You actually end up sewing 1/2" from the edge of your fabric, but when the zipper is closed, 5/8" rolls under.

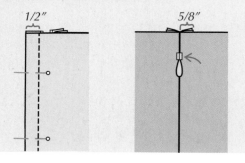

6. Unzip the zipper and sew the other side the same way.

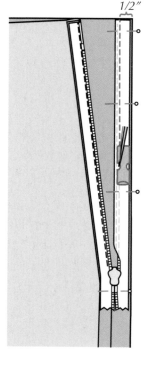

7. Sew the rest of the seam below the zipper, right sides together, using a zipper foot.

TIP: To avoid a pucker at the base of the zipper, start sewing 1/2" above and 1/8" out from the end of the zipper stitching (on the 5/8" stitching line)

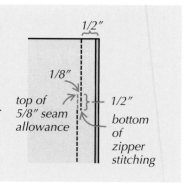

TIP No. 2: With presser foot up and zipper teeth standing on their side, lower needle into exact spot you want to start sewing. DO NOT BACKSTITCH. Lower the presser foot and stitch to the end of the seam. Pull threads to one side at the beginning of the seam and tie a knot.

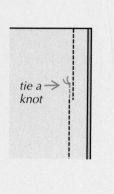

8. To strengthen the zipper, sew the bottom of the tape to the seam allowances ONLY, using your machine.

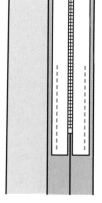

NOTE: Invisible zippers are shortened from the bottom. Zigzag over the teeth with a short, wide stitch to lock the end and trim away extra length.

CHAPTER 14
The Perfect Non-Roll Waistband

Monofilament nylon waistband interfacing is lightweight, will not stretch, and won't roll (even after lunch!). "The Perfect Waistband Interfacing" is 1" wide and comes in a 5 yard package with instructions. (Armoflexx and Ban-rol are no longer available . However, "Perfect Waistband" is still called Armoflexx in Australia.) Some patterns are changing the standard width to 1" from 1¼" when using this interfacing.

Tissue-Fit

Wrap the tissue around your waist and mark where it meets. Leave a 3" extension on each end in case you need it.

If you don't have a waistband pattern piece or one that fits, use the gridded Perfect Pattern Paper or tissue. Cut your pattern piece 6" longer than your waist measurement and twice the finished width, plus 1 1/4" for seam allowances.

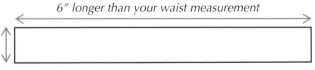

6" longer than your waist measurement

3¼" wide for 1"-wide interfacing

Cut Out Fabric

TIP: For lightweight fabrics, fuse lightweight interfacing to the wrong side of the waistband for a little more body, then apply waistband interfacing as usual. If you can't find the non-roll interfacing, fuse to the wrong side with a heavier weight fusible.

Sew

1. Mark the 5/8" stitching line on one long edge of your band with machine basting. (Now it's marked on both right and wrong sides of the fabric!)

seamline

2. Place the interfacing next to the stitching line on the WRONG SIDE of the band. Stitch interfacing to the seam allowance.

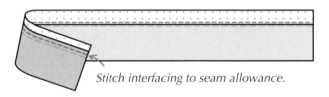

Stitch interfacing to seam allowance.

TIP: The finished waistband needs to be 1/2" to 1½" bigger than your waistline to allow for the layers of fabrics in the waistband seam and tucked-in tops. Don't fit your pants too tight!

3. We have a WONDERFUL new way to fit a waistband. Try on the pant without the waistband pinned to it. Fold the waistband over the interfacing and wrap the waistband around your waist JUST AS IT WILL BE SEWN. When the waistband feels comfortably snug, pin the ends together. Distribute the ease at the top of the pants under the waistband until smooth. Chalk all matching points such as center front and back, darts, tucks, pockets, and side seams. Now you will know where to pin the band to the pants, making it fit perfectly, even if your right and left sides are different! We call it the QUICK FIT BAND TRICK! (See page 86, Sue.)

Before you chalk-mark, look for the following:

Pull the pants up above any dimples, and if wrinkles are pointing to the side waistband, pull pants down at the sides until all wrinkles are gone.

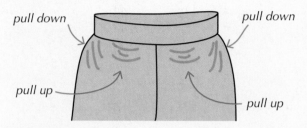

pull down   *pull down*

pull up   *pull up*

Horizontal wrinkles below the waistband mean the pant is too tight in the high hip area so it creeps up seeking more room. Let out the side seams just below the waistband.

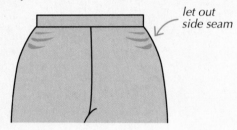

let out side seam

If you have uneven hips, adjust so more ease is above the fuller areas.

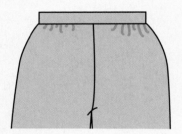

If your high hip is considerably larger than your waistline, you will end up with lots of ease or several curved darts and a curved side seam. (See darts page 104.)

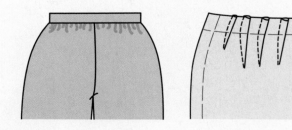

4. Pin band to pants, lining up chalk marks to matching points and matching the top edges of interfacing and pants. (You should have trimmed your pant waist seam allowance to an even 1".) Marta pins horizontally and removes pins as she sews. Pati pins vertically anchoring floppy seams.

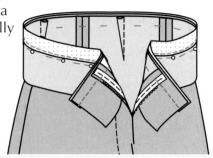

TIP: Unless your sides are straight up and down with no waist indentation, the pant will be a little larger than the band, allowing the pants to fall more gracefully over your hips. Your feed dogs will help ease the pant to the band.

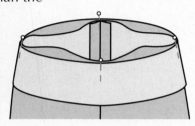

If you need to ease a lot of the pant into your waistband, hold the waistline over your hand as you pin. If the pant is on top of the band, the ease will disappear, making pinning a breeze. Use LOTS of pins! Remove pins as you sew or VERY CAREFULLY sew over them slowly so you don't break your needle.

waistband

5. With the waistband on top, sew just below the interfacing. Your feed dogs will help ease the pant to the band.

NOTE: If you are lining the pants, before step 6 sew the lining into pants, wrong sides together. (See page 157.)

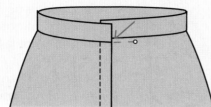

7. To make the ends firm so that the hooks won't pull out and show, fuse everything together. Use a 1" x 2" rectangle of fusible web. Wrap it over the interfacing. Turn band to the right side. Press until the web melts.

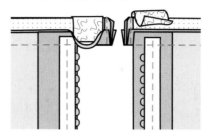

6. Fold band in half right sides together with seams turned up.

   Don't sew through the monofilament nylon interfacing as it will be too bulky. Trim the interfacing just inside the stitching line.

   Stitch the ends, backstitching at the beginning and the end of the seam. After stitching, trim the seam to 1/4" and cut corners diagonally.

Stitch next to interfacing.　　　*Trim away interfacing.*

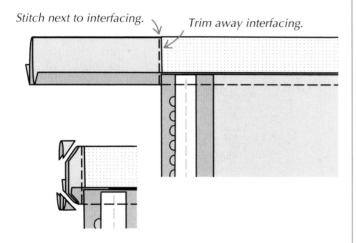

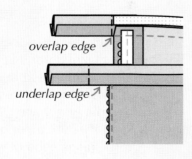

overlap edge

underlap edge

8. Clip the seam allowance on the underside of the band about 1½" from the zipper teeth. Hand slipstitch the seam allowance at the ends of the band together.

9. Finish the long edge of the underside of the band with zigzagging or serging, leaving at least a 1/4" seam allowance. (Finish earlier if you wish.)

   Then fold the band tightly over the interfacing and pin flat. Note that the interfacing acts as a cushion for the seam allowances, making the right side of the waistband very flat and smooth.

edge finish

interfacing

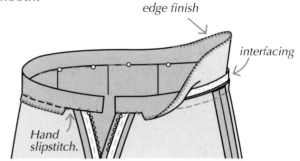

Hand slipstitch.

10. Now stitch from the right side in the well- of-the-seam to hold the band in place. This is less bulky than turning under the seam allowance.

Stitch in the well of the seam. (Hint: use edgestitch foot.)

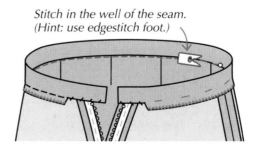

11. Sew on the hooks and eyes. A double set will hold better. Try sewing them on by machine if you are covering your band with a belt or if the fabric is dark and the stitches won't show. Tape them in place with Scotch Tape and use a narrow zigzag stitch. Or use a snap in place of a second set of hooks and eyes.

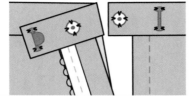

TIP: Do you get this pull at the top? Reposition hook or eye to tighten waistband and instantly solve the problem!

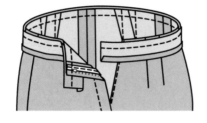

Wrapped Seam Allowance Waistband

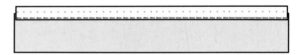

If you are short waisted or like a softer waistband, the bound waist-band seam is for YOU! Because it is narrow and filled with seam allowances, it won't roll.

Use your fashion fabric on the lengthwise grain (least stretch). If your fabric is a natural fiber or a stretchy fabric, fuse a strip of interfacing to the wrong side with the stable direction the length of the waistband. Or, sew a strip of seam tape or Stay-tape in the seam.

1. Cut the binding four times your seam allowance. If it is 5/8", the binding is 2½" wide.

2. Press under a seam allowance along one long edge, or serge, trimming 1/4" off.

3. Pin binding to pants RIGHT SIDES TOGETHER. Stitch.

4. Fold binding in half RIGHT SIDES TOGETHER with seam allowances both turned up.

5. Stitch left back end even with center back.

6. Stitch right back end, leaving an extension for fasteners.

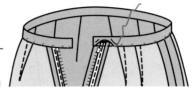

7. Trim seam and cut diagonally at corners.

8. Turn right sides out and slipstitch fold-ed edge to pant, or stitch in the well-of-the-seam as on previous band (page 113).

9. Sew on hooks and eyes or a hook and snap at the ends.

Shaped Non-Roll Waistband

If you are smaller in the waist than your high hip area, or if you want to have the waistband sit below your waist, you might need to shape it. It will shape better if cut on crosswise grain.

Sew the monofilament nylon waistband interfacing to the seam allowance of the waistband (page 111).

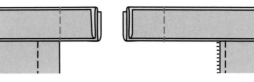

Wrap the waistband tightly over the interfacing and press. Then shape it with an iron using steam and a press cloth if the fabric might shine.

As you press, curve the band.

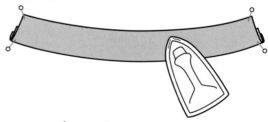

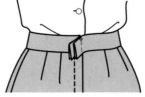

Shape it a little at a time and try it on to make sure you don't over-shape it. Sew to pant as shown on page 112.

CHAPTER 15

Belts Loops The Easy Way

Belt loops are great if your waistline changes size throughout the day. Wear a belt and adjust it!!

1. Cut one long strip of fashion fabric 1¼"-wide. Press under 1/4" on each long edge and fold in half. Press.

2. Edgestitch along each long edge.

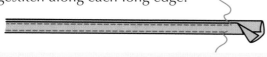

> **TIP:** Cut one edge on selvage and make strip 1" wide. Fold under 1/4" on raw edge. Fold in half.
>
>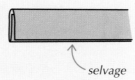
>
> *selvage*

Quick Tip The easiest way to make and sew belt carriers is to cut a 1¼"-wide strip of fabric and run it through the 18mm bias tape maker, pressing as the fabric comes out the other end. This helps you evenly press 1/4" toward center. Then fold in half and press. If you can't force your fabric through the tape maker, use a pin. Belt loops are generally on the straight of grain, but they can be bias, depending on the look you want.

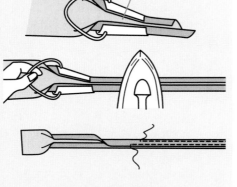

3. Cut carriers a length that can accommodate the width of the belt you plan to wear plus about 1/4" for ease and another 3/4" for plenty to turn under on each end.

4. Pin or baste them to the side seams, center back, and between center front and side on each side of the front so top edge is 1/4" above waistline seam.

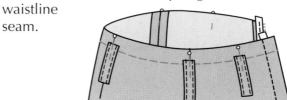

5. Sew waist-band to pants.

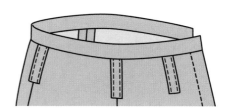

6. Bring belt carriers over the top of band to wrong side and hand stitch in place or machine edgestitch through all layers at top.

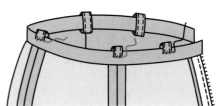

> **TIP:** If you have already finished the waistband, turn under each end of carrier and topstitch to pant about 1/4" below waistband and at top edge.
>
>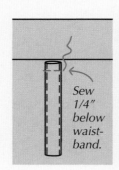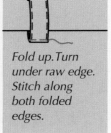
>
> *Sew 1/4" below waistband.*
>
> *Fold up. Turn under raw edge. Stitch along both folded edges.*

NOTE: For a wider belt, use a longer strip and sew it further below the waistband

CHAPTER 16

Comfortable, Expandable Waistbands

If you fluctuate in weight throughout the day, you can use elastic as your waistband interfacing or in combination with a non-roll interfacing. Or, if you use the non-roll waistband in the previous chapter, fit when your figure is the fullest. If you fluctuate a lot, add belt loops and a belt so you can tighten or loosen your belt as needed.

Elastic Waistband in a Zippered Pant

Choose 3/4"- to 1"-wide non-roll elastic. Wider elastic will tend to fold in half inside the band.

1. Fit the pants 1"-2" looser in the waist by sewing narrower side seams or narrowing or eliminating darts. Sew the band to the pant.

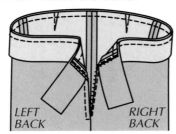

LEFT BACK   RIGHT BACK

TIP: Rather than cutting elastic to fit you perfectly ahead of time, use an extra long piece (for example, whatever is in the package) as it is MUCH EASIER!

2. Place elastic on the seam allowance of the waistband piece (not pant side of seam allowance). Start with the end that will be the UNDERLAP with elastic next to where you will sew the seam at the end of the band.

3. Zigzag elastic to seam allowances through all layers for 2".

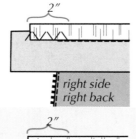

right side right back

TIP: Or use a honeycomb stitch. It flattens the bulk better.

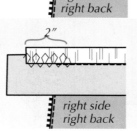

right side right back

4. Fold band at this end in half right sides together, with seam allowances turned up. Stitch next to elastic. Backstitch at beginning and end. Trim seam and turn. Now elastic is caught in ONE end of the band.

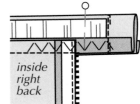

inside right back

5. Clip the seam allowance of the band underside 2" from each end. Turn under the seam allowance near the underlap end and slip stitch the folded edges together. Serge-finish and trim the remaining inside waistband seam allowance to 1/4"-1/2". (Or, trim and zigzag.)

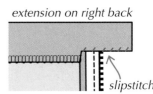

extension on right back

slipstitch

6. Fold rest of waistband over elastic tightly and pin. Stitch in the well-of-the-seam from the right side to within 5" of the other end.

Stitch in well-of-the-seam to here.

TIP: Use your edge-stitch foot to help stay in the well of the seam.

7. Try on pants. Pull on elastic to tighten it until comfortable.

8. Zigzag the elastic to the seam allowances from OVERLAP END for 2". Cut off extra elastic even with edge of pant.

Outside LEFT BACK

9. Finish OVERLAP end by stitching as you did for UNDERLAP end.

10. Finish stitching in the well-of-the-seam. Slipstitch folded edge in place.

11. Sew on hooks and eyes.

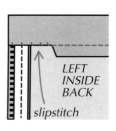

LEFT INSIDE BACK

slipstitch

Elastic-Back Waistbands

If you want a band that won't roll in the front when you sit but has a little give for expanding waistlines, try these techniques.

Non-Roll Combined with Elastic

The elastic sewn to each end of a piece of non-roll interfacing will be a total of 2" shorter than the waistband, but any gathers will occur only across the back until your waist expands, making the elastic the same size as the band.

1. Determine length of finished waistband and add 2". Measure from side to side across your front. Cut non-roll interfacing that length plus 1" for lapping each end 1/2" over elastic. Measure from side to center back and cut two pieces of 1" elastic that length less 1".

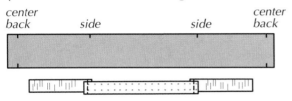

center back   side   side   center back

2. Lap ends of non-roll interfacing 1/2" over each piece of elastic and stitch ends together.

3. Apply as in previous elastic application.

Non-Roll Front, Elastic Back

For even more give, use a non-roll interfacing across the front and elastic across the back. Since the non-roll interfacing is 1" wide, use 1"-wide elastic. Side seams are finished after waistband pieces are applied.

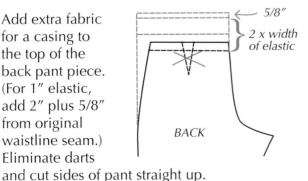

1. Add extra fabric for a casing to the top of the back pant piece. (For 1" elastic, add 2" plus 5/8" from original waistline seam.) Eliminate darts and cut sides of pant straight up.

5/8"

2 x width of elastic

BACK

2. Stitch center back crotch seam. Finish top edge of waistband. Fold casing down and stitch. (For 1" elastic, stitch about 1 1/8" from fold.)

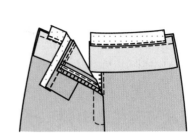

casing

finished edge

3. Apply non-roll interfacing to front waistband pieces (see page 111).

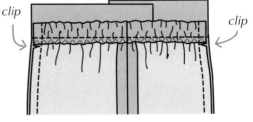

4. Insert elastic in back casing. Pin elastic ends to anchor them. Pin front and back side seams together.

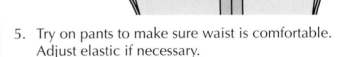

5. Try on pants to make sure waist is comfortable. Adjust elastic if necessary.

6. Sew side seams through waistband and elastic. Backstitch at top. Clip back side seam allowances to seamline. Press seam allowances above waistline toward front. (Or, press side seams toward front.)

clip   clip

7. Finish the ends of the waistband (see page 113.)

8. Fold front waistband over elastic. Stitch in the well-of-the-seam from the right side to anchor the front bands.

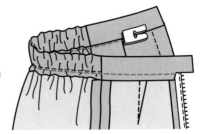

9. Slipstitch front ends of waistband and side seams. Stretch back waistband until smooth and stitch one or more rows of stitching through all layers.

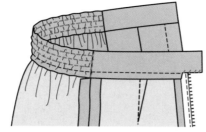

TIP: If including elastic in the seams is too bulky, sew an inch square of lightweight non-ravelly fabric to ends of elastic and include that in the seams instead. If you use seam tape or Stay-tape, zigzag two pieces together.

← seam tape

Shirred Elastic

If you want a pull-on pant that is non-bulky and very comfortable to wear, try Stitch & Stretch™, a polyester woven band with rows of spandex elastic cording drawn through it. It comes in 1″, 1½″, and 2½″ widths. It is so non-binding that it would be comfortable over the tummy of someone nine months pregnant, if ANYTHING could be comfortable that is!

Pati likes this technique in soft rayon print pants either combined with a non-roll front or as a pull-on pant. **First decide if you want to wear this soft elastic above or below your waist and what width you'd like to use.** The wider widths give a nice shirred look. Add length you need for a cut-on waistband; then cut an extra 1/2″ onto the top of the pant.

1. Sew your pants, but leave 5″ of the back crotch seam unstitched.

2. Finish the back seam allowances with zig-zagging or serging.

3. Cut a piece of Stitch & Stretch the length of the top of the pants.

4. Press under 1/2″ around the top of the pants.

5. Pin Stitch & Stretch to the wrong side of the fabric, positioning it 1/8″ from the fold.

6. Sew it to the wrong side of the fabric along each of the blue lines on Stitch & Stretch.

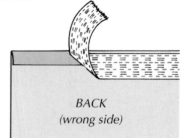

BACK
(wrong side)

7. On one end of the center back, sew two rows of very narrow satin zigzag stitches, 1/4″ and 1/2″ from the edge to secure the elastic cords. Use a stitch length of 1.5mm and a width of .3mm. It is hard to stitch through the cords, but you should catch them with two rows of satin stitching.

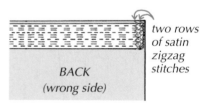

BACK
(wrong side)

two rows of satin zigzag stitches

8. On the other side of the center back, grab all four of the elastic cords in each row at one time and pull on them EVENLY until the waist-line comfortably fits your body.

9. Anchor the elastic cords just as you did on the other side of the center back.

Trim excess cords. ↘

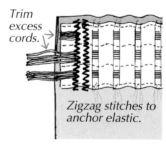

10. Trim off excess cords and smooth the gathers around the top of the pant evenly.

Zigzag stitches to anchor elastic.

11. Now finish stitching the center back seam through the stitch and stretch.

12. Press the seam open and hand catch the seam allowances down to the Stitch & Stretch to anchor them.

Pull-on Pants in Any Fabric — Knits or Wovens

If you want pull-on pants, the waistline will need to be large enough to fit over your hips. If you have a small waist and large hips, you will have a lot of gathers at the waistline. The extra bulk won't be flattering unless the fabric is very soft.

If you are straight up and down, pull-on pants work great. There will be hardly any gathering at your waistline.

Cut-on Fold-over Casing

If you are converting a pant with darts, eliminate darts and cut the side seams straight up. For 1" elastic you will need 2⁵⁄₈" extra fabric above WAISTLINE seam for casing.

1. Sew crotch seams to within 1½" of inseams.

2. Pin side seams and inseams WRONG SIDES TOGETHER. Try on with 1/4" elastic around your waist.

3. Pin-fit deeper or shallower side seams. Pull pants up or down evenly all the way around until the crotch is comfortable. Mark new waistline seam.

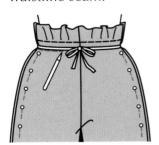 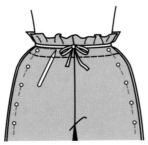

NOTE: Ease may depend on fabric.

	Hip Ease	Crotch Depth Ease
Knits or lightweight, soft fabrics	1"-3"	1/4"-1/2"
Wovens or heavier, stiffer fabrics	2"-4"	1/3"-3/4"

FIT Tip

If you want a smooth fit instead of a more gathered appearance, try to fit as close to the body as possible, but remember the pants must "pull on and off." Get rid of extra bulk at the waistline by pinning side seams deeper at the top and then try to pull pants down over your hips. The amount of fullness you can eliminate depends on your shape and the give of the fabric. The less waist indentation on your body, the more excess fullness you will be able to eliminate and still get pants off.

4. Take pants off and mark where pins are on wrong side. Unpin, place right sides together, and sew side seams and inseams. Trim seams to an even 5/8". Press open.

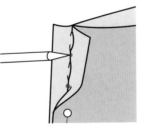

5. Turn one leg inside out and put the other leg inside. Finish sewing crotch seam. Finish crotch as in fitted pant, page 40.

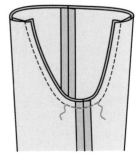

6. Trim seams in casing area to 1/4" and fuse down with a strip of fusible web so the seams won't get in the way when threading elastic through casing.

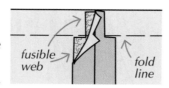
fusible web
fold line

7. Zigzag or serge top edge, or turn under 1/4".

8. Fold casing to inside and topstitch 1 1/8" from top, leaving a 1" opening at center back, through which elastic may be threaded.

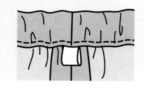
1" opening

9. Wrap elastic around your waist until snugly comfortable. Allow an extra inch for lapping ends of elastic.

10. Thread elastic through casing and finish off ends by overlapping 1" and stitching them together in an "X" as shown.

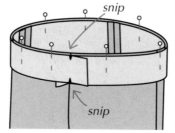

TIP: Sew a loop of seam tape at center back. Pin it in place before stitching opening closed. Then you can always tell the front from the back.

11. Sew remainder of casing seam.

Sew-on Casing in Any Weight Fabric

This method works best if you have a very "wavy" or uneven waistline. To turn under a casing unevenly all the way around would be difficult. This casing also gives the pull-on pants the look of a waistband.

1. Cut waistband to fit top of pants and twice as wide as the elastic, plus two seam allowances. Measure the top of the pant to determine the length.

2. Pin the waistband to the pant, RIGHT SIDES TOGETHER, lapping ends at center back. Snip waistband ends where they cross the center back seam at the top and bottom edges.

snip
snip

3. Match snips and sew center back seam RIGHT SIDES TOGETHER. Trim seam to 1/4" and press open.

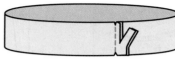

4. Sew band to pants.

5. Finish the inside edge of the waistband casing, leaving a 3/8"-1/2" seam allowance.

6. Cut a piece of elastic the same length as the waistband plus 4". Pin one end on waistband seam allowance at center back with lower edge on seamline.

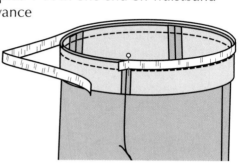

TIP: If you use a very long piece of elastic, and cut it to fit after you have stitched most of the casing, you won't have so many gathers to contend with. Cut off excess after fitting.

7. About 2" from the pin, wrap waistband tightly over the elastic and pin in place to hold. Pin all the way around or until you run out of elastic (if you didn't cut an extra-long piece). If your elastic is shorter, you will need to sew part way and then pull on the elastic to have enough more to fold the casing over.

8. From the right side of the pant, stitch in the well of the seam, catching the underside of the band. Start and stop 2" on either side of the center back.

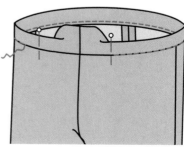

9. Try on pants and pull loose end of elastic until comfortable.

10. Lap 1" of elastic over the end pinned at center back. Pin. Stitch lapped ends as shown (or use honeycomb stitch).

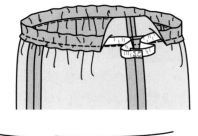

11. Wrap band over center back and finish stitching casing.

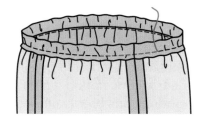

TIP: To keep elastic from rolling, stitch in the well of the seams at center back and sides.

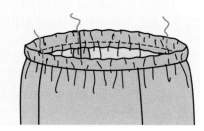

Sew-on Casing for Lightweight Fabrics

This is the quickest method and works well with a serger, but three seam allowances stitched together would be too bulky in heavy fabrics.

1. Make a waistband to exactly fit the the top of the pants. Stitch center back seam, backstitching just past fold, leaving an opening. Press open and fold band wrong sides together.

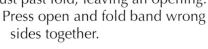

backstitch

2. Pin band to outside of pants.

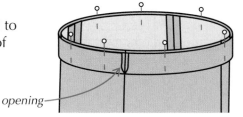

opening

3. Stitch waistband to pant and serge seam allowances together, trimming to a narrow width. Or, trim, then zigzag all seam allowances together to make them neater and flat.

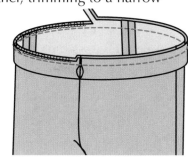

4. Thread elastic through opening. Pin ends together and try on to fit. Finish ends as previously shown. (Or, leave ends of elastic safety-pinned for adjustability!!)

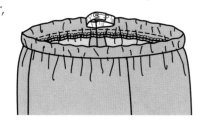

Design Ideas for Waistband Stitching

For pleated pull-on pants, smooth out fullness in casing over front and topstitch through all layers vertically at side seam or front pleat closest to side seam.

Then distribute fullness throughout remainder of casing evenly by pulling on elastic.

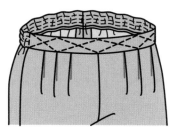

Across back, sew several rows of stitching through all layers while stretching elastic to flatten the fabric. A longer stitch length will allow elastic to recover better.

Then, be your own designer. Sew diamond, zigzag, or swirly or wavy stitching across the smooth area in front, through all layers.

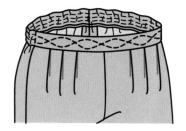

No-side-seam Pull-on Pant

This pant is great out of slinky knits or silky wovens for evening or summer casual wear.

1. Unless you are using a knit, make sure the pattern measures at least 2" larger than body in the hip area, because you will have no side seam to let out. Lap front and back pattern pieces at sides, matching seamlines. Leave out darts and add a cut-on casing (page 117).

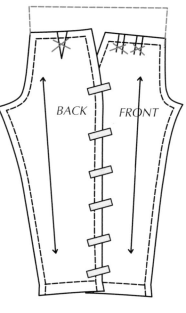

2. Sew inseams. Press open

TIP: For lightweight fabrics, serge the seams.

3. Turn one leg inside out and put other leg in it. Stitch crotch seam.

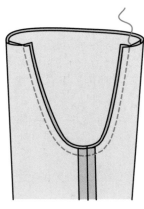

4. Finish casing as in pull-on pant page 120.

Drawstring Waistline Pants

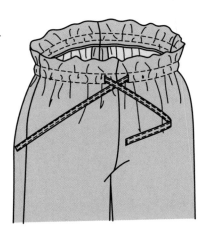

This is a casual look with a comfortable adjustable drawstring.

Usually, a purchased cord is used as the drawstring. However, it can be bulky and won't match your fabric. Sue Neall from Australia uses this technique. She makes a self-fabric cord as if making a belt loop (page 115). It is flat, firm so it won't roll, and of matching fabric.

She likes the "ruffled" look at the top edge of the pant, so she makes her casing wider than what is needed for the drawstring. There is a row of stitching at the waistline and another above it, leaving a ruffled top edge. The inside is nonbulky because the 1/4" seam allowance at the bottom edge is left flat, being serged or zigzagged.

1. Add 3" above the waistline for a casing.

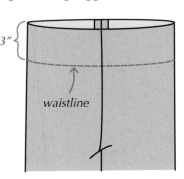

waistline

2. Sew a 5/8"-long vertical buttonhole 3/8" from either side of the center front seam, beginning 1/8" above the waistline.

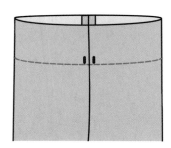

TIP: If you make the upper center front seam allowance 3/4" wide, the buttonhole will be sturdier because it will go through two layers of fabric.

3. Trim seam allowances in casing area to 1/4" to reduce bulk, and fuse them down with a strip of fusible web so they don't stop the drawstring when you thread it through. (See page 120.)

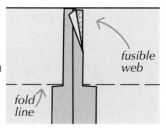

4. Finish top raw edge with serging or other method.

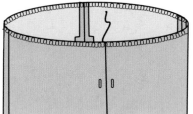

5. Fold 1⅝" to inside of pants and press. Pin close to raw edge of casing.

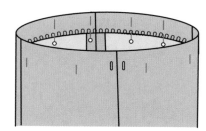

6. Stitch 1/2" from fold.

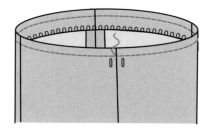

7. Stitch again 7/8" below first line of stitching.

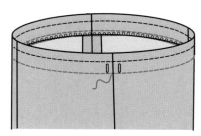

8. Make your cord, belt-loop style. Cut a 2"-wide strip of fabric your waist measurement plus about 30" more to tie into a bow.

9. Press ends under 1/2". Press long edges to the middle and then press in half again. Edgestitch along all edges.

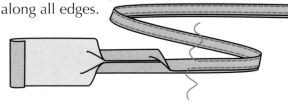

Alternately, see Quick Tip, page 115.

TIP: For comfort, you could insert 1/2" elastic in the middle of the cord for give.

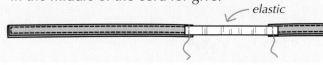

10. Thread your "belt loop" cord through one buttonhole around the pant through the casing and bring it out the other buttonhole.

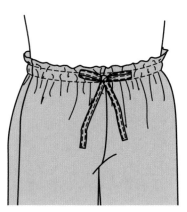

11. After centering your drawstring, stitch in the well of the center back seam through all layers to keep the drawstring from pulling out.

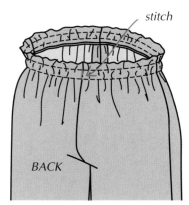

Drawcord Sport Elastic

This product is an elastic with a stretchy cord encased in the center that acts like a drawstring. It allows you to tighten up a sport garment at the waist. It is used in expensive ready-to-wear.

We like the 1" width, but you may find it in other widths.

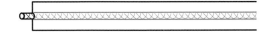

1. Cut a 2" casing above the waistline of a pull-on pant. (Cut a 3/4" wide center front seam. See tip page 122.)

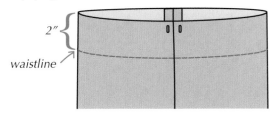

2. Sew a 1/4"-long buttonhole 3/8" from top edge and 3/8" from each side of the center front.

3. Pull the drawcord out of the elastic for about 5" from one end.

   The honeycomb tube elongates easily.

4. Determine the amount of elastic length you need by wrapping it comfortably around your waist. With a pin, lift a loop of cord and cut elastic and cord. Pull about 5" of cord out of that end as well.

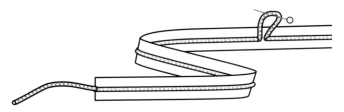

5. Pull a loop of drawcord out about 1/2" from each end. Pull until cord comes out of mesh at that point.

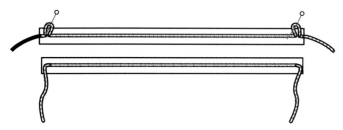

6. Lap ends of elastic and zigzag together.

7. Pants will be larger than elastic. Pin elastic to pants with drawcords at center front. Pull cords through buttonholes. Fold elastic in half and pin halfway point to center back. Evenly pin remainder to pants.

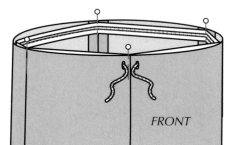

FRONT

8. Zigzag or serge elastic to pant, stretching elastic to fit pants.

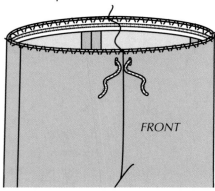

FRONT

9. Turn to inside and stitch casing to pant along lower edge.

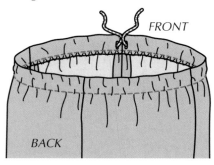

FRONT

BACK

10. Stitch again 1/4" from folded edge and again 1/4" above casing stitching line, being sure not to stitch through cord.

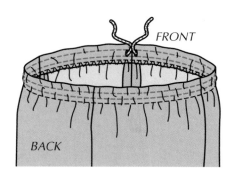

FRONT

BACK

CHAPTER 18

Faced and Contour Waistlines

Faced Waistlines

With Invisible Zipper

If you are short-waisted or you like low-rise pants, this is the waistline treatment for you.

Using an invisible zipper with the faced waistline is by far the easiest method for getting a nice finish at the top of the zipper. If you want a lapped zipper, we would suggest binding the waistline instead of facing it for the neatest look.

Fit the pants and sew and press all seams before applying facing.

> **TIP:** If you are converting a pattern with a waistband to one with a facing, fold out darts. Measure 3″ down from the top edge of the pattern. This section will be the pattern for the facing.

1. Apply invisible zipper following directions on page 109. To avoid bulk, be sure the zipper stop or top of teeth is 3/8″ below the waistline seam.

2. Fuse interfacing to wrong side of facing. Have stable direction of interfacing going around your body.

> **TIP:** So that the facing fits the pant exactly, lap front and back at sides and snip where they lap at side seams. This marks where you will sew facing side seams.

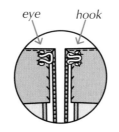

snip

snip

snip

3. Sew facing side seams. Trim to 1/4″ and press open. Finish lower edge.

4. Sew facing to pant, right sides together. Sew through a stabilizing tape such as twill tape, seam tape, Stay-tape™, or the selvage of a lightweight lining fabric. Trim and grade seam.

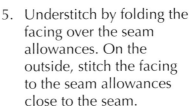

5. Understitch by folding the facing over the seam allowances. On the outside, stitch the facing to the seam allowances close to the seam.

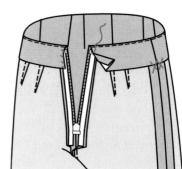

6. Turn facing to inside and press. Hand-stitch facings to zipper tapes and tack to seam allowance.

eye   hook

7. Sew hook and eye above zipper.

> **TIP:** If your invisible zipper tab doesn't match your fabric, paint it. You can find small quantities of paint colors in craft stores. Or, sew a fabric tab to the outside of the pant that can be buttoned over the zipper tab.

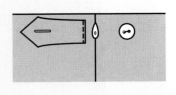

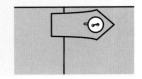

An Alternate Way to Apply Facing

1. Trim 5/8" off center back seam allowances of back facings.

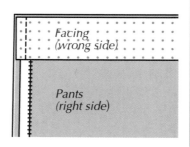

2. Pin facing and pants right sides together. Stitch 3/8" from edge through facing, zipper tape, and pants.

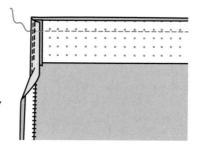

Facing (wrong side)

Pants (right side)

3. Fold 5/8" back, pulling facing out of the way until side seams are lined up. Stitch across top on 5/8" seamline.

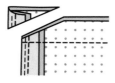

4. Slash corners, trim and grade seams to 1/4".

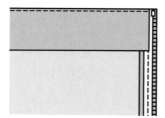

5. Turn, understitch, and press.

Contour Waistlines

The contour waistline has the look of the faced waistline, but it shapes the top of the pant with a separate curved band fitted to the body rather than being shaped with darts. Usually the contour waistline sits below your actual waist. (See Melissa, page 60.)

Fitting a Contour Waistline

A pattern's curve may not match yours. To fit, try on the tissue.

1. If you do not have a full front and back pattern piece, make one so you can fit both sides of your body.

2. Pin the side seams together with seams sticking out.

3. Alter the pattern to fit your shape.

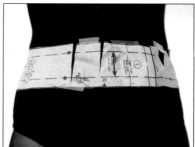

If your waist is larger than the pattern measurement, slash from the top to, but not through, the bottom in several places and spread. Have someone else help you. Tape over the slashes right to your body to hold the spread.

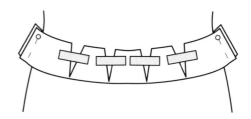

After altering, take the waistband off and place it on tissue. The tape will stick. Add more tape as necessary and trim away excess tissue.

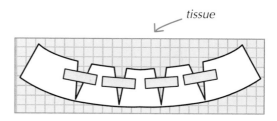

tissue

If your waist is smaller than the pattern, slash from the top and lap the pattern pieces. Pin or tape.

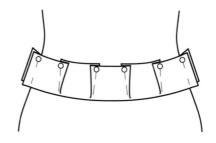

If your high hip/tummy area is larger than the pattern, slash from the bottom and spread. Tape.

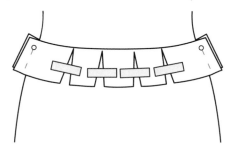

If your high hip/stomach area is smaller than the pattern, but the waist fits, slash from the bottom up and lap. Pin or tape.

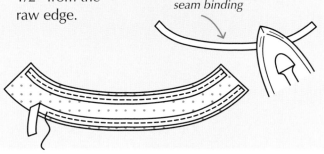

Sewing a Contour Waistband

1. Cut two front and back pieces for the band and its facing.

2. Fuse interfacing to wrong side of band with stable direction going around your body.

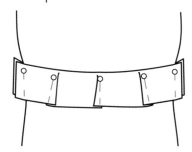

PRO Tip Prevent stretch by taping upper and lower edges of waistband on wrong side with a stay tape centered over the 5/8" seamline. Shape seam binding first by curving it under the iron as you press. Machine-baste in place 1/2" from the raw edge.

seam binding

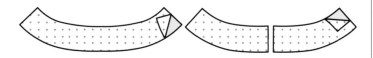

3. Pin waistband sections right sides together, with pins parallel to the edge in the seamline. Wrap band around your waist to make sure you like the fit. Adjust sides seams as necessary.

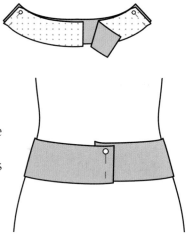

4. Sew the band side seams and press open.

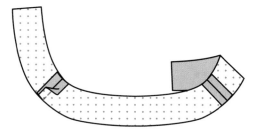

5. Sew band to pants. Press seam allowances toward band.

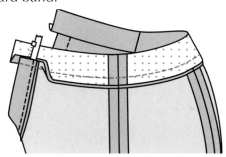

6. Sew facing (which you cut from same altered pattern piece) to band.

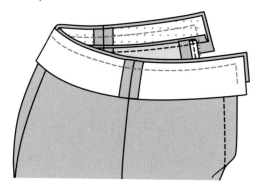

7. Trim, turn and press. Turn under lower edge of facing and slip-stitch in place.

CHAPTER 19
Side Seam and Patch Pockets

Pockets add style to pants and there are many different shape and style possibilities. Side seam and patch pockets are easy to sew. Slanted trouser pockets have a few more steps, but are still easy to sew. The most complex pockets are the welt styles so popular today.

Simple Side Seam Pockets

You must fit pants before adding pocket bags.

TIP: In general, pocket bags can be made from your fashion fabric unless it is too bulky. To reduce bulk, use lining for the bag attached to the pants front. For light-colored pant fabrics, use skin-tone lining for pocket bags.

1. Mark waist seam.

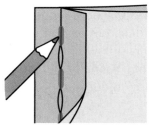

2. Mark side seam final stitching lines. Trim to an even 5/8".

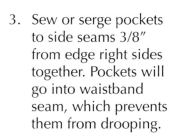

3. Sew or serge pockets to side seams 3/8" from edge right sides together. Pockets will go into waistband seam, which prevents them from drooping.

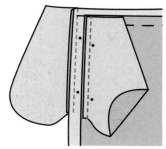

TIP: Pocket bags will not droop if they are caught in waistline stitching. However, they might be too bulky if included in the entire casing in a pull-on pant, so make sure pockets will be just barely caught in the casing seam.

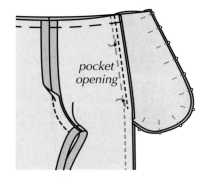

4. Pin pant front to back at sides.

5. Stitch side seams from lower edge to pocket opening; backstitch. Baste pocket opening closed, backstitch at upper opening and continue stitching to top edge. (The pocket opening averages 5½"- 6½".)

6. Press pockets toward front. Pin edges together. (Edges may not match.) Stitch around pocket edges.

pocket opening

7. Clip back seam allowances below pockets. Press side seams open. On most fabrics you can press the seam open without clipping. Then if you need to let out the seam, you can.

8. Baste upper edge of pockets to front.

clip

TIP: On lightweight fabrics, serge all seams together and press toward the front.

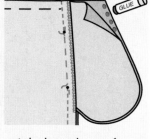

- First, serge pockets to garment. Straight stitch from top to circle. Backstitch. Change to a longer stitch and machine baste to lower circle. Backstitch and continue on to 3"–4". Glue-stick the edges of the pockets together, especially if they are out of a slippery lining.

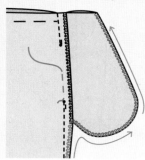

- Now serge side seam from the lower edge up to the straight stitching, then angle off toward pocket. Serge around pocket. Press pocket and seam toward front. Remove basting to open the pocket.

Sporty Designer Side Seam Pockets

This technique is used when you want the entire side seam edgestitched as you see in expensive designer chinos or cotton pants.

1. Cut four pocket pieces, two from fashion fabric and two from a lightweight cotton if fashion fabric is too heavy.

2. Fit pants and mark waistline and side seams as shown on the simple pocket, page 128.

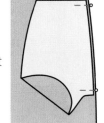

3. Place the lighter weight pocket pieces on the front of the pant, right sides together.

4. 2" below the waistline, using a stitch length of 1.5 mm, sew in from the edge of the side seam for 5/8"; pivot; sew along side seam 5½"–6"; pivot; sew to edge again. Trim seam to 1/4" and clip to corners.

clip seam

trim 1/4"

5. Turn pocket to wrong side. Press. Edgestitch.

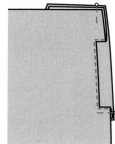

6. Place fashion fabric pocket under front. Pin to front and pin pocket bag edges together.

7. Stitch pocket bag edges together. (Edges may not match. Don't worry!)

8. Stitch pocket to pant across the top and along the sides.

9. Sew pant side seams, being careful not to catch the pocket edge.

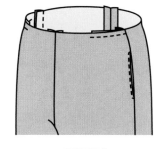

10. Press seams toward the front. Only the edge-stitching on the pocket front will show.

11. Edgestitch next to the seam on the pant front above and below the pocket.

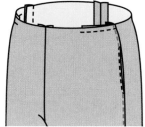

Single-Layer Topstitched Pocket

We've adapted this technique from Roberta Carr's book *Couture, the Art of Fine Sewing*. We recommend reading this book as it improves the quality of all of your sewing, even if you don't consider yourself a "couture" sewer.

1. From fashion fabric, cut one rectangle 7″ X 11″ for each pocket. Serge or zigzag all edges.

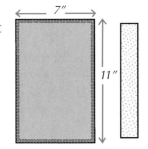

2. For each pocket cut a lightweight strip of fusible interfacing 1½″ X 10″ with the stable direction the length of the strip.

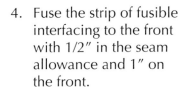

TIP: PerfectFuse Sheer is an excellent choice.

3. Sew side seams after perfecting fit. Use a stitch length of 1.5 mm from top of pant to 3″ down. Backstitch; baste for 6″-6½″ (pocket opening); backstitch. Sew remaining seam with a regular stitch length.

4. Fuse the strip of fusible interfacing to the front with 1/2″ in the seam allowance and 1″ on the front.

5. Press seams open. Finish seam allowances if necessary.

6. Topstitch the front seam allowance from the right side. Start at top of pant and stitch to the bottom of the pocket opening (or continue down entire side seam for a sporty look). If you stop at bottom of pocket, pull threads to the wrong side and tie a knot to anchor the ends.

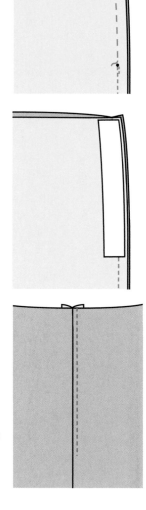

7. Stitch the rectangle pocket piece to the back seam allowance right sides together as close to the seamline as possible.

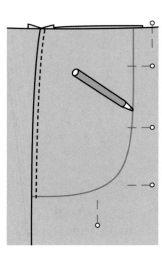

8. Pin pocket flat to front of pant.

9. Draw shape of pocket topstitching (any shape you desire) with chalk on outside of pant. If fabric is slippery, it is wise to hand-baste all the layers together along these stitching lines to prevent slippage. Or, use 505 Temporary Spray Adhesive to hold them in place.

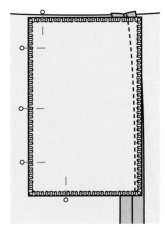

10. From right side, topstitch with one or two rows of stitching.

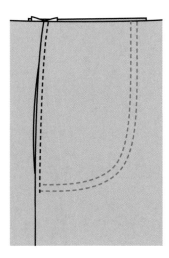

11. Remove basting from pocket opening.

Traditional Patch Pockets

Patch pockets are generally sporty and machine sewn in place on the pant back.

1. Finish upper edge of pocket by serging, zigzagging, or turning under 1/4″ and edgestitching.

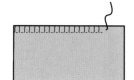

2. Turn upper edge of pocket to right side along hemline.

TIP: You can shape the pocket facing for variety.

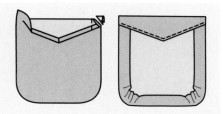

3. Starting at facing fold, stitch around raw edge 5/8″ from edge. To ease fullness on curves, machine baste 1/4″ from raw edges.

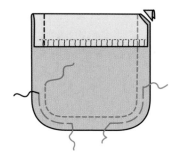

4. Turn facing to inside. Press under seam allowance on line of stitching, pulling up basting to ease in fullness on curves. Trim seam allowances to 1/4″. Steam-shrink bulk at corners until flat.

TIP: A quick way to get perfect curves is to use a pocket template. Pick the shape of the pocket curve from the template and insert it so edge is along stitching line. Attach clip section to hold pocket seam allowance in place. Press.

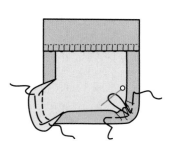

5. Stitch across facing 1½″ from top fold.

6. Pin pockets to pants. Edgestitch and then topstitch 1/4″ from the edge along sides and lower edge.

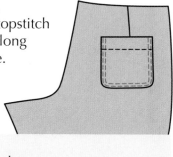

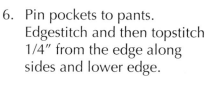

Use strips of fusible web or a temporary adhesive to hold pocket in place.

Pocket Flap

If you want to add a flap to the patch pocket, cut it 1/8″ wider than the top edge of the pocket. It can be sewn from two layers of fashion fabric or if too bulky, line it.

1. Stitch flap pieces right sides together along sides and lower edge. Trim seams to 1/4″ and trim diagonally across corners. Turn right side out and press. You may edgestitch close to edges and if you topstitched your pocket, topstitch 1/4″ away.

2. Make a buttonhole in the center if you wish to add a button. This is a good idea if the pocket is large.

3. With flap right sides together on pant and edge along top of pocket, sew 5/8″ seam. Trim to 1/8″.

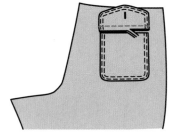

4. Press down over pocket and edgestitch 1/8″ from fold through all layers to hold flap down.

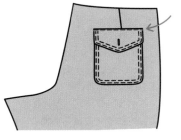

5. Sew on button.

Cargo Pockets

Cargo pockets are like patch pockets with a pleat in the center (to hold more cargo!). Usually they have square corners. Often they are placed over the side seams just above the knee.

1. To add a pleat to a plain patch pocket, add 1½" to center of pocket.

2. Fold pocket in half length-wise. Place a pin 2½" from top edge and 1⅛" from bottom edge.

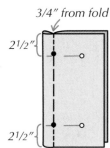

3/4" from fold

2½"

2½"

3. Sew 3/4" from fold, using a 2mm stitch length, to the first pin. Backstitch; baste between pins; backstitch; sew 2mm stitch length to bottom.

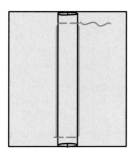

4. Press, centering pleat. Hold pleat in position with hand basting.

5. Finish upper edge of pocket with zigzagging, serging, or turning under 1/4" and edgestitching.

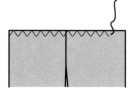

6. Turn upper edge of pocket to right side along facing fold line. Stitch hem to pocket at sides and continue around pocket if you want a guide for turning under the 5/8" seam allowances. Cut upper corners diagonally.

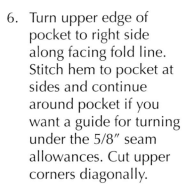

7. Turn hem to inside. Press under 5/8" on sides and lower edge, folding in corners.

8. Stitch facing in place 1¼" from upper edge.

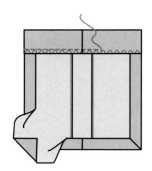

9. Pin pockets in place and stitch close to side and lower edge. You may also top-stitch 1/4" from edge. Pull out basting stitches in the pleat.

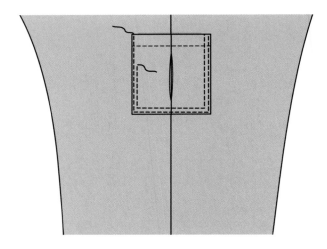

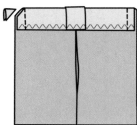

Quick Tip

Use strips of fusible web or a temporary adhesive to hold pocket in place.

TIP: Add a flap if desired. A flap with a button will keep large pockets from sagging.

CHAPTER 20

Classic Trouser Pockets

Trouser pockets are slanted pockets. The pant can be with or without pleats in the front. We will show a pleated pant because it requires a few more tips.

Incorporating a Front Stay

Turn your pocket into a front stay! The stay will be caught in the zipper, keeping the tucks and pocket bags flat.

If your pocket pattern piece doesn't extend into the center front, it is not a stay.

To create the stay, place pocket on front as shown. Fold out the pleat closest to the center front. Use the depth of the second pleat to form a dart in the stay. Draw a line from side seam to front edge on your front pattern piece and you have the pattern for the stay. Cut the stay out of lining.

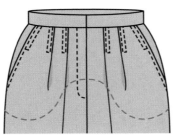

BEFORE SEWING TROUSER POCKET, sew and press pleats in pant front. Press front crease in pant as well (see page 80, 102, and 103).

Sewing the Trouser Pocket

1. Sew the dart in each stay. Press in the opposite direction of the pleats to reduce bulk.

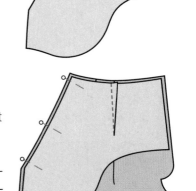

2. Pin stay to front pocket edge, right sides together. To keep this bias edge from stretching, place the pattern on top and make the fabric the same size. (Often it will have already grown. Simply ease it back to the length of the pattern.)

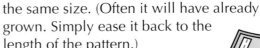

3. To stabilize, sew seam tape or the lighter weight Stay-tape into the seam. (The selvage of lining can also be used as tape.)

TIP: If your pockets always gap, center a stay tape over the stitching line and pin at one end. Mark a dot on the tape at the other end and one on the stay 1/8" away. Pull tape until the marks line up. Pin, distributing fullness. Sew with tape on top; feed dogs will ease fabric to tape. (Don't shorten the tape if your fabric is firmly woven and won't ease well.)

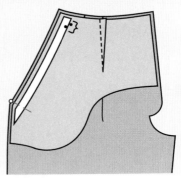

4. Trim and grade the seam.

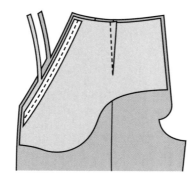

5. Press the lining over the seam allowances toward the side.

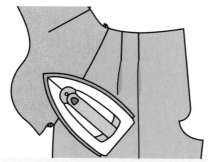

TIP: You can understitch lining to seam allowances, which helps keep the lining from showing.

6. Turn the stay to the inside and press.

TIP: Roll the seam 1/8″ to the inside when pressing so the lining won't show. Pressing on a ham allows you to pin the pocket to the ham, anchoring it as you press.

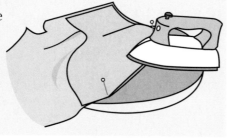

7. Pin to prevent the layers from slipping and causing a puckered edge. Edgestitch the finished slanted edge 1/8″ from the edge.

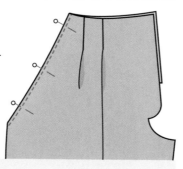

TIP: If fabric is slippery, hand-baste through all layers first to prevent a puckered edge. OR, use a temporary spray fabric adhesive to hold all of the layers together while you stitch.

8. Topstitch edge again 1/4″ away for a sporty look. If you do this, also topstitch pleats through all layers.

Add Side Inset

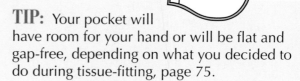

9. Finish upper straight edge as shown with serging or zigzagging.

10. Put pattern piece on side inset and put pins into circles. Lift tissue off pins.

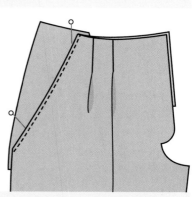

TIP: Your pocket will have room for your hand or will be flat and gap-free, depending on what you decided to do during tissue-fitting, page 75.

11. On a flat surface, with pants right side up, pin front to inset matching pocket edge to pins. Pin inset in place.

TIP: Check both sides before sewing. To ensure right and left trouser fronts are identical, check insets before attaching permanently to make sure they are lapped under the front exactly the same on both sides. The distances at the arrows should be the same.

If your hips are uneven, you will lower the waistband on one side and that will make one pocket shorter, but at this point, make sure they are even.

uneven

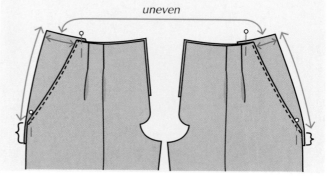

12. Flip front of pant out of way and pin edges of side inset and stay together. Don't match edges if they are uneven. Just make sure pocket bags are flat with no bubbles.

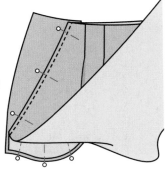

13. Fold pant front toward side seam. Stitch pocket sections together. Finish lower edge of pocket bags if desired.

14. To make sure your lining will be caught and held by the zipper, machine-baste *right* front along center front.

15. Machine base *left* front 5/8" from center front (at fly-front underlap fold line snip).

16. Baste front to side inset along seam-lines at top and at sides.

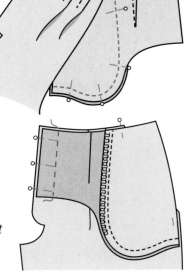

baste

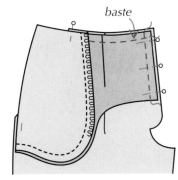

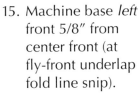

TIP: To prevent the pocket from gapping or pulling just below the waistband, topstitch on top of the original stitching for 3/4" below waistline seam through all layers.

If you used two rows of stitching on pocket edge, stitch a "U" at the top of the pocket (page 133).

topstitch

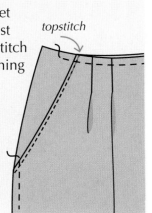

Ready-to-wear Variations on the Classic Trouser Pocket

Fashion Fabric Facing

If you want to have fashion fabric facing at the edge of the pocket, follow steps two to eight on page 136.

Side Inset/Stay

In addition to the faced edge, above, designers often like the side inset to become the stay as it covers up the pocket pieces on the inside and makes unlined pants look neater.

Simply add the stay section to the inset pattern piece. Fold pleats out of front and place inset on top, matching circles and notches. Add tissue from side edge of inset to front edge.

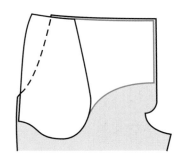

If you want a little play in the stay, make a small dart at the waistline before trimming the tissue even with front and top edges.

Draw a line that will be at least 1½" from the front of the pocket.

Cut your new side panel stay out of lining.

Cut a piece of fashion fabric that will go from the side seam to the line you drew and stitch it to the lining. (Use this combination inset/stay in place of the standard side inset in previous instructions.)

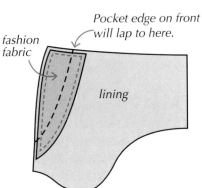

fashion fabric

Pocket edge on front will lap to here.

lining

135

Sporty Topstitched Trouser Pockets

This is a sturdy pocket for a cotton pant. We've added a facing to add strength.

1. Square the corner of the pocket lining pattern piece while cutting lining out of a lightweight cotton or self-fabric.

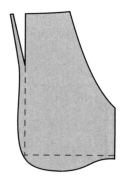

2. Cut a facing 1½" wide using the pocket pattern piece as a guide.

3. Finish lower edge of facing.

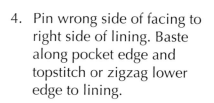

4. Pin wrong side of facing to right side of lining. Baste along pocket edge and topstitch or zigzag lower edge to lining.

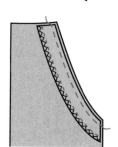

5. Pin pocket lining to pants right sides together. Stitch.

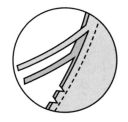

6. Trim and grade seam. If pocket edge is curved, clip if necessary.

7. Press lining over seam allowances.

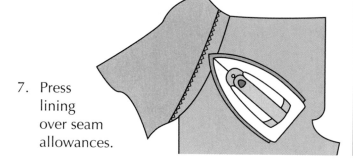

8. Turn lining to inside and press.

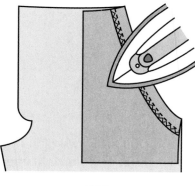

9. Edgestitch and/or topstitch outer pocket edge.

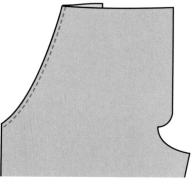

10. Pin inset to front.

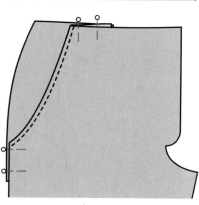

11. Stitch pocket edges together.

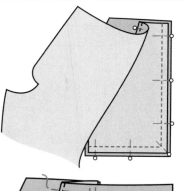

12. Hand baste top and side edges of pocket to pant front. Topstitch with one or two rows through all layers.

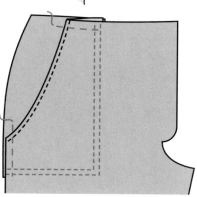

CHAPTER 21
Welt Pockets

There are many variations of single and double welt pockets which may be either horizontal or vertical. Some pants have back welts on both sides, some on just the left back, others only the right back. For women's pants, we prefer a fake welt in the back without the pocket bag that adds bulk.

Fake double-welt—just a big bound buttonhole with the lips stitched closed. Or, if the lips are not stitched closed, then a button and loop are added to keep the buttonhole closed and a fabric piece is stitched under the lips for modesty.

Double-welt—horizontal in the back and generally vertical or diagonal on the front. However, Pati bought an Anne Klein pant with a tiny horizontal double welt pocket sewn over front pleats.

Single-welt—horizontal on the back and generally vertical on the front, but can be horizontal or diagonal on the front.

There is also the single welt with a wider welt constructed separately and inserted into a faced hole. (Traditional welts are sewn to the hole.)

Fake Double-welt Pocket

This can be done two ways. You can use the windowpane bound buttonhole method as follows or the double-welt pocket on page 147, but leave out the pocket parts and add a facing for modesty.

1. To face the hole, cut a rectangle of lightweight crisp fabric like silk organza. Or, stiffen a lightweight or sheer cotton with Perfect Sew liquid stabilizer. Draw a box on this facing fabric 1/2" by 4" or 5" using a pencil.

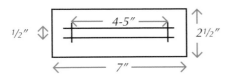

2. Pin facing on right side of fabric placing marked box where you want pocket. Sew around the box beginning in the middle and using a stitch length of 1.5mm at the corners and ends.

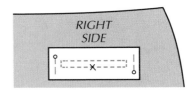

RIGHT SIDE

3. Cut through the center of the box through all layers, stopping 1/2" - 3/4" from the ends. Carefully cut to the corner stitching.

4. Push facing through the cut to wrong side. Press.

RIGHT SIDE

TIP: An easy way to press is to anchor facing by pinning to a pressing ham.

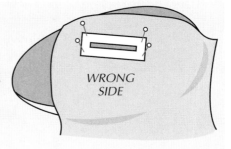

WRONG SIDE

5. Prepare welts. Cut two pieces of fashion fabric 2" X 7". Welts should be on straight of grain unless fashion fabric is plaid— then use bias for interest. Stitch right sides together, through the center of the long side. Press open.

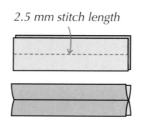

2.5 mm stitch length

TIP: To hold welts in place, use fusible web strips on the facing edges. Lightly steam to hold in place. Or, use paper backed fusible web like Steam-A-Seam2®. Stick it around the window and peel away the paper.

6. From the right side, center welts under the faced window. If you used a fusible web, fuse using a press cloth. Welts will now stay in place without slipping while stitching.

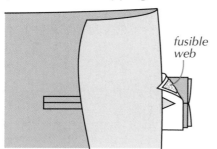

fusible web

7. Fold pant away and sew long sides on original stitching line.

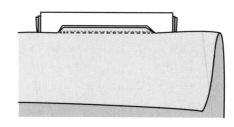

8. Fold back fashion fabric, exposing ends. Stitch on original stitching line and again over triangle.

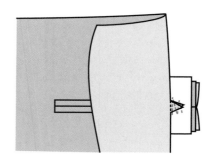

Vertical Double-welt Front Pockets

After looking at how these pockets were made in many ready-to-wear pants, we've adapted a method that will never gap open because one pocket bag is a stay that is sewn into the center front and side seams. The finished pocket opening is 5"-5½" long by 1/2" wide.

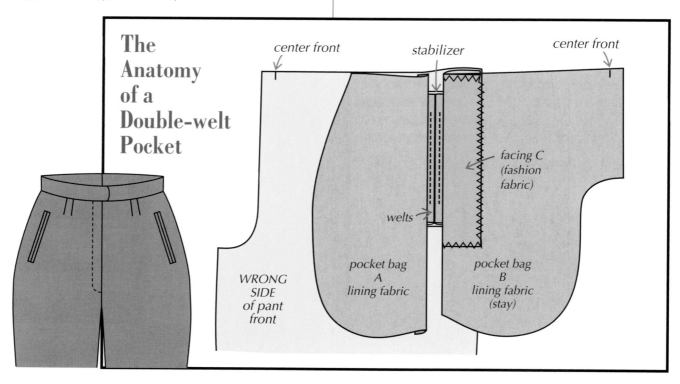

The Anatomy of a Double-welt Pocket

center front

stabilizer

center front

facing C (fashion fabric)

welts

WRONG SIDE of pant front

pocket bag A lining fabric

pocket bag B lining fabric (stay)

Pocket Placement

With crotch and inseams sewn, try pant on RIGHT SIDES OUT with side seams pinned WRONG SIDES together. Adjust pins until pants fit like you want. If your hips are uneven, one side may need to be let out or taken in more than the other. Now determine pocket placement:

- To find where welts look best on your body, pin 5" to 5½" by 1/2"rectangles of paper straight or at an angle to pant front.

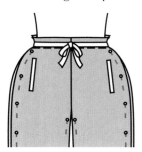

- For uneven hips, keep the lower edge of the pockets level. Keep the pockets equal distance from the center front.

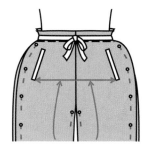

equal distance

Mark Side Seams and Pocket Placement

Mark side seams and welt placement lines on the WRONG sides of fabric. The pockets shouldn't be closer than 1½" from the side seam and about 2" from the waist seam. Use chalk or a washable marker.

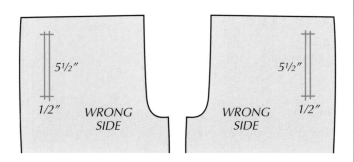

5½" — 5½"
1/2" — WRONG SIDE — WRONG SIDE — 1/2"

NOTE: The following instructions are for ONE standard 5"-5½" pocket. For two pockets cut TWO of everything!

Transfer Pocket Placement and Side Seams to Tissue

Before creating pocket pattern pieces, place the front tissue on top of fabric fronts. If you made changes during pin-fitting, mark new side seam stitching lines on tissue.

Draw pocket placement on the front pattern tissue.

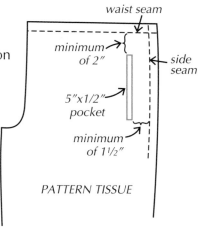

waist seam
minimum of 2"
side seam
5"x1/2" pocket
minimum of 1½"

PATTERN TISSUE

Create the Pattern Pieces

Make your pocket pattern pieces from a gridded tissue like Perfect Pattern Paper, using your altered pattern. **First pin darts or tucks out of the pattern front. Smoosh the tissue flat.**

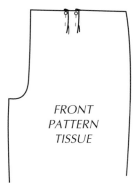

FRONT PATTERN TISSUE

Pocket Bag "A" — to be cut from LINING

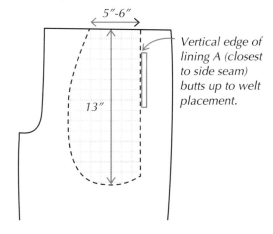

5"-6"

Vertical edge of lining A (closest to side seam) butts up to welt placement.

13"

Pocket Bag "B" — To be cut from LINING.

Create as shown at the right. (It extends to center front in pleated trousers, but doesn't have to in plain front pants.) Transfer the pocket placement onto "B." This welt shape will vary depending on placement/tilt of welt and size of pattern.

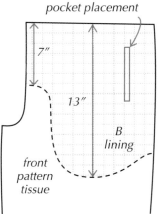

pocket placement

7"

13"

B lining

front pattern tissue

Pocket Facing "C" — To be cut from FASHION FABRIC.

This piece will go under welts, so if pocket opens, you will see fashion fabric.

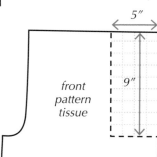

5"

front pattern tissue

9"

Welt — to be cut from FASHION FABRIC on straight grain or bias (nice for plaids).

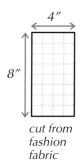

4"

8"

cut from fashion fabric

Welt Stabilizer — to be cut from a medium weight NON-WOVEN sew-in interfacing such as Pellon®.

4"

8"

cut from stabilizer

With a pencil, draw a box 1/2" by 5" to 5½" using a gridded see-through ruler.

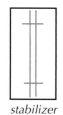

stabilizer

NOTE: If your fabric is soft or loosely woven, interface welts with PerfectFuse™ Light fusible interfacing.

Sewing Directions

Sew darts and pleats in pants before starting welts.

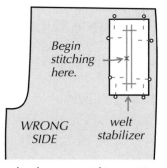

Begin stitching here.

WRONG SIDE

welt stabilizer

1. Place and Stitch Welt Stabilizer

Place one welt stabilizer on the **wrong side of fabric**, matching welt placement lines. Pin.

Starting in the center of a long side at the "X," sew around the box using short stitches. Count the stitches at one end of the box. The other end should use the same number of stitches. Turn the fly wheel by hand near the corners, especially if you have a computerized machine.

From the right side of the pant, you will see only a stitched rectangular box.

TIP for perfect placement on both sides of pant:

(This assumes your hips are the same on both sides.) Place second piece of welt stabilizer on top of the first piece.

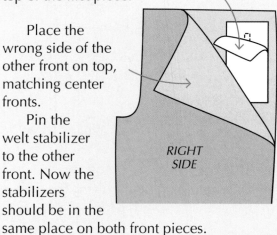

RIGHT SIDE

Place the wrong side of the other front on top, matching center fronts.

Pin the welt stabilizer to the other front. Now the stabilizers should be in the same place on both front pieces.

Sew the second welt stabilizer in place. First, compare both front pieces to make sure the stitching is in the exact same place. Now is the time to rip if they aren't! (This doesn't apply if your hips are uneven!)

2. Position the Welt Fabric

On the right side of the pant fabric, center the fashion fabric welt piece over stitches and pin (right sides together).

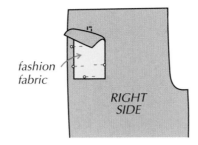

fashion fabric

RIGHT SIDE

3. Stitch the Long Sides Only

From wrong side of fabric, stitch on top of stitching lines on LONG sides of box only. Start and stop at ends. Carefully, turning the fly wheel by hand, backstitch on top of last stitch at both ends.

Remove pins.

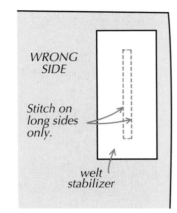

WRONG SIDE

Stitch on long sides only.

welt stabilizer

4. Basting Determines the Widths of the Welts

Continuing on the wrong side, make two rows of machine basting stitches 1/4" outside of each side of the box on the long sides through all layers. Stitches should start 1" before the end of the box and extend 1" beyond the box.

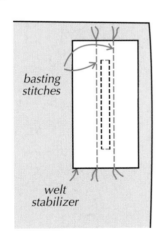

basting stitches

welt stabilizer

TIP: Don't cut basting thread. Sew one line, pull slack in thread and sew other line. This makes a loop to pull out stitches later.

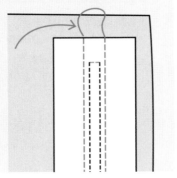

5. Create the Welts

From the right side, fold one side of the welt up firmly against the basting line. Finger press. Pin in place taking a small "bite" through two layers only. For a better stitching line, points of pins should not extend into the seamline area. DO NOT IRON! Press firmly with your fingers.

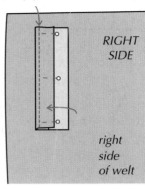

stitching line area (Keep pins free from area.)

RIGHT SIDE

right side of welt

From the wrong side, stitch on the one long side of the box (where you pinned) on top of previous stitching, ending exactly at the end of the box. Back stitch carefully. Remove pins.

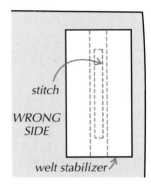

stitch

WRONG SIDE

welt stabilizer

From the right side, fold other side of welt over stitching and repeat the previous step. (Fold and pin edge of first welt out of the way.)

You have created the "welt lips."

6. Cut and Turn the Welts

Remove the basting threads. From the right side, carefully cut through the center of the WELT ONLY. **Do not cut through pant yet.**

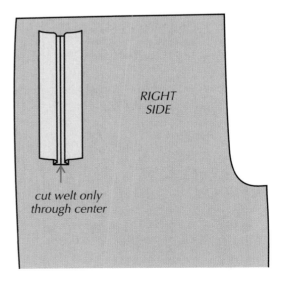

RIGHT SIDE

cut welt only through center

From the wrong side, cut through the center of the welt stabilizer "box" and through pant fabric to 3/4" from the end. Angle cut to the corners right up to the stitches. Use your fingers underneath as a guide to make sure you don't cut the welts.

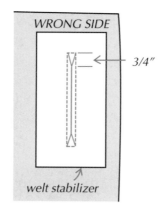

WRONG SIDE

3/4"

welt stabilizer

Turn or pull welts through to the wrong side.

To avoid imprints from all of the underneath layers, steam the welts over a ham from the wrong side.

Catch-stitch the welts together from the right side.

Don't worry if welts lap at ends a little, they won't after you stitch them later.

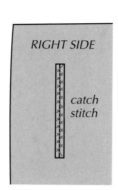

RIGHT SIDE

catch stitch

7. Prepare and Add the Pocket Lining

Center and pin the wrong side of the fashion fabric ("C") over the welt placement lines on lining "B." Zigzag in place using a 2mm length and 3mm width. This ensures that instead of seeing the lining peaking through the finished welt, you will see the fashion fabric.

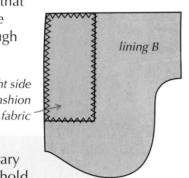

lining B

right side of fashion fabric

TIP: Use temporary spray adhesive to hold layers together while you stitch.

TIP: If fabric is bulky like some corduroys, trim "C" so it is only under the pocket area (1" x 6½"). Zigzag to the lining along all edges.

Trim.

lining B

C

8. Attach Lining Pieces "A" and "B"

Lining "A" will be attached to the LONG edge of the welt that is closest to the center front of the pant. Match edge of lining with wrong side of top of pant fabric. Fold pant and stabilizer as shown. Stitch to the welt using a 1/4" seam allowance. Sew with the lining on top, so the feed dogs won't gather the lining. Press toward the center front.

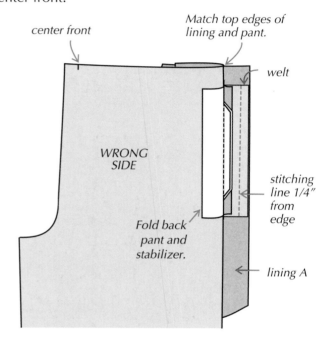

center front

Match top edges of lining and pant.

welt

WRONG SIDE

Fold back pant and stabilizer.

stitching line 1/4" from edge

lining A

Place lining B under pant front and line up top and sides. Fold pant fabric and stabilizer back. Stitch lining to the other side of the welt 1/4" from the edge of the welt. Zigzag the welt seam allowances through all layers to flatten them, making them less bulky.

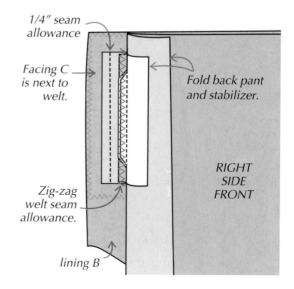

1/4" seam allowance

Facing C is next to welt.

Fold back pant and stabilizer.

Zig-zag welt seam allowance.

RIGHT SIDE FRONT

lining B

Now both pocket bags have been attached.

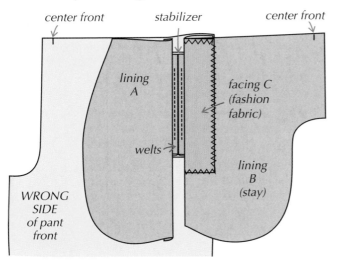

Fold lining B over pant to match center fronts.

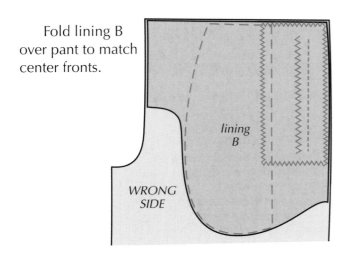

This is how it looks from the right side.

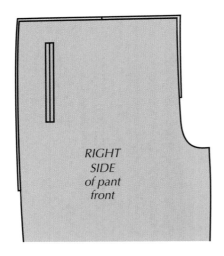

NOTE: If there is a pucker at the ends, check to see if you clipped all the way to the stitching at the corners.

9. Sew Across Top Triangle

With the right side of the pant fabric facing up, fold down the top of pant fabric and the stabilizer as shown until you see the triangle. Sew directly on top of the first stitching line. Continue sewing back and forth over the triangle through all layers. Repeat on the lower triangle.

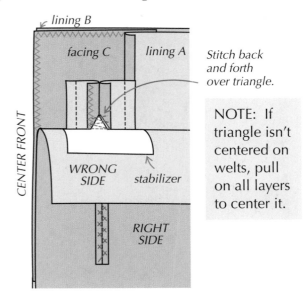

NOTE: If triangle isn't centered on welts, pull on all layers to center it.

10. Sew Pocket Bag

Fold pant away and to the side as shown. Pin pocket bags together. Sew linings with 5/8" seam along edge of lining "A." Stitch up to the welt stitching line, continuing at or just above triangle point and across to edge of welt.

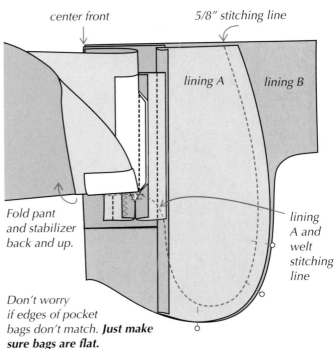

Fold pant and stabilizer back and up.

Don't worry if edges of pocket bags don't match. **Just make sure bags are flat.**

143

Stitch linings/pocket to the pant 1/2" from edges where shown. If you are using a fly front, baste to fold lines for overlap and underlap edges.

Be sure to trim stabilizer out of side seam allowances.

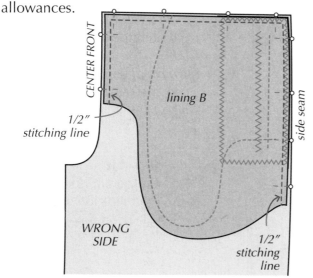

CENTER FRONT

1/2" stitching line

lining B

side seam

WRONG SIDE

1/2" stitching line

NOTE: The stay that goes to the center front **should not have any play** in it if you want to keep pockets from gapping.

Single-welt Front Pockets

This wonderful technique starts like the double-welt pocket using the same fabric pieces and a non-woven stabilizer. You may want to interface the welt piece on softer fabrics with Perfect Fuse Sheer interfacing. (Read pages 138 and 139 in double-welt pocket section for size and placement of pocket pieces.)

1. Draw a rectangle 1/2" by 5" to 5½" on stabilizer. Place stabilizer on the wrong side, centered over pocket location. Stitch around the box using a short stitch length beginning in the middle of a long side. Then draw a pencil line 1/2" from the box toward the center front. Machine baste on the line.

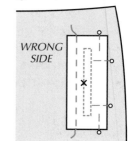

WRONG SIDE

2. Fold welt in half, wrong sides together, and crease with iron.

3. Place folded edge of welt along the basting on the right side of the pant. Pin as shown.

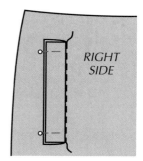

RIGHT SIDE

4. From WRONG side, stitch on side of box closest to the center front and the basting. Backstitch carefully at each end. Remove basting.

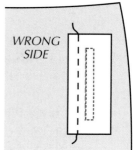

WRONG SIDE

5. Fold welt out of way so you can sew pocket bag "B" to other side of box. Pin to hold.

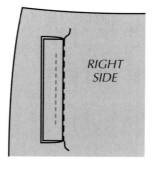

RIGHT SIDE

RIGHT SIDE

6. Place pocket bag "B" (with facing "C" sewn to it) flat on table.

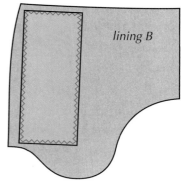

lining B

7. Place pant front on top of pocket. Put pins in each corner.

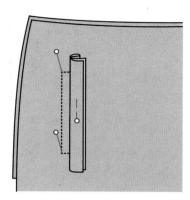

8. Lift front and mark where pins go into pocket bag.

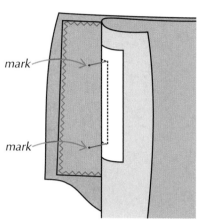

mark

mark

9. Place pocket bag "B" on RIGHT side of pant matching marks to corners of box closest to the side seam. Pin.

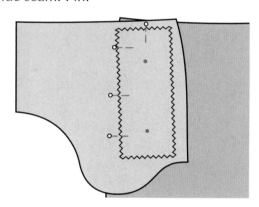

10. From WRONG side, stitch along side of box closest to side seam to catch pocket bag lining "B".

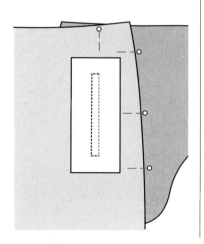

11. From stabilizer side, slash through center of box to corners in a "pie" shape.

12. Pull pocket bag and welt to wrong side. Carefully press.

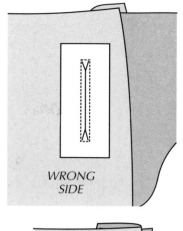

WRONG SIDE

13. Match edge of pocket bag lining "A" to edge of welt seam allowance. Stitch pocket bag "A" to welt seam allowance on original stitching line of long side of box.

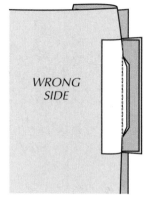

WRONG SIDE

14. Stitch triangle ends of box on original stitching line and then through triangle.

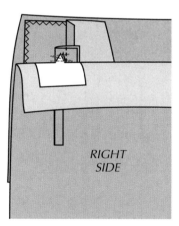

RIGHT SIDE

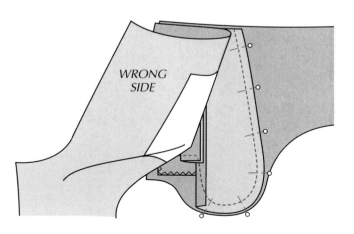

WRONG SIDE

145

15. Sew pocket bags together. Do not worry if the pocket bag edges don't match.

Sporty Single-welt Front Pocket

The finished single-welt should measure about 1/2" to 1 1/2" x 6" and the opening should be about 2"-2 1/2" from the side seam.

1. On WRONG SIDE of pant front, mark pocket stitching lines 1/2" apart. The one closest to the SIDE is 5 1/2" long and the other is 6" long. Mark the same lines on a piece of stabilizer 4" x 8". Pin stabilizer to pant matching lines.

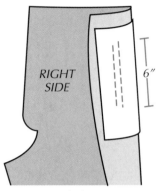

2. Make welt.
   3" x 7" = 1 1/4"-wide welt
   2 1/2" x 7" = 1"-wide welt
   1 1/2" x 7" = 1/2"-wide welt

   Fold in half right sides together and sew a 1/2" seam at each end. Trim seams to 1/4" Press seams open over a point presser. Turn to right side. Press. Baste raw edges 1/4" from raw edge.

3. On right side of pants, place welt right side down on pocket marking closest to center front with welt fold toward center front. Line up stitching lines on welt and pant front. Stitch on right side from one end to the other. Do not stitch off end of welt. Backstitch.

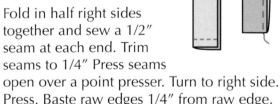

4. Create pocket bags using same instructions as double-welt pocket page 139 and 140. Place pocket bag A over welt with raw edge of pocket in middle of box. **Stitch on same stitching line from wrong side.** Backstitch at each end.

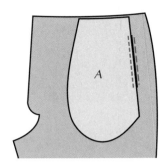

5. See page 145 for marking placement line on pocket bag B. Match these marks to second shorter line on right side of front. From wrong side, stitch carefully on this line. This row of stitching is 1/4" shorter at each end than the first row.

Use a 1/4" foot or move needle to left to avoid ridge of welt.

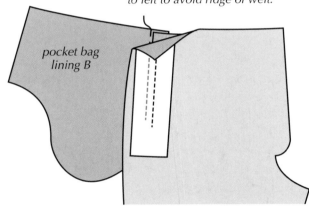

6. From wrong side, slit pant front between stitching lines to within 1/2" from ends. Snip to each corner.

7. Pull pocket bags to wrong side. Place on a ham and lightly press. The welt will end up with fold toward side seam.

8. From wrong side, stitch pocket bags together. Don't worry if edges of pocket bags don't match, just be sure everything is flat!

9. Baste top and side of bags to pant front.

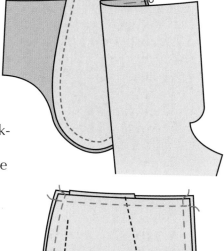

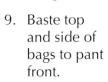

10. From right side, stitch top and bottom edges of welt through all layers, backstitching at each end. The "pies" at each end will be caught in the stitching.

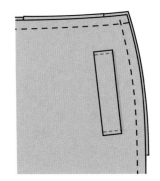

Double-welt Back Pocket

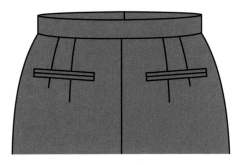

1. Stitch darts and press toward the center.

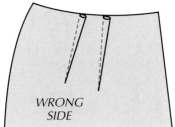

WRONG SIDE

2. Cut two pieces of fashion fabric 7" x 3" for welts.

   One will become the welt and is sewn to top end on lining. The other becomes the facing and is placed 2" from the other end of lining.

   Cut one piece of lining 7" x 15" for pocket bag.

7"

3"

7"

15"

3. Turn under one edge of each fashion fabric welt and edge stitch to lining, or, if fabric is bulky, zigzag it flat to lining.

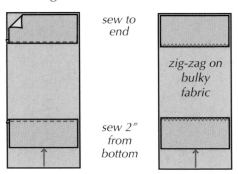

sew to end

sew 2" from bottom

zig-zag on bulky fabric

4. Cut pocket stay from a non-woven interfacing 7" x 3". Draw a box 1/2" by 4" to 5" long.

3"

7"

5. On wrong side, place box you drew on stabilizer where you want pocket on either left or right or both backs, 2"-3" below waist seamline.

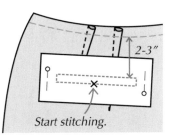

2-3"

Start stitching.

6. Stitch along dotted lines, using small stitches, forming a "box." Start and stop at the center of a long side.

7. Pin pocket to back, right sides together, centering welt over stitched box.

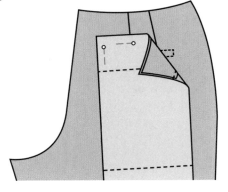

147

8. On INSIDE, stitch over previous stitching on LONG sides of box ONLY, back-stitching carefully at corners. Do not stitch short sides of box at this time.

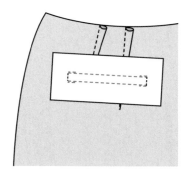

9. On INSIDE, machine-baste exactly 1/4" above and below long sides of box.

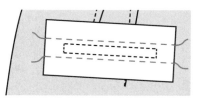

10. On OUTSIDE, fold pocket up firmly against basting line. Pin in place.

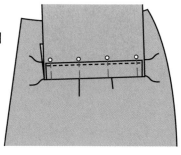

11. On INSIDE, stitch again over previous stitching on LOWER long side of box, backstitching at corners. (This stitching creates the welt.)

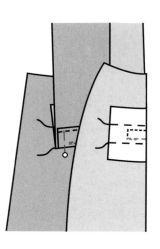

12. On OUTSIDE, fold upper edge of pocket down firmly against top basting line. Pin in place. Be sure first welt is out of the way.

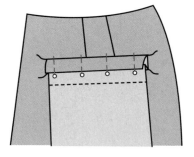

13. Flip once more to INSIDE and stitch on upper line of box; backstitch carefully.

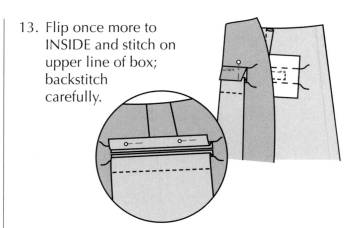

14. On OUTSIDE, slash through welt/pocket ONLY. DO NOT slash through pants yet. Remove basting threads.

15. For pocket opening, on INSIDE, slash along solid line and diagonally to corners as shown. Have your finger underneath as a guide to be sure you don't cut the welts.

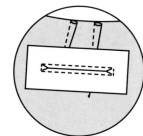

16. Turn pocket to INSIDE through opening. Whipstitch edges of welts together. Press.

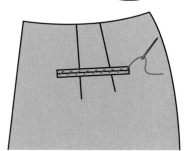

17. Fold back pant and stabilizer and stitch through triangle on original stitching line and a few more times to stabilize ends.

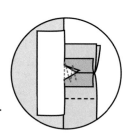

18. On OUTSIDE, edgestitch along lower edge through all thicknesses.

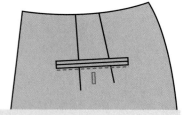

NOTE: If not making a tab, sew a buttonhole through pant and one layer of pocket before sewing bag to waistline.

Optional Pocket Tab

NOTE: Sew and insert tab before you attach pocket bag to waistline and sew sides.

1. Cut two pieces of fabric the shape of a tab. Interface wrong side of tab if needed.

2. Pin the pieces right sides together and stitch tab edges.

3. Trim, slash corners, turn and press.

4. Edgestitch if desired.

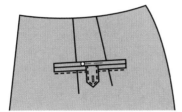

5. Sew buttonhole in center of tab.

6. Slip tab into center of opening. Pin.

7. On INSIDE stitch tab to top welt over welt stitching.

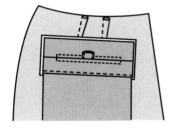

19. Fold pocket up with facing under welts. Stitch edges of pocket bag together. Shape top edge of pocket lining to match pant waist edge. Baste together 1/2" from waist edge.

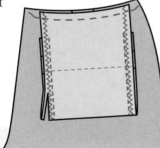

TIP: Round the lower corners if you wish, so less lint will collect.

20. If you made a buttonhole, sew button to inside of pocket.

Optional Loop Technique

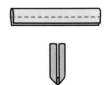

If you want a loop-type tab, sew the loop, turn, and fold into a tab.

Stitch it to the upper center of the box before making pocket.

It will be included in the welt seam and will go over the upper welt rather than under as in the previous tab.

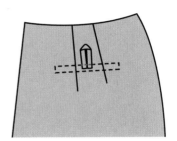

Horizontal Single-welt Pocket

The narrow single-welt pocket is a variation of our easy double welt. This is usually shown in the back, but we have seen it in the front of pants too.

The pocket section is prepared like the double welt, then cut in half.

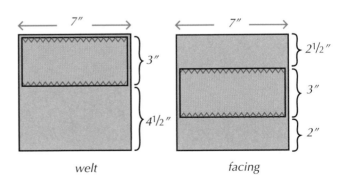

welt   *facing*

1. Mark on a 3″ x 7″ piece of non-woven stabilizer a 1/2″ by 4″ to 5″ box. Place it on wrong side where you want the pocket—2″-3″ below the waist if a back pocket. Beginning in the middle, stitch around the box, stitching corners accurately.

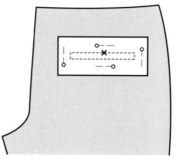

2. Center the welt section over the box on the right side.

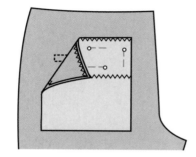

3. From the stabilizer side, stitch on the bottom line of the box.

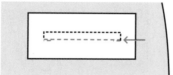

4. Baste 1/2″ below the bottom line.

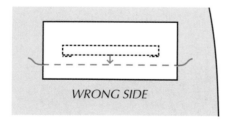

WRONG SIDE

RIGHT SIDE

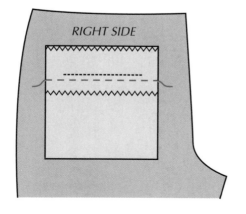

5. On OUTSIDE, fold the welt over basting. On INSIDE, stitch again on the lower long side of the box.

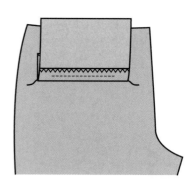

6. Carefully fold the back pocket so you won't stitch through it when you sew on the top line.

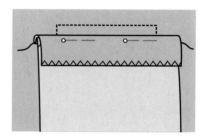

7. Place facing piece on right side, centering over box with the longer section of the pocket toward the waist. Stitch carefully from WRONG SIDE along top line of box. Remove basting.

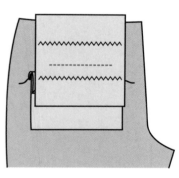

8. Slash though stabilizer and pant, cutting to corners.

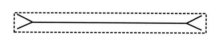

9. Pull pockets through opening to wrong side and press. Lower section will form the welt.

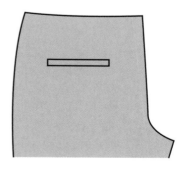

OPTIONAL: Hold pocket facing section away and edge stitch pant just below bottom of welt. Make a buttonhole in pant just below the center of the welt.

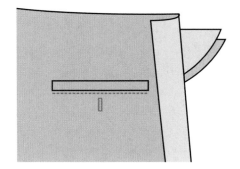

10. Fold back fabric and stabilizer. Sew triangles at ends to welt. Stitch through triangle on original stitching line and a few more times to flatten and stabilize ends.

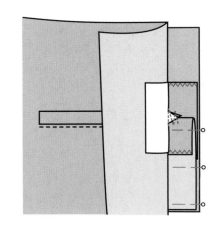

11. Fold back pant and stabilizer and sew seam at upper edge to welts.

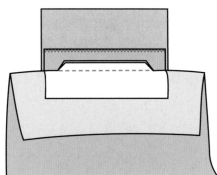

12. Sew pocket bags from triangle to bottom edge on each side and across bottom. Upper edge of pocket bag will be caught in waistline seam.

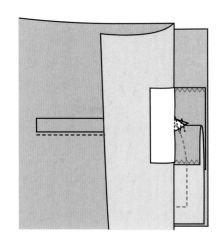

OPTIONAL: If you edgestitched the bottom, now edge stitch ends and above welt on pant.

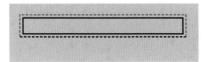

13. If you sewed a buttonhole, sew button to inside of pocket bag.

CHAPTER 22

Easy Hems and Cuffs

Leg Width and Pant Length

The longer the pant leg, the longer your legs will appear. Length of pants varies with fashion and with leg width. Length also varies with the height of the heel you wear. When establishing length, try pants on with the shoes you plan to wear with them. Pati's friend Cleo used to call out, "Your pants are too short!" when she would see Pati walking out the door wearing a trouser for a seminar she was about to teach. Standing, the pants touched the front of Pati's shoe, but walking exposed a lot of ankle. Now you will see Pati with pants that break on the front of her shoe. It is however, personal preference.

Length of Pants

During tissue-fitting, you should have determined your approximate length leaving at least 1¼" to 1½" hem allowance. If you are not sure of the shoe, make the hem allowance 2½" for safety.

Now is the time to fine-tune the length. Pin up the hem and try the pants on with shoes you plan to wear with them.

A slight break on the front of the shoe is nice. The slight extra length helps keep ankles from showing when you sit. Also, the break disappears when you bend your knee while walking.

If your pants fit properly, you can turn up the same amount of hem on both legs. If one leg is longer, compensate at the waistline, not at the hemline.

Hem depth should be 1¼"-1½". If the pant has a side slit, the hem allowance needs to be the length of the slit plus about 1".

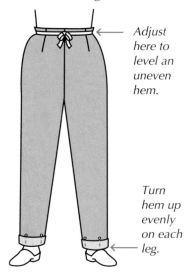

Adjust here to level an uneven hem.

Turn hem up evenly on each leg.

Narrow legs must be shorter in length.

Narrow legs can be made longer in back.

Straight legs can touch the top of the shoe in front.

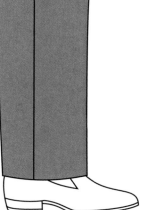

Straight legs can break on top of the shoe so that when you sit and cross your legs, less leg shows.

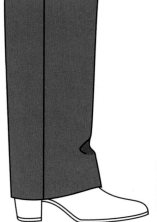

Wide legs can go nearly to the floor.

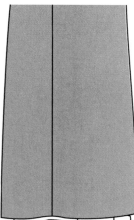

Four Rules for an Invisible Hem

1. Trim seam allowance in hem area to 1/4" to eliminate bulk.

2. Never press over the top edge of a hem. You'll get a ridge on the right side. Press from the fold to within 1/2" of the hem edge.

3. Finish the raw edge ONLY if necessary. Pinking is second best and zig-zagging or serging is fine if the threads won't show through. Use a 2-thread serger stitch for less thread bulk.

4. Use a quality thread and a fine needle.

Different Hems for Different Pants

Designer Hem

This is the most invisible and nicest on fine fabrics. Use a long

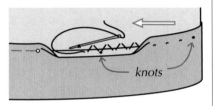

knots

loose blind stitch under the hem edge staggered between hem and pant. Catch only a single fiber of your outside fabric. You can do this if you use the smallest needle you can thread—a size 10 sharp is best, but we now use a larger size 8—because of our AGE!

NOTE: Every 6", pull to loosen stitches so they will be more invisible and secure by knotting in hem allowance. This protects you in case you accidentally step into your hem.

Catchstitch

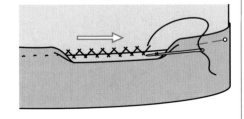

Using a catchstitch or herringbone stitch instead of a running stitch adds a little more strength and for knits is quite flexible. It can show more if you pull your thread too tight. Stay loose!

Machine Blind Hem

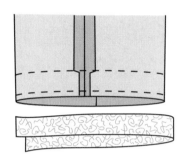

blind hem foot

This makes a very sturdy hem for activewear or children's clothing. You will need to fold the pant back, instead of the hem allowance, as shown, making a crease that can show on the outside. It will show less on medium- to heavy-weight fabrics. (See your machine's manual for complete blind hemming instructions.)

Fused Hem

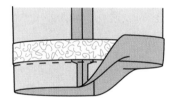

Use fusible web for a very fast hem. It works nicely on doubleknits.

Cut web 1/2" narrower than the hem width. Fuse 10-15 seconds in each spot to within 1/4" of top edge. Test on a scrap first to make sure fusible web won't be too stiff.

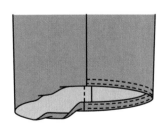

Topstitched Hem

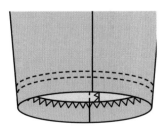

Jeans are usually hemmed by turning up 1/4" and then 3/8" and topstitching, then edgestitching.

Topstitching with a twin needle works well on knits as it creates a zigzag on the underside that will give, preventing popped hem stitches. It also gives wovens a sporty look.

Tapered Hems

If you taper your legs, you will need to mark your hemline, fold up hem, and mark new stitching lines. Use a pen that will go through both layers of tissue. Unfold and trim away excess tissue. Now the hem will fit the pant leg when turned up.

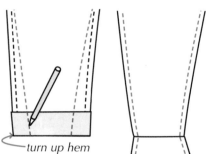

Side Slit at Ankle

A 2" hem depth is better when you have a slit.

Mark hemline. Make a dot 1½" above and below hemline at side seam.

Stitch side seams to first dot, backstitch. Backstitch at second dot and stitch to lower edge.

Turn hem to outside matching dots. Stitch opening on each side of slit. Trim seam and cut corners diagonally.

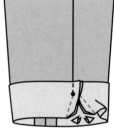

Turn hem to inside. Press. Finish hem edge. Hem pants.

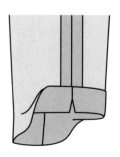

Deep Side Slits

These won't be faced as you won't want that deep a hem.

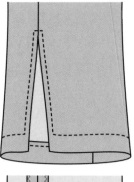

Finish hem and seam allowances.

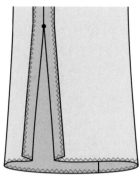

Mark hem, allowing a 1¼" hem allowance.
Turn up 1¼" to outside and stitch seam.
Trim seam, cut corners diagonally, turn to right side, and press.

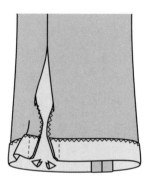

Stitch 1" from lower edge, pivoting at corners and stitch 1/4" from opening edges, squaring stitching above slit.

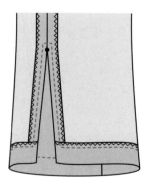

Cuffs

Cuffs come and go in popularity. They show up on any leg width and in many cuff widths. For correct hem allowance, double the finished width of cuff and add a 1″ hem. Here is a handy chart to help you add enough hem allowance for the cuff width you choose.

Width of Finished Cuff	Hem Allowance
1″	3″
1¼″	3½″
1½″	4″
2″	5″
3″	7″

1. Before hemming, try on pants and mark desired finished length. Cut away any extra length.

2. Turn under the following amount:

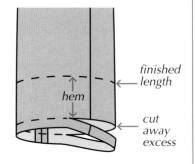

finished length

hem

cut away excess

Cuff Width	First Turn Up
1″	2″
1¼″	2¼″
1½″	2½″
2″	3″
3″	4″

3. Crease slightly with an iron.

4. Trim seam allowances in hem area to 1/4″ to eliminate bulk.

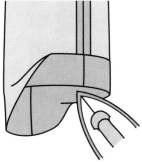

5. Finish hem edge.

6. Hand sew hem.

7. Turn up cuff. Press.

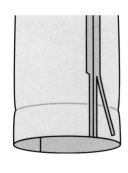

TIP: To hold in place, make a swing tack at side seams between cuff and pant.

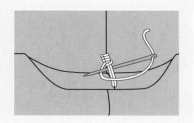

Stirrups

Since stirrups are generally in pants that stretch, make sure that when you are barefoot, the pant will stretch comfortably to the floor on both sides of your feet.

1. Cut an arch from side to side for front and back with the front cut higher than the back.

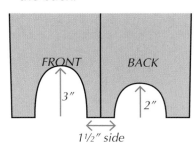

FRONT   BACK

3″   2″

1½″ side

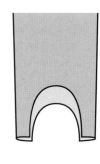

2. Hem the arch by turning up 1/4″ and topstitching. Or, you can serge and turn up 1/4″ and top-stitch.

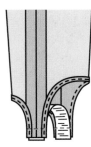

3. Stitch 3/4″ or 1″ wide elastic to ends.

4. Press seam allowances toward pant and topstitch 1/4″ from seamed edge.

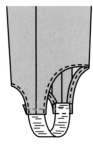

CHAPTER 23

Lining & Underlining

When Should We Use a Lining or Underlining?

1. To prevent seams from showing through light colored fabrics. Underlining does this better and it also camouflages seam allowances.

2. To keep wools from scratching or causing skin irritations. Lining gives more protection.

3. To strengthen loosely woven or fragile fabrics. Underlining works better because it is sewn into all seams next to the outer fabric.

4. To prevent baggy knees and seat. Underlining is better for the same reason as above.

5. To prevent wrinkling—either will do the job.

Line With...

• Polyester lining

• Rayon lining

Lining at a Glance

Make a pant out of fashion fabric and lining.

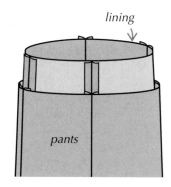

Place the two pants wrong sides together and sew them together at waist. (Save time by sewing waistband on first, then after checking fit, add the lining.)

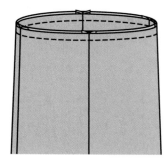

Underline With...

• Cotton or poly/cotton batiste or lightweight broadcloth

• Polyester lining

• Rayon lining

• Silk organza

• China silk

Underlining at a Glance

Baste underlining to wrong side of fashion fabric.

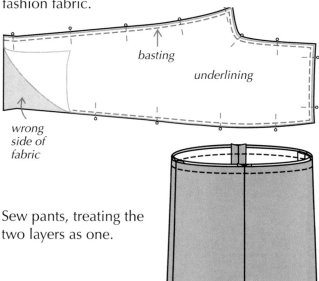

Sew pants, treating the two layers as one.

How to Underline— The Glue and Fold Method

Use a fabric glue that dries soft and flexible like Sobo or Tacky. Sobo is permanent, so use only on the seam allowances.

1. Cut underlining and fashion fabric from the same pattern pieces.

2. Mark darts on underlining only.

3. Steam press the two layers together to remove wrinkles and excess shrinkage caused by steam.

underlining

4. Lift the underlining and dot glue (open nozzle only 1/4 turn for small dots) on the seam allowances close to the edge of fabric. Don't glue hem edge!

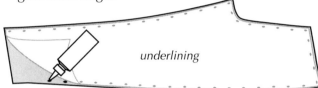

underlining

5. Because the underlining is like an inner cylinder when on the body, it must be made smaller or it will sag. Quickly, before the glue dries, fold each leg lengthwise toward the center front or back. A small bubble will form in the underlining.

bubbles in underlining

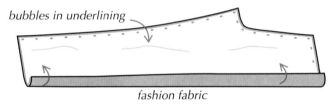

fashion fabric

6. Fold again and the bubble will get larger.

7. Scoot excess underlining (the bubble) off the edge while glue is still wet. Let each leg remain folded until dry (five minutes). Cut off excess underlining if it gets in your way.

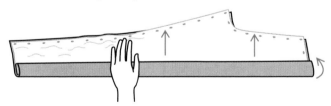

8. After glue dries, baste through center of darts, 1/2" past dart point in order to catch both layers when stitching darts.

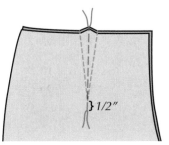

3 1/2"

NOTE: The dart may have moved a small amount toward the center during folding. It's not enough to worry about.

9. Sew pants together, treating the two layers as one. When you turn up the hem, the underlining will scoot out a bit as another inner cylinder is created. This is why you don't glue the hem edge. Hem, catching underlining only for an invisible hem.

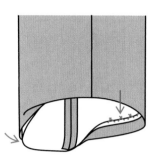

Tips for Linings

Quick Tip

Wait to cut lining until after you have pin-fitted your pant. Mark any changes on your fabric. Unpin pant and place pattern on top of each front and back. Transfer final stitching lines to tissue. If your right and left sides differ, use two colors of ink, one for each side. Cut all seam allowances an even width. We prefer 1" seam allowances. Use adjusted tissue to cut the lining.

Cut lining the length of the finished pant. This will allow for a hem in the lining.

Also, note that you will be dropping the lining into pant AFTER the waistband is attached, but not finished on the inside. That way, if the waistband is too tight or loose and you have to make adjustments to the pants seams or darts, you don't have to take the lining out.

Sewing and Fitting Tips

Sew crotch seams of lining front and back, beginning 1½" from inseams, stopping at zipper opening.

TIP: In lower crotch curve, sew lining with a 3/8" seam allowance instead of 5/8" to allow room for the pant seam allowance.

Pin lining right sides together and try on wrong side out (the same way it will be worn when in your pants). Adjust pins if necessary.
Sew lining seams. Press toward front. Pink edges. Or serge seams together and press toward front.

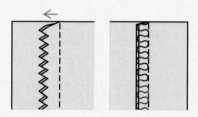

Press darts or pleats in the opposite direction of those in the fashion fabric.

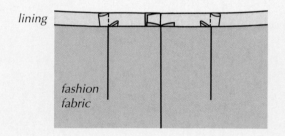

lining

fashion fabric

After sewing and fitting waistband, drop lining into pant and pin to waistline. Machine baste.

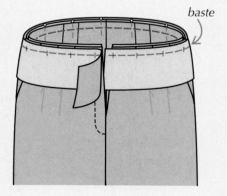

baste

Trouser Tip

Don't sew tucks in lining. Simply pin to fit when you drop lining into pant and pin to waistline. Pin in the opposite direction of pleats.

Then complete your waistband.

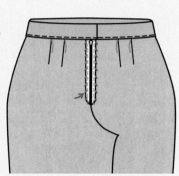

pin

Finishing Tips

Hand slipstitch lining to zipper tape.

TIP: In fitted pants, leave lining loose around zipper to keep it from ripping when you bend.

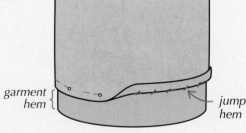

A "jump hem" is a tidy way to finish lined pants. Hem the garment first, then turn under lining hem so the fold is about 1/2" from bottom of pant. Pin horizontally near lining raw edge. Fold lining back to pins and slip stitch lining to garment hem.

garment hem *jump hem*

Pant Liners

Some people like to have one pant "liner" to wear with all pants. You can purchase them in lingerie departments or sew one from lining. However, if you've ever owned lined pants, you will no doubt prefer a lining sewn into a pant. There will be only one waistband around your waist!

CHAPTER 24
Jumpsuits and Culottes

Jumpsuits

Fitting a jumpsuit is the same as fitting a bodice and pants, except the two are joined at the waist.

Pattern Size

Buy a jumpsuit pattern to fit your bustline. It is much easier to alter the pant portion than it is to alter the bodice.

Jumpsuit Styles

If you've never sewn a jump-suit, choose a pattern with a waistline seam. Cut a 1″ seam allowance onto the waist of the bodice and the pant pieces.

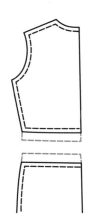

With the larger waistline seam allowances, you can easily alter for all the following:

1. **Sway back**—Sew a deeper waistline seam at center back, tapering to normal seamline at sides.

2. **Full tummy**—Let out waistline at center front, tapering to normal seamline at sides.

3. **Jumpsuit too long in crotch**—Sew deeper waist seam all the way around.

4. **Jumpsuit too short in crotch**—Sew shallower waist seam all the way around.

NOTE: Raise your arms for the true comfort test of jumpsuit body length. A jumpsuit with sleeves needs more body length than one without sleeves.

Fit Bodice Length

1. Pin tissue pattern together—shoulder seams, side seams down to waist, and darts.

2. Tie 1/4″ elastic around waist. Try on tissue pattern over elastic. Check to see if pattern waist markings come down to bottom of elastic.

3. If waist markings do not meet bottom edge of elastic, lengthen or shorten front and back the necessary amount as shown. This also gives you an opportunity to check dart position, neckline depth, and other details.

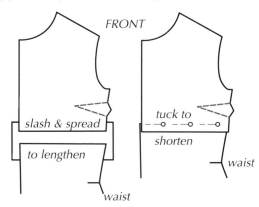

FRONT

slash & spread
to lengthen

tuck to
shorten

waist

waist

159

Fit Width

Try on the tissue and check waist and hip width. If you need to make width smaller, pin side seams in deeper. If waist or hips are too small, add tissue to the sides.

If you only need more waist room, sew narrower darts or eliminate them entirely.

NOTE: Cut 1" side seam allowances (rather than 5/8") if you are not sure how much ease you will need.

Fit Crotch

A jumpsuit needs to be long enough in the crotch so you can bend. And, if it has sleeves, you need to pin them in while tissue fitting and carefully raise your arms. Lengthen or shorten the crotch depth if necessary the same way you would on a pant (pg. 28).

FABRIC TIP:

Recommended crotch depth ease for jumpsuits with sleeves.

Woven fabrics:	3/4"-1"ease
Moderate stretch knits:	1/2" ease
Very stretchy knits:	1/4" ease

(If knits are SUPER stretchy like velours, you may be better off with no ease.)

NOTE: The chart applies to jumpsuits with sleeves. Sleeveless jumpsuits would have the same amount of crotch depth ease as pants.

NOTE: It is worse to make a jumpsuit too long in the crotch than too short. If too long, wear a belt to shorten it a little, or take a horizontal tuck at the waist and cover it with a belt. If it is too short, just sew a deeper crotch seam as shown. Sew crotch seam deeper 1/4" at a time, trim, and try on until comfortable. You can lower the crotch up to 2" in a straightleg jumpsuit without affecting width of legs. However, the legs will get shorter, so check hem allowance!

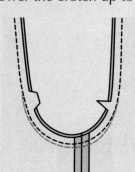

Culottes

Culottes are cut fuller than pants, more like a skirt. Pattern companies automatically make the crotch of culottes 1/2"-3/4" longer than a basic style pant. The hip width may be wider also, because the culotte is usually fuller than most pants. Try on the tissue and alter as for a pant pattern, then fit-as-you-sew!

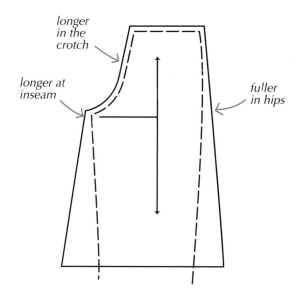

longer in the crotch

longer at inseam

fuller in hips

CHAPTER 25
Jeans for the Whole Family

Three Reasons to Sew Jeans

1. **Fit**—Sew them to fit your shape! If, when you buy jeans, the waist is always too big, and the crotch too tight, you are a sew-them-yourself jeans body. (See page 8 for more on ease in jeans.)

2. **Price**—Now that jeans (even kids') cost as much as the weekly grocery bill, it will behoove you to learn to copy these easy-to-sew-once-you-learn-how, money-savers.

3. **Creativity**—Go beyond denim; try velveteen, satin, synthetic suedes, or stretch denim. Embroider on the pocket—why wear some other designer's name!

Don't Let All the Pockets Scare You

Follow this simple order:

| Create SIDE INSET. Sew coin pocket to side piece, then side piece to side inset (usually lining). | FACE FRONT. Sew pocket facing (lining) to front. | Turn and press. Topstitch. | SEW POCKET BAGS. Place side unit under front and stitch side unit to side inset. |

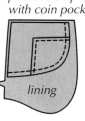

pocket side piece with coin pocket

lining

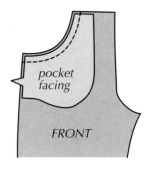

pocket facing

FRONT

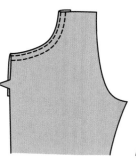

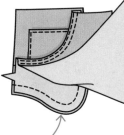

Edges may not match.

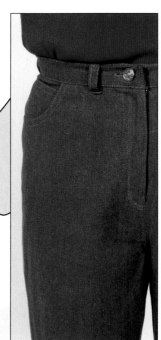

TIP: The side inset can be made from fashion fabric if it is not too heavy.

Special "Fit-As-You-Sew" Order for Jeans

We designed a jeans pattern that allows you to fit even those with flat-felled side seams. We added "in-case" seam allowances at the upper inseam (for full thighs), side seams (for hip width), and waist (for crotch depth) because jeans are made with less ease in these areas. You can make these changes on any jeans pattern. After all pocket, zipper, and yoke construction is done on flat pieces, assemble as shown.

Stitch crotch seams. Machine baste inseam. (Note larger seam allowances.)

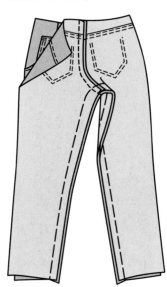

Pin side seams right sides out, and pin band onto pants. Try on and fit.

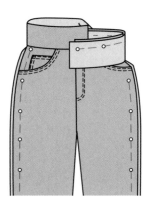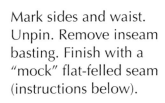

Mark sides and waist. Unpin. Remove inseam basting. Finish with a "mock" flat-felled seam (instructions below).

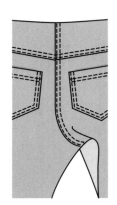

Stitch side seams with mock flat-felled seam.

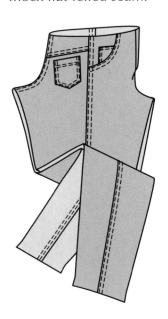

Stitch inseams. Trim to 3/8". Zigzag seam allowances together. Press toward back.

Now apply waistband.

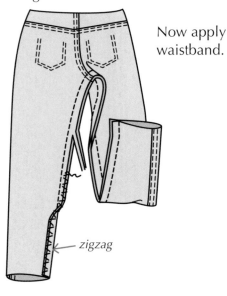

zigzag

Mock Flat-Felled Seam
(faster, easier, and less bulky)

Sew seam. Trim one side to 1/2". Zigzag or serge other edge.

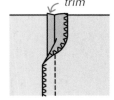

trim

Press to one side, long seam over short. Edgestitch close to seam and topstitch 1/4" away.

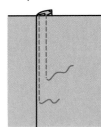

NOTE: Some ready-made jeans have flat-felled inseams and regular side seams. YOU CHOOSE!

CHAPTER 26
Pants for Men

Since we are both selfish seamsters treasuring our precious sewing time, when we sew for men it can only be termed "a labor of love!" We try to use fast and easy, yet still professional looking, sewing techniques.

We avoid the traditional fly front which has a center front seam instead of a fold at the edge of the overlap. Also, a fly protector is less necessary now that we have soft nylon zippers.

Our secret—we use the same techniques that we use to sew our own pants:

1. The non-roll waistband technique (page 111).

2. The simple fly front zipper technique sewn the same as the one used in women's pants, just a mirror image (page 107).

3. Patch pockets on pant back rather than welt pockets.

Once you master fitting men's pants, then you can elaborate more on sewing techniques.

Men's Pants Patterns

Buy a pant pattern by hip size for a better pant leg shape. Add to the waist if necessary. If the pattern includes a jacket, buy by the chest size. It's easier to alter pants than a jacket.

Measure waist, hip, and length from waist to floor at sides, and crotch to floor at inseam. You may find it easier to measure a pair of ready-made pants that fit reasonably well. Measure the pant waist, hip, inseam, and outseam. Subtract the inseam from the outseam for crotch depth measurement.

Or, better yet, tissue-fit a man the same as you would a woman. You'll instantly see the necessary alterations and be assured of a good fit.

Common Alterations

There are two very common fitting problems in pants for men over 40 years of age. One is the flat derriere and the other is the full tummy, commonly called the "bay window."

"Bay Window"   **"Flat Derriere"**

Patterns altered for men commonly look like this:

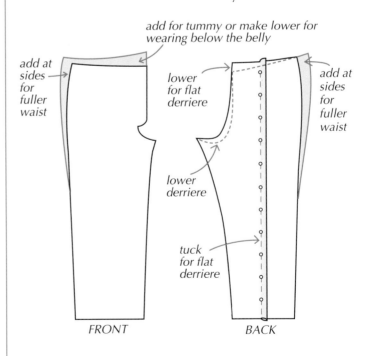

add for tummy or make lower for wearing below the belly

add at sides for fuller waist

lower for flat derriere

add at sides for fuller waist

lower derriere

tuck for flat derriere

FRONT   *BACK*

Fitting Pants for Men

Altering Ready-made Pants

- Men's ready-to-wear pants have a center back seam in the waistband for easy altering. If you sew to fit him, you don't need that seam.

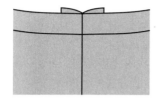 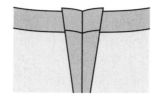

- If a man has a **full derriere**, taking in the waist at the center back in ready-made pants works.

- If he has a **flat derriere** and he needs the waist to be **taken in**, an angled seam, like a dart, is created at the center back which causes bagginess.

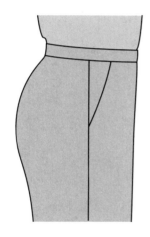 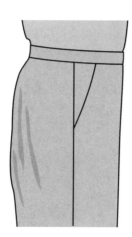

- However, if he is flat, and he needs the waist **let out,** the angle goes away and the pants will fit better.

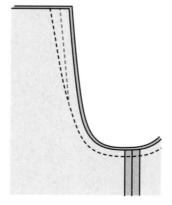

Sewing Men's Pants

NOTE: Men's pant patterns usually appear very complicated because of all the pocket pieces (often including a front "watch pocket"). The easiest way to figure out how they are assembled is to pin the tissue pattern pieces together before you cut and sew. This helps you organize all those little pieces and understand where they go.

Men's Fly Front Zipper

- A fly front zipper is like a lapped zipper. A woman's fly laps right over left (page 107) and a man's fly laps left over right. Also, a fly protector is added as the last step.

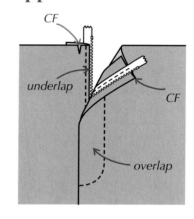

A fly front zipper has an overlap and an underlap. The fold line on the overlap side is the center front (CF).

- Check your pattern before cutting. The fly front extension should measure at least 1½" wide so it will be caught in top-stitching. If fly front is not 1½" wide, add width when cutting.

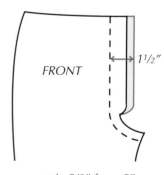

- Snip-mark fold lines. Snip CF for overlap, snip 5/8" from CF for underlap. (This fold is even with crotch cut edge.)

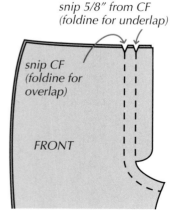

- Use a 12" conventional zipper. Let the excess extend above the top edge and into waistband and cut off later. With the deep underlap, the zipper won't show so a perfect color match isn't necessary.

TIP: Length of the fly opening is important to men. Pati once made the opening too short. Eventually her husband explained why this didn't work for him.

Sewing Men's Fly Front Zipper

1. Stitch crotch seam 1½" from inseam to zipper opening. Backstitch.

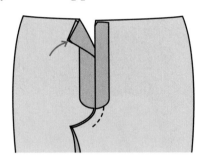

2. Fold left front under from crotch seam to center front (CF) snip. Press. Fold right front under from underlap snip to edge of crotch seam allowance.

3. Place basting tape on underlap side of zipper. Peel away protective paper and stick to underlap. Stitch next to fold.

4. Place basting tape on edge of overlap. Peel away protective paper.

5. Line up CF snips and stick overlap in place.

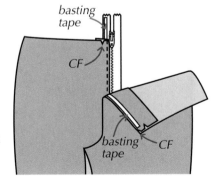

6. Lay fronts on flat surface. Pin overlap side through all layers to prevent scooting of fabric. Using Scotch Magic Tape as a stitching guide, topstitch 1" from CF. When you get to the curve, step on the accelerator and go. It's easier when you stitch fast. Remove tapes.

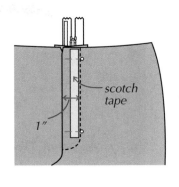

NOTE: For a perfectly curved topstitching, use washable marker or chalk to draw around a paper template traced from the pattern tissue stitching line. Tuck template back in pattern envelope to use again.

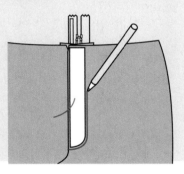

7. Insurance for men! Cut fly protector according to pattern and sew lining fabric to rounded edge. Turn and press. Sew fly protector to extension on underlap side. Since nylon zippers are now stronger than metal and they don't scratch, ask him if the fly protector is now optional. It is one less step if he doesn't care! But DO MAKE THE ZIPPER OPENING LONG ENOUGH!!

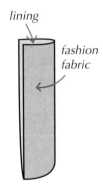

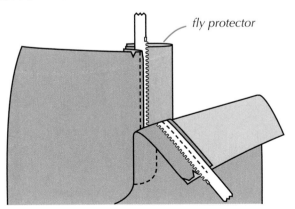

CHAPTER 27

Altering Pants for Weight Changes

Altering What You Have Sewn

If you have a pattern that you've altered to fit and then your weight changes, can you still sew from the same pattern? Can you adjust pants you've already made? Yes and yes! You can adjust most pants within the seam allowances for 10 to 15 pounds of weight change.

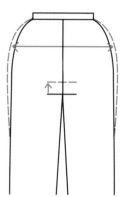

If you gain weight, your body expands. As you fill out the pants the crotch gets shorter. If you lose weight, you "deflate" in width and the crotch hangs lower.

Gained Weight

Take waistband off and side seams out. Try pants on with elastic tied around your waist to hold them up. Pin sides to fit. Adjust crotch depth until comfortable by pulling pants down under elastic. Mark new side and waist seams.

mark new seams

NOTE: This may not work if the pants have side-seam pockets.

If you don't have enough waist seam allowance to make the crotch comfortable, deepen the crotch. Sew it lower, trim seam to 1/4". Now you have a longer crotch.

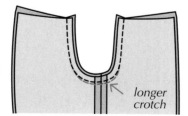

longer crotch

Lost Weight

Take the waistband off. Sew side seams deeper. Lower the waistband by pulling pants up under elastic until crotch is comfortable. Mark bottom of elastic and sew waistband back on. Lowering the waistline seam will shorten the pant so hopefully you will have enough hem allowance to adjust the length.

Pati has succeeded in losing many pounds in recent months. These trousers were worth saving, so she's pinned them to her new figure.

Altering Ready-to-Wear

You can alter ready-made clothes, but some alterations are just not worth the time. The following are in order of how easy the alteration is:

1. **Length**—See page 153 for invisible hems.

2. **Width**—if pants are a little too tight but don't have wide seam allowances, buy the next size larger and take in the side seams. You may need to remove the waistband first. Too loose? Take in the side seams.

3. **Crotch too short**—sew crotch deeper (page 160) . Check hem allowance.

4. **Crotch too long**—remove waistband and sew it lower all the way around. This will definitely shorten legs. Check hem allowance.

5. **Smiles in the crotch**—let out inseams as much as possible. Extreme smiles? Definitely don't buy them or toss if you own them.

6. **Baggy in the back**—remove waistband from side seam to side seam and sew it lower at the center back. Still baggy? Take in inseams.

Marta's quickie method—just take a tuck right at waistband edge at center back tapering to nothing at side seams. Press toward band.

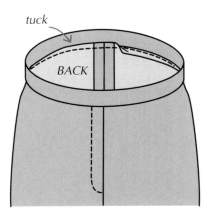

tuck

BACK

Maternity Pants

Gail Brown, maternity expert and author, has these pant suggestions for mothers-to-be.

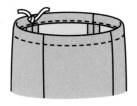

- Since pregnancy is many different sizes, adjustable pants are a must. Pull-on pants with elastic tied at the side seam can grow with you.

  Sew pull-on pants (page 119). To convert to a maternity pant, add tissue as shown when cutting. (This is very similar to a large tummy alteration on page 30.)

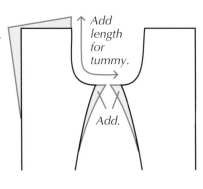

Add length for tummy.

Add.

- Stretch panels are best for when you are biggest, or for converting conventional pants into maternity pants. Some patterns allow for a stretch panel but the panel may not be where you are the largest. Hold the pant front pattern piece up to you and mark around your tummy. Stitch the panel to that marking. Remember, the lower the panel, the longer your tops must be to cover it.

  To convert conventional pants to maternity pants, try on pants, chalk mark around your tummy. Stitch the panel to that marking. Again, remember, the lower the panel, the longer your tops must be to cover it.

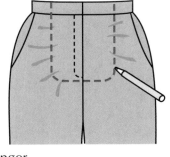

  If the stretch panel is too large in the early stages of pregnancy, take tucks at the top or tighten the elastic.

"Be gorgeous," says Gail, who sewed a wool gabardine pant with a stretch panel front! "I got so tired of the stretch pajama look that I craved crisp fabrics for a change. They made me feel terrific!"

CHAPTER 28

Design Ideas for the Creative

Designer Pants

It's the details that make the clothing of ready-to-wear designers unique. Study them...and then do it yourself!

Anne Klein Wool Crepe Pants

FRONT

seam at top of waistband

fusible interfacing in waistband

short, very narrow double-welt pocket over tucks

piped, very narrow double welt pocket openings

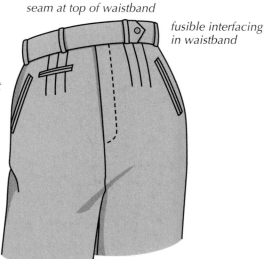

BACK

inside fly protector

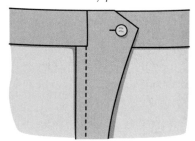

Escada Trousers

topstitched 2" waistband

FRONT

pleats pressed toward center

1½" cuffs at hem

1/2" topstitching

BACK

very short back darts

single welt with edgestitching

side seams pressed toward back and edgestitched

Liz Claiborne Shorts

FRONT

BACK

Dana Buchman Pant

FRONT

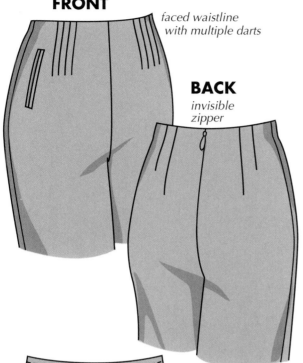

faced waistline with multiple darts

BACK
invisible zipper

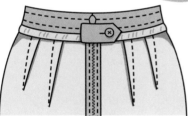

INSIDE BACK

two back darts

lining folded over elastic

Pati's Linen Trousers

FRONT

BACK

fake

Escada Pants

FRONT

pleats turn toward side

vertical welts

edgestitched band

BACK

menswear-look seam at center back of waistband

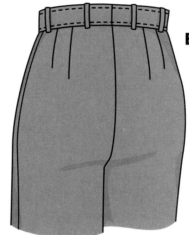

wide seam allowance from crotch through waistband

INSIDE BACK

extra button sewn to label

two narrow darts

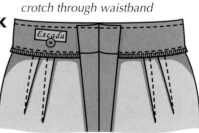

Escada

zipper to top of waistband

darts in stay, which goes into side seam

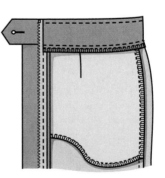

Waistline and Pocket Designs and Details

Add Design Lines

If you would like to make minor design changes or create a look you can't find in the pattern books, it is as easy as drawing a line! Create any design line by cutting the pattern and adding seam allowances. Sew the new seam and you have an instant design line.

Vertical Seaming

For pants that form-fit your derriere (great if you are flat in back), cut through center of dart to hemline. Add seam allowances.

Fold darts out of tissue.

Design a Yoke

Draw a straight or curved line. Fold dart out of yoke before cutting fabric; add seam allowances.

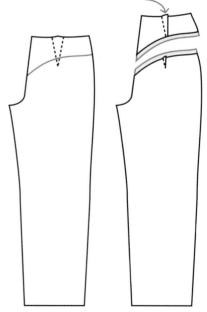

Knee Seaming

Draw an upside down "V" at knee in front and back (great for leather and suede, real or synthetic). Add seam allowances.

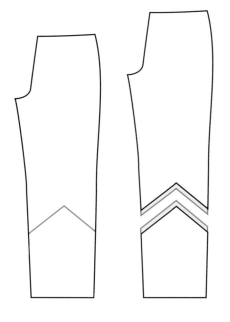

Color Splicing

A fun idea for summer cottons, evening pants, jeans, and children's clothes. Cut pattern, add seam allowances. Cut sections out of various colors of fabrics and seam together.

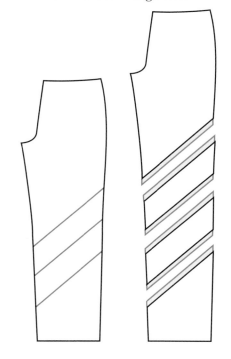

Metric Conversion Chart

inches	centimeters	inches	centimeters	inches	centimeters
$\frac{1}{8}$	.3	7	18	29	73.5
$\frac{1}{4}$	.6	8	20.5	30	76
$\frac{3}{8}$	1	9	23	31	78.5
$\frac{1}{2}$	1.3	10	25.5	32	81.5
$\frac{5}{8}$	1.5	11	28	33	84
$\frac{3}{4}$	2	12	30.5	34	86.5
$\frac{7}{8}$	2.2	13	33	35	89
1	2.5	14	35.5	36	91.5
$1\frac{1}{4}$	3.2	15	38	37	94
$1\frac{1}{2}$	3.8	16	40.5	38	96.5
$1\frac{3}{4}$	4.5	17	43	39	99
2	5	18	46	40	102
$2\frac{1}{2}$	6.3	19	48.5	41	104
3	7.5	20	51	42	107
$3\frac{1}{2}$	9	21	53.5	43	109
4	10	22	56	44	112
		23	58.5	45	115
$4\frac{1}{2}$	11.5	24	61	46	117
5	12.5	25	63.5	47	120
		26	66	48	122
$5\frac{1}{2}$	14	27	68.5	49	125
6	15	28	71	50	127

Index

Palmer/Pletsch PRODUCTS

These ready-to-use, information-filled sewing how-to books, manuals and videos can be found in local book and fabric stores or ordered through Palmer/Pletsch Publishing (see address on last page).

LARGE BOOKS

❑ **The BUSINE$$ of Teaching Sewing** *Second Edition, by Marcy Miller and Pati Palmer, 112 pages plus downloadable business forms, $24.95* Be in the BUSINESS of teaching sewing. This book covers: Appearance and Image; Getting Started; The Lesson Plan; Class Formats; Location; Marketing, Promotion & Advertising; Pricing; Teaching Techniques; and Continuing Education—Where To Find It.

❑ **Couture—The Art of Fine Sewing** *by Roberta C. Carr, 208 pages, $29.95* How-tos for couture techniques and secrets, brought to life with illustrations and dozens of garments photographed in full color.

❑ **Creative Serging for the Home and Other Quick Decorating Ideas** *by Lynette Ranney Black and Linda Wisner, 160 pages, $19.95* Color photos and how-to's of dozens of rooms help you transform your home into the place YOU want it to be.

❑ **Dream Sewing Spaces—Design and Organization for Spaces Large and Small** *Second Edition, by Lynette Ranney Black, 128 pages, $24.95* Make your dream a reality. Analyze your needs and your space, then learn to plan and put it together. Lots of color photos!

❑ **Fit for Real People: Sew Great Clothes Using ANY Pattern** *Second Edition, by Marta Alto and Pati Palmer, 256 pages, $24.95* This practical approach is explained in a simple, logical style. Learn to buy the right size, and then learn to tissue-fit to determine alterations. Special sections include fitting young teen girls, the history of sizing, and fitting REAL people.

❑ **Hand Mending Made Easy** *by Nan Ides, 60 pages, $14.95* Written specifically for the non-sewer. See how easy it is to do your own mending–a skill that anyone old enough to hold a needle can learn to do.

❑ **Looking Good— A Comprehensive Guide to Wardrobe Planning, Color and Personal Style Development** *by Nancy Nix-Rice, 160 pages, $24.95* Everything women need to look their personal best—not by following what fashion dictates, but by spotlighting their best features to create the most flattering, effective look possible.

❑ **Pants for Real People: Fit and Sew for ANY Body** *by Marta Alto and Pati Palmer, 176 pages, $24.95* The most detailed pant fitting and sewing book available, integrating "real people" photos with easy how-to illustrations and instructions. Includes trouser and pull-on techniques, non-roll waistbands, pockets, zippers, linings, plus design ideas, maternity men's pants, and more.

❑ **Sewing Ultrasuede® Brand Fabrics—Ultrasuede®, Ultrasuede Light™, Caress™, Ultraleather™** *by Marta Alto, Pati Palmer and Barbara Weiland, 128 pages, $16.95* Color photo section, plus the newest techniques to master these luxurious fabrics.

For more details visit www.palmerpletsch.com

Note: these books are all softcover. Most are available with coil binding: $5 additional for large books, $3 for small.

❑ **Théâtre de la Mode— Fashion Dolls: The Survival of Haute Couture** *Second Edition, edited by Susan Train, 192 pages, $29.95* The story of the event...and the 27" high dolls...that resurrected the global haute couture and fashion industry after WWII. The book features historic black & white photos plus color photos of all 172 dolls, their theater sets, and the fashion photographs of David Seidner.

AND A COOKBOOK!

❑ **The Food Nanny Recues Dinner—Easy Family Meals for Every Day of the Week** *by Liz Edmunds, 288 pages, $24.95* With over 200 delicious kid- and budget-friendly recipes plus strategies for successful family dinnertimes, this 288-page book is *more* than a cook book.

SMALL BOOKS

❏ **Mother Pletsch's Painless Sewing,** *NEW Revised Edition, by Pati Palmer and Susan Pletsch, 128 pgs., $10.95* The most uncomplicated sewing book of the century! Lots of tips on how to sew FAST!

❏ **Sewing With Sergers—
The Complete Handbook for Overlock Sewing,** *Revised Edition, by Pati Palmer and Gail Brown, 128 pages, $10.95* Learn easy threading tips, stitch types, rolled edging, and flatlocking.

❏ **Creative Serging—The Complete Handbook for Decorative Overlock Sewing** *by Pati Palmer, Gail Brown and Sue Green, 128 pages, $10.95* In-depth information and creative uses of your serger.

❏ **Pants For Any Body,** *Fourth Edition, by Pati Palmer and Susan Pletsch, 128 pages, $8.95* Learn to fit pants following clear problem-and-solution illustrations.

❏ **The Shade Book,** *New Revised Edition, by Judy Lindahl, 140 pages, $11.95* Everything you need to know to make six major shade types.

❏ **Smart Packing,** *New Revised Edition, Susan (Pletsch) Foster, 240 pages, $19.95* Pack less but have more to wear! Learn how to travel in comfort and style— no matter where you're headed or who's traveling with you. Plan and pack for any trip from business to pleasure.

MY FIRST SEWING BOOK KITS

My First Sewing Books, *by Winky Cherry,* are available packaged as kits with materials for a first project. With a Teaching Manual & Video, they offer a complete, thoroughly tested sewing program for young children, 5 to 11 years old. They'll learn patience, manners, creativity, completion, and how to follow rules—all through the enjoyment of sewing. Each book follows a project from start to finish with clever rhymes and clear illustrations. *Each book, 8½" x 8½", 40 pages*

HAND SEWING SERIES

*each book alone $10.95
book with kit $14.95*

❏ **My First Sewing Book**
Children as young as five can learn to hand sew and stuff a felt bird shape. Also available in Spanish.

❏ **My First Embroidery Book** Beginners learn the importance of accuracy by making straight stitches and using a chart and gingham to make a name sampler. *(electronic download of book only; no kit available)*

❏ **My First Doll Book**
Felt dolls have embroidered faces, yarn hair, and clothes. Children use the overstitch and skills learned in Levels I and II.

MACHINE SEWING SERIES

*each book alone $10.95
book with kit $12.95*

❏ **My First Machine Sewing Book** With practice pages, then a fabric star, children learn about the machine, seam allowances, tapering, snips, clips and stitching and turning a shape right side out.

❏ **My First Patchwork Book**
Children use a template to make a fourpatch block and can make the entire alphabet of patchwork flags used by sailors, soldiers, pilots, and astronauts.

❏ **My First Quilt Book**
Children machine stitch a quilt pieced with strips and squares and finish it with yarn ties or optional hand quilting.

TEACHING MATERIALS

❏ **Teaching Children to Sew Manual and Video,** *$29.95*
The 112-page, 8½" x 11" **Teaching Manual** shows you exactly how to teach young children, including preparing the environment, workshop space, class control, and the importance of incorporating other life skills along with sewing skills. In the **DVD Video** *(1 hour),* see Winky Cherry teach six 6-to-8-year olds how to sew in a true-life classroom setting. She introduces herself and explains the rules, then shows them how to sew. Then, see close-ups of a child sewing the project in double-time. (Show this to your students.) Finally, Winky gives you a tour of an ideal classroom setup. She also talks about the tools, patterns and sewing supplies you will need.

❏ **Teacher's Supplies** Additional kit supplies, patterns and teaching materials for The Winky Cherry System of Sewing are available. Call for a catalog.

DVD VIDEOS

The styles and techniques in our books are brought to life and expanded on by Marta Alto and Pati Palmer in these interactive DVD videos.

Serger Basics Learn to master serger basics, and the practical reasons for using your serger on garments. Based on the best-selling *Sewing With Sergers* book. *2 hours $19.95*

Creative Serging Maximize your serger and have FUN using it. You'll see close-ups of all the tips that make decorative threads work on YOUR sergers, PLUS a fashion show of creative ideas. Based on the book *Creative Serging. 2 hours $19.95*

21st Century Sewing Tips and techniques to make sewing fun, fast, and trouble-free, including products that make sewing easier and/or better. *1 hour $19.95*

Pants for Real People, Fitting Techniques Pati Palmer teaches you to fit a fitted and trouser-style pant. *90 minutes $19.95*

Pants for Real People, Sewing Techniques Marta Alto shows you how to sew a fitted pant and a trouser. *90 minutes $19.95*

Fit for Real People: BASICS Learn the basics of choosing the right size, fitting, and altering, including the most common alterations for bust, back, shoulders, and sleeves. *90 minutes $19.95*

Full Busted? Sew Clothes That Fit! Buy patterns to fit your upper chest, neck, and shoulders and easily learn to alter the front to fit your larger cup size. *2 hours $19.95*

Jackets for Real People Follow along as Marta sews a lapel-style jacket. *2 hours, 45 minutes $24.95*

Learn to Sew a Shirt or Blouse Learn how to fit, cut, mark, and sew two styles of shirts. *1 hour $19.95*

Looking Good, Live! Look like a million...for considerably less. What you need to know about style, line, design, and color to flatter *you. 1 hour, 40 minutes $19.95*

Sew an Ultrasuede® Jacket Clear, step-by-step demonstrations on how to sew an Ultrasuede jacket, plus a fashion show of other garments. *1 hour $19.95*

Sewing...Good To Great. It's in the Details The most difficult sewing details demystified. The techniques demonstrated will improve your skills in making beautiful finished garments. *1 hour $19.95*

Perfect Fusing. Interfacing decision making simplified. *45 minutes $14.95*

INTERFACINGS

Our extra-wide fusible weft **PerfectFuse™ Interfacings** are available in four weights. *1-yard and 3-yard packages charcoal black and ecru-white*

Perfect WAISTBANDS™
1" x 5 yds $4.95 a non-roll interfacing

PerfectFuse **SHEER** *$7.95/$23.50*
PerfectFuse **LIGHT** *$7.95/$23.50*
PerfectFuse **MEDIUM** *$8.95/$26.50*
PerfectFuse **TAILOR** *$12.95/$38.50*

Needle Threader for hand & machine needles. *$4.95*

FOR PERFECT SEWING...

Perfect Sew liquid wash-away stabilizer *8.5 oz. spray $11.95 35 oz. refill $24.95*

Perfect Pattern Paper *two 84" x 48" sheets $6.95*

PALMER/PLETSCH WORKSHOPS

Our "Sewing Vacations" are offered on a variety of topics, including *Pant Fit, Fit, Tailoring, Creative Serging, Ultrasuede, Couture, Sewing Update, Beginning Sewing Teacher Training, Intermediate Sewing, Sewing Camp,* and more. Workshops are held at the Palmer/Pletsch International Training Center in Portland, Oregon.

Teacher training sessions are also available on some topics. They include: practice teaching sessions, up to 300 digital slides and teaching script; camera-ready workbook handouts, and publicity flyer.

Check your local fabric and book stores for Palmer/Pletsch books and products or contact Palmer/Pletsch Publishing, 1801 N.W. Upshur Street, Suite 100, Portland, OR 97209
(503) 274-0687 or fax (503) 274-1377
or 1-800-728-3784 (orders)
info@palmerpletsch.com

For more details on these and other products, workshops, and teacher training, please visit our website:

www.palmerpletsch.com